# A RHETORIC OF BECOMING

Studies in Rhetorics and Feminisms
Series Editors: Cheryl Glenn and Shirley Wilson Logan

The series promotes and amplifies the interdisciplinarity of rhetorics and feminisms, connecting rhetorical inquiry with contemporary academic, sociopolitical, and economic concerns. Books in the series explore such enduring questions of rhetoric's rich and complex histories (globally and locally) as well as rhetoric's relevance to current public exigencies of social justice, power, opportunity, inclusion, equity, and diversity. This attention to interdisciplinarity has already transformed the rhetorical tradition as we have known it (upper-class, public, powerful, mostly political, antagonistic, and delivered by men) into regendered, inclusionary rhetorics (democratic, deliberative, diverse, collaborative, private, intersectional, and delivered by all people). Our cultural, political, and intellectual advancements will be enriched by exploring the varied ways rhetorics and feminisms intersect and animate one another (and take us in new political, cultural, scientific, communicative, and pedagogical directions).

## BOOKS IN THE SERIES

*A Rhetoric of Becoming: USAmerican Women in Qatar* by Nancy Small (2022)

*Rhetorical Listening in Action: A Concept-Tactic Approach* by Krista Ratcliffe and Kyle Jensen (2022)

# A RHETORIC OF BECOMING

## USAmerican Women in Qatar

Nancy Small

Parlor Press
*Anderson, South Carolina*
www.parlorpress.com

Parlor Press LLC, Anderson, South Carolina, USA
© 2022 by Parlor Press.
All rights reserved.
Printed in the United States of America on acid-free paper.

S A N: 2 5 4 - 8 8 7 9

Library of Congress Cataloging-in-Publication Data on File

1 2 3 4 5

978-1-64317-319-1 (paperback)
978-1-64317-320-7 (hardcover)
978-1-64317-321-4 (PDF)
978-1-64317-322-1 (EPUB)

Cover design by David Blakesley.
Cover photo by Nancy Small. Used by permission.

Parlor Press, LLC is an independent publisher of scholarly and trade titles in print and multimedia formats. This book is available in paper and ebook formats from Parlor Press on the World Wide Web at www.parlorpress.com or through online and brick-and-mortar bookstores. For submission information or to find out about Parlor Press publications, write to Parlor Press, 3015 Brackenberry Drive, Anderson, South Carolina, 29621, or email editor@parlorpress.com.

# Contents

*To*

*Nannie Hart McClinton, a mother*

*Nancy Estelle Watson, a writer*

*Ann Watson Stevens, an adventurer*

*Hannah Grace Small, a storied life just beginning*

# Acknowledgments

On a former plantation in Red River County, Texas, my maternal great-grandmother, Nannie Hart McClintock, died in childbirth as my grandmother, Nancy Estelle Watson, entered the world in 1906. Nancy Watson grew up through the Great Depression and aspired to be a writer but was turned away from newspapers where she applied. They told her that she could be a secretary but that reporting was "men's work." She went on to write stories and submit them to publications via the mail but was never successful. She destroyed her writings, so we cannot know anything of her genres, style, concerns, or imagination. Nannie and Nancy, along with my paternal grandmother from the Frio County borderlands, Ruth Era Collins, persisted through hardscrabble times and went on about the business of living (and dying) as best they could. My mom, Ann Watson Stevens, turned hard times into opportunities for adventure. She taught me to leverage the openings I can find, to make my own space. These women were loving yet pragmatic, and their tenacity resides in me as a stubborn willfulness. *Thank you, Grandmothers and Mom, for this gift.*

In 1995, shortly after a bloodless coup in which he seized power from his father and became Emir of Qatar, Sheik Hamad bin Khalifa and his second wife, Sheikha Moza bint Nasser, founded the Qatar Foundation for Education, Science, and Community Development. One story of this founding has them sitting under a Sidra tree, a symbol of perseverance in the face of extreme adversity, having a conversation that would change the lives of thousands of students, educators, and knowledge-makers. *Thank you, Sheikha Moza and Sheikh Hamad, for pursuing these dreams and for wrapping us up in them.*

Sometime back in 2008, my partner John and I were chatting, and he asked me if I would ever consider living abroad. With images of the

Scottish countryside in my mind, I immediately said yes, I would like to spend time outside the USA; the change in perspective would be educational. John set to work applying to be the first Director of Development for Texas A&M at Qatar, and about two years later, we packed up our lives to move to Doha. This expatriate life certainly was different than what I imagined in Scotland. More than educational, it was radically transformative. *Thank you, John, for being a co-traveler and risk-taker, and for opening the doors for me and our family to enter transformative places.*

In 2012, I proposed this project as a doctoral dissertation to my committee chair, Dr. Rebecca Rickly. In our conversations, I asked to write something beyond the traditional genre of the dissertation, based in storytelling and meditative in style, quite at odds with what others in our program seemed willing to accept. Becky let me go just feral enough to bump up against my own struggles and failures, then offered guidance and support to help me get back on track. *Thank you, Becky, for trusting me enough to let me roam, for directing me just when I needed it, for listening, and for being my advocate.*

At the 2014 Conference on College Composition and Communication, we were waiting to hear Angela Davis deliver the keynote, when my friend and former professor Dr. Amanda Booher leaned over and whispered, "You wanted to meet Cheryl Glenn? She's sitting one person over from us." Having just read Glenn's *Unspoken: A Rhetoric of Silence*, I jumped at the chance. Upon being introduced, Cheryl asked me where I worked, and when I answered Qatar, she enthusiastically responded with something like "that sounds fantastic!" In my typical social awkwardness, I blurted out "Come visit us!" At that moment, Angela Davis began speaking, and our brief exchange ended. A few minutes later, Cheryl put her business card in my hand, and indeed made the twenty-four-hour journey to Doha some months later. On that visit, she grilled me about my dissertation, knowing I was interested in converting it to a book, and since then, she has proven to be a powerfully influential mentor. *Thank you, Amanda, for the caring initiative in helping me learn to network. And thank you, Cheryl, for lifting up our community of scholars at TAMUQ, for believing in me, and for coaching me through this process—this intimidating, challenging process—of moving from dissertation to book.*

I could share dozens, maybe thousands, more of these stories, all contributing to a narrative of how this project came to be, but I'll stop here and offer the typical sort of notes instead. Thank you to my Cohearts and purveyors of silent judgment from Texas Tech—Laura Cunningham, Russell Kirkscey, Ashlynn Reynolds-Dyk, Charity Tran, and Virginia Tucker—for being the best friends I never expected to make upon returning to graduate school at forty years old. Thank you to my dissertation committee members, Joyce Locke Carter and Kristen Moore, for the smart questioning and feedback. Thank you to my colleagues in Qatar, particularly Leslie Seawright, Mysti Rudd, Bea Amaya, Kelly Wilson, Amy Hodges, Brenda Kent, Sara Hillman, Deanna Rasmussen, Sherri Ward, Michael Telafici, Joseph Williams, the faculty in Liberal Arts, and the members of the Women's Faculty Forum for the beautiful, compelling community you created. Thank you to the students and staff at the branch campus, for you taught me more about life in the Arabian Gulf than any books or study could ever teach. Leaving my colleagues and students to return to the USA was beyond difficult, but now in retrospect, I see those years together were an exceptional yet temporary moment in time.

Thank you to my University of Wyoming family, who received me in 2016 with open arms. To Kelly Kinney, Tracey Patton, Julia Obert, Arielle Zibrak, Mike Edson, Michael Knievel, Mimi Fenton, Susan Aaronstein, Kent Drummond, Susan Frye, Allison Gernant, Shelby Hutson, Joyce Stewart, and all my smart, kind colleagues: I appreciate that you have created a space where I feel I belong. A special thank you to Monica Wesley for her generous friendship, knitting advice, and help teaching me how to be a Wyomingite. Thank you to the Studies in Rhetorics and Feminisms editors, Cheryl Glenn and Shirley Logan, as well as to the outside reader and to editor David Blakesley. I appreciate you supporting me through these revisions and for all the ways you have made this project better. And finally, thank you to the Department of English and the Wyoming Institute for Humanities Research for their funding in support of this book's publication processes.

I close with large debts of gratitude, first to my interviewees—here referred to as Amanda, Amy, Ashley, Emily, Jessica, Mary, Melissa, Michelle, Lisa, Patricia, Sarah, Susan—for sharing their lives with me. Most of you didn't know me before our conversations, and I appreciate you trusting me with your stories. Your reflections, wisdom, and humor taught me how to persist amid paradox and how to appreciate the wonderful complexities of our Doha lives. I hope I have done you justice.

And last but never least, to my sassy, smart, funny, loving kids: Hank, Jack, and Hannah. Thank you for engaging in debates about rhetoric, for being patient with times when I was gone for weeks at a time for graduate school and professional development, and for giving me the generous space to grow into this life. I love you.

# Preface

اللي بده يعمل جمال لازم يعلي باب داره

*Who wants to be a camel rider must raise the door of his house.*
—Arab Proverb

In the bright sun and heavy heat of late June 2010, we embarked[1] on an expatriate experience in the Middle East. We are a family of five: three children—then ages four, nine, and twelve—my partner, and me. We come from a long line of Texans and Americans, tracing our ancestry back to the earliest colonialists, and we are from modest families of ranchers, farmers, and homegrown businesses. At the time, my partner and I worked for a state university, he as a development officer and I as a faculty member. We had limited international travel experience but had never lived outside of our home state. Our children had been raised in a rural town of less than three thousand people, and most of our friends had not heard of Qatar. To be honest, I had not heard of Qatar before our university opened a branch campus there in 2009. Those friends and family who had heard of it knew little more than that it is in the Middle East. In earnest curiosity, one friend asked me if Qataris ride camels to work. Since then, I have been asked if Texans ride horses to work. A strange parity exists. As we prepared to depart, any mention we made of our plans to live in the Arab and Islamic nation usually was met with looks of bewilderment. A few friends were supportive ("You're

---

1. Because my study is situated in a particular time (2010–2016), I use past-tense verbs when talking about past experiences. When quoting a participant, I use the tense used in their interviews (generally present tense). The awkwardness of shifting verb tenses throughout reinforces the liminal and highly contextualized nature of this study.

going to learn so much!"); others were indignant ("Why would you want to do *that* to yourselves and your children?"). Responses at work were similar. We were headed seemingly a world away, not only in time zones but also in culture, religion, and politics.

Learning to live as a guest in the Middle East, as the Arab proverb above proclaims, indeed required raising my doors, my ways of viewing, interacting with, and of making sense of daily life.[2] My perceptions of "normal" and "comfortable" would be shifted sometimes in quiet ways but other times through loud disruptions. As a faculty member at a USAmerican university's international branch campus, I had privileged access to conversations with Qatari and international students, so I had a special insider status for exploring the hybrid intercultural worlds of the branch campus and the state. Movement within and across new places and spaces provoked transformative shifts as I struggled to make sense of a new "here" in terms of my previous home "there." Then when traveling back to the USA to visit, the vertigo of reframing my "here" back at home in terms of my expat life "there" would start again.

"Tell me what it's like . . . ": this frequently heard phrase was the specific catalyst for my research. Soon after my expatriate days began and even now, years after it ended, people ask me to tell them "what it's like" to live and work in the Arabian Gulf. The phrase invites troped storytelling because the *like* invites comparisons ("like Houston with dust!") based on concepts relatable and relationships interpretable to the hearer or receiver. The assumption is that the situation or experience is so *unlike* anything the listener has experienced that a direct telling ("what it *is*") is not feasible. Always tainting the conversation is the USAmerican media's harsh and stereotypical portrayals of the homogenized "Arab world" or "Middle East."

This project also grew out of a curiosity, about myself and others like me and what we consciously and unconsciously relate when we tell "what it's like." The descriptions, comparisons, and stories we tell here—as a collective of white, USAmerican women living and working in Qatar—form narratives, and those narratives have significant rhetorical consequences. They not only influence how the location and experiences are portrayed; they also set terms for how expatriates

---

2. Credit goes to Primrose Arnander and Ashkhain Skipwith for the sayings here and at the start of chapter 5. Thank you to Khadija ElCadi for her help writing them in Arabic.

perceive ourselves and for what behaviors and beliefs constitute community belonging. Telling stories about "what it's like" is a political act, revealing how the individual sees her own positioning, commenting on how USAmerican communities abroad think and behave, and contrasting (and/or complementing) the stereotypical media narrative. Intrigued by stories I heard other expats tell and by stories that flew out of my own mouth when others asked me to tell them what it was like to live in the Middle East, I decided to formally research everyday conversational storytelling as a community-making activity. Although the project began in the workplace, it quickly transcended those bounds to encompass the broader "narrative lifeworld" (A. Gross) rising up as our stories converged.

Although my white USAmerican expatriate colleagues and I were not aware of it in daily conversation, study of our storytelling revealed that we lived within a series of dissonance-producing paradoxes, where two opposing conditions simultaneously existed, trapping us in uncertainties with no clear way forward. But also emerging from our stories were insights into unexpected sources of agency resulting from that same paradoxical positioning, as well as an intense and sustained learning about the implications of being white, being USAmerican, being women, and being white USAmerican women in transnational spaces. My status as an insider to the expatriate community as well as an outsider to the host community certainly shaped my role and perspectives on this project. My choice of feminist lens for interpretation is no accident either: as I both appreciated the privileges and persisted through the challenges of daily life, I could not deny that feminism's core concerns of gender, power, and justice were undeniably central to being an expat in Qatar.

## White, USAmerican, Woman

This book does not center on Qatari or Arab people. I do not pretend to be an expert in gender or anything else *within* Qatari society and do not want to speak for and/or (mis)represent a group of people— particularly Arab and Islamic women—that has been so persistently misrepresented and silenced. Instead, my inquiry is grounded in the storytelling of a group of *outsiders* living in the Qatari scene, a group whose general identity and positionality I shared: white, USAmerican women. Rather than entering a foreign space and pondering the difference of Others, this project narrates how entering a foreign space led to a re-examination of our individual and collective selves.

*White USAmerican woman*: each of these identity signifiers is a trope, a product of social construction and performance. *Woman* is used in a cisgender stereotypical way, creating an obviously flawed gender binary of female/male, an admittedly false oversimplification. *Whiteness* is a complex concept associated with unearned privilege, bias, and potential supremacist attitudes. In transnational spaces, colorism is alive and well, making whiteness just as problematic as it is in the USA, perhaps more so. While I recognize the limitations of these tropes, this project is about women who identify with them. When asked if being an expatriate impacted their identities as women and as white people, all participants accepted those categories of identity. The *USAmerican* trope engages stereotypes of the driven, innovative, individualistic, risk-taking, confident patriot represented in the international media.[3] Even if discussion of being USAmerican inspired complicated reflections and storytelling, all of my participants and I readily identified with it as well.

The white, USAmerican woman identity is intersecting, yet in contrast to the interlocking oppressions addressed by Kimberlé Crenshaw's intersectionality, the identity foregrounded here is often associated with layered privilege. Whereas intersectional critique attends to marginalization and injustice, our expatriate combination of USAmerican passport, light skin, and female gender presentation often opened doors and created opportunities grounded in transnational white privilege. It did so because, as Cheryl Glenn affirms, "identity conditions rhetorical relationships" (*Rhetorical Feminism* 29). At the same time, however,

---

3. Barak Obama was President of the USA during the entirety of my stay in Qatar. In fact, the first few months of our time in the country included frequent smiles, thumbs up, and cheers for "Obama!" when store clerks or other daily interactions included conversations about where we were from. During the spring 2016 semester, as I taught my final courses and as the presidential race was heating up, the tone had begun to shift. My students began asking me why some Americans hated them, why they would be banned from visiting a country they felt a kinship to through their time at the USAmerican branch campus. I listened to their worries, tried to unpack the political situation in the USA, and shared their misgivings. If my study had taken place later in time, following that 2016 election and in the proceeding years as the world's views of the USA shifted, expatriate experiences and storytelling certainly would have reflected that change in how others perceive USAmericans.

our layered identities also created barriers by marking its bearers as outsiders (and sometimes as an inferior). Experiencing simultaneous unearned advantage and disadvantage, along with the uncertainty of expatriate life in general, proved transformative in positive ways. By choosing to focus on the experiences of those acting from this identity intersection, I acknowledge that I am also strategically essentializing my participants and myself as members of the group. Patricia Hill Collins and Sirma Bilge address the critique of essentializing (124–25) and turn to Gayatri Spivak's strategic essentialism as a means of adapting identity to context and as "an important political tactic" (133). In other words, our gendered and racialized identities were bound up in our daily experiences and practices because our identities were irrefutably at the forefront of everything we did. We could not separate our strategies and tactics from our positioning as privileged outsiders.

## ACKNOWLEDGING AND STUDYING PRIVILEGE

Any inquiry into transnational performances and relationships must acknowledge the world-wide privilege assigned to being Western, a label typically conflated with being white. White expatriate women certainly carried a "knapsack of special provisions" in Qatar, but it differed from Peggy McIntosh's description in that it was not "weightless" ("White Privilege: Unpacking"). Stark socio-economic stratification among various national and labor groups was part of daily life. The "golden ghettos" of Western expatriate life formed bubbles of ease (and entitlement) around us that would have made for a blissful, willful ignorance. However, because I had been invited to participate in the building of Qatar, I felt an "ethical imperative to study whiteness (1) as [a transnational] racial category that marks some people's bodies and (2) as [an international] cultural code that socializes all people's bodies" (Kennedy, Middleton, and Ratcliffe 365). Whiteness is a rhetorical and relational force. It is rhetorical because it is suasive through symbolic systems that advantage it over other external identity markers, and it is relational because it bonds some people together as insiders and/or advantaged while simultaneously marking others as outsiders and/or disadvantaged. As a relational force, whiteness pushes and pulls in the creation of policies, laws, and norms.

Other identity markers are assumed and not overtly addressed here. My participants and I did not identify in ourselves any neurological, physical, or psychological differences at the time of the study. As far as I understood, we shared similar socio-economic statuses as well. Therefore, the focus of this project by necessity raises as many questions as it seeks to answer. USAmerican women of color, women of other national or ethnic identities, folx of different gender identities and sexual orientations, people with visible and/or invisible disabilities, and others would likely experience Qatar differently than my participants and I did.[4]

A glaringly important question lingers as I write: Why do we need yet another text about white women? I readily admit that writings by women of color, as well as by people of different gender and embodied identities, deserve much more space at the table. Therefore, I write with a strong dose of that reality and humility. What I offer in my own defense, however, is that in this contemporary context, white US-American women in professional roles are finally getting opportunities to take on transnational assignments. Even just twenty years ago, the vast majority of expatriates were white males, as women were not seen as prepared for the challenges of international assignments and were assumed to be less valued by international stakeholders. The following chapters also offer a narrative of coming to awareness, of unlearning and relearning, and of accountability by women who did not identify themselves as feminist and who did not have social justice agendas. They were neither activists nor academics but were everyday women striving to function in the world.

Thinking about how my interviewees and I—as representatives of one group of everyday (white, middle-class, USAmerican women) rhetors—grew to understand forces of politics and power perhaps can help us, as scholars of rhetoric and feminism, to locate more strategies for building more inclusive worlds and to find better ways of framing our challenges and sharing what Glenn identifies as our "rhetorical feminist tactics" (*Rhetorical Feminism*).

## EXTENDING RHETORICAL FEMINIST THEORY

Set in women's work and social spaces, this project highlights lived experiences and unpacks how overlapping identities—including gender,

---

4. Ashley Butterfield's first-hand account provides a useful counternarrative of what it's like to be a USAmerican Black woman traveling in similar spaces (Mohan).

race,[5] nationality, and professional status—create specific rhetorical positioning associated with privileges and disadvantages. Although many people identify feminism through its "loud acts of refusal and rebellion," this study is more about "the quiet ways we might have of not holding onto things that diminish us" (Ahmed, *Living* 1) and about how being displaced makes "everything into something that is questionable" (2). Although I identify as a feminist, most of my participants did not because they associated being feminist with "making people feel bad about their desires and investments" (2). Despite their nonidentification, however, their activities, stories, and reflections had a strong collective feminist twist. Although they denied affiliating themselves with the label, their actions revealed a collective—though individually designed—set of feminist practices filled "with hope, with energy" (1).

Focusing on contemporary, everyday women moves this study out of the literary, media, and archival realms where studies of feminist rhetorics have previously flourished. For some readers, this study will be unconventional, but I argue that it only extends previous compelling work by reframing what appear to be the mundane aspects of modern daily life as sources of feminist and rhetorical discovery.

Ultimately, what surfaces is a transnational application and extension of Glenn's "rhetorical feminism." In *Rhetorical Feminism and This Thing Called Hope*, Glenn differentiates between "feminist rhetoric" and "rhetorical feminism." Feminist rhetoric is "a set of long-established practices that advocates a political position of rights and responsibilities that certainly includes the equality of women and Others" (3). It engages Western rhetorical concepts—audiences, purpose, exigence, argument, and appeals—yet expands to acknowledge that rhetoric is embodied, works in public and private spheres, and has a wide range of mechanisms including listening and silence. Beyond analysis and advice concerning the tools feminists use to get things done, "rhetorical feminism is a tactic (actually a set of tactics)—a theoretical stance—that is responsive to the ideology that is feminism and to the key strat-

---

5. By "race," I mean the social construction (rather than any biological distinction) of groups based on outward phenotypic markers. Although being "white" is not technically a race, "whiteness" as a racial construct clearly assigns hierarchies to different people based on how they look. Race is a shifting and "slippery" term (Ratcliffe, *Rhetorical Listening* 14–16) that links to assumptions of difference.

egy that is feminist rhetoric" (4). Rhetorical feminist tactics emphasize "a constant state of response, reassessment, and self-correction" as they reject and resist the traditional masculinist singularity of the Western rhetorical tradition (4). As Ahmed writes, "To live a feminist life is to make everything into something that is questionable" (*Living* 2).

Glenn's rhetorical feminism motivates us to re-view and re-configure our shared tactics for being in the world and for getting things done as rhetorical agents. As Ahmed writes, "To build feminist dwellings, we need to dismantle what has already been assembled; we need to ask what it is we are against, what it is we are for . . ." (*Living* 2). In other words, "Feminism is DIY: a form of self-assembly" (27). As a do-it-yourself project of creating and claiming our spaces, rhetorical feminism re-locates persuasion in dialogue (and storytelling) rather than in the power of the individual speaker over his passive audience and reconceives of the artistic appeals as "a reshaped logos based on dialogue and understanding, a reshaped ethos rooted in experience, and a reshaped pathos that values emotion" (Glenn, *Rhetorical Feminism* 4). Rhetorical feminism provides the tactics that operationalize the feminist rhetorical strategies thus promoting the goals of feminist ideology.

Drawing theory from everyday life practices, Ahmed paints a portrait of feminism at work in mundane locations such as university committee meetings and family dinner tables. Her meditation is a strategic contemplation that describes the becoming of a feminist. That becoming begins with a re-awakening, a process of unlearning and relearning: "To become a feminist is to stay a student" (Ahmed, *Living* 11). The process continues via recognition of undeniable inequities previously ignored: we become "even more conscious of the world in this process of becoming conscious of injustices because we had been taught to overlook so much" (31). Ahmed's "feminist becoming" is a process of developing willfulness in the face of systematic restraint and experiencing an estranging from what was once comfortable, in order to perceive and be in the world anew.

My participants' stories reveal them to be in an Ahmed-style process of becoming feminist, a process based not on explicit intent but instead resulting from living in patriarchal spaces paradoxically both privileged and oppressive. Becoming feminist was a result of confronting that privilege while simultaneously resisting oppression. Located in complicated and sometimes risky transnational scenes, my participants and I found "other [feminist] ways of living in [our bodies]" (Ahmed,

*Living* 30). Those ways of living were not the overtly willful and disruptive ways of Ahmed's killjoy. In contrast, we developed quiet and sometimes subversive rhetorical feminist tactics to resist hegemonic forces and reshape what we recognized as hopeful and possible in our daily lives. Our tactics included listening in complex ways, engaging in strategic silences, and silencing ourselves, as well as micro-level acts of resistance located under the radar of the host country's oppressive systems. Not all of these tactics were successful or ideal, however, and reflection (another rhetorical feminist tactic) in the upcoming chapters will address those tensions.

## STRUCTURE AND OVERVIEW

The upcoming introductory chapter provides additional feminist and rhetorical framing to support the remainder of the book. In it, I argue that this book's central concerns—paradox and sensemaking— are rhetorical feminist terms as well as feminist rhetorical practices. Further rhetorical feminist grounding is established via Sara Ahmed's *Living a Feminist Life* and Glenn's *Rhetorical Feminism and This Thing Called Hope.* At the conclusion of the introduction, I review my data collection and analytical methods in preparation for the interpretive work that makes up the rest of the text.

Chapter 1 sets the scene as the foundational substance affecting all other aspects of expatriate life. Qatar and the Western university branch campus are examined as locations both traditional and modern, serving both host and home authorities, set in idealistic and realistic terms, where the private blends into the public. However, rather than accepting the scene as conflicted and confusing, expat women recast it in rhetorical feminist terms as a space of potential learning, creative thinking, and professional growth. The paradoxical scenes and culturally complex locations in which we re-established our footing proved alchemical sites where our understanding of how to live *and* resist living in a foreign space was transformed.

Moving from scene to agent, chapter 2 tacks in to focus more narrowly on stories of expatriate women as paradoxically hypervisible and invisible due to externally ascribed gender and white/Western identities. In feminist terms, this chapter inspires questions about the power and vulnerability of the agent being visibly present, especially when the scene is complicated by hegemonic whiteness and intercultural relationality. Out of these stories sprouts a connection between Rosemarie Garland-Thomson's generative staring and Krista Ratcliffe's rhetorical listening. As an alternative mode of rhetorical feminist interaction, the "transnational stare" offers opportunities to confront the injustices of globalization and reassess complicity in the system.

Chapter 3 argues that movement itself is a primary form of agency for white USAmerican expatriate women living and working in Qatar. Agency is located in crossing literal and intercultural borders, learning to navigate complex transnational spaces, and a growing concern over justice as a "right." These coalesce to reveal yet another paradox of transnational life: being both freed and restrained. Additional paradoxes of being permanently temporary, of being located amid both the familiar and the unfamiliar, and of living in certain uncertainty drive broader perceptions of being simultaneously empowered and disempowered.

Chapter 4 tacks out to read across expatriate women's stories and by attending more carefully to their intentional and unintentional metaphoric language and to the broader narrative that emerged. Previous work on expatriate life draws close parallels to Joseph Campbell's heroic monomyth, and this chapter demonstrates points of alignment and departure for white USAmerican expatriate women in Qatar. Proceeding beyond that narrative, this chapter next reveals what participants experience when they engage in one of the inherent flows of transnational life, temporarily returning to visit their families and friends in the USA. Rather than successfully bringing home the transformative lessons learned from living abroad, expat women are met with and engage in strategic silences that undermine their roles as rhetors and lead to a disillusioning with their home communities. The paradoxical positioning here is that participants keenly felt the strain of simultaneous belonging and estranging.

Chapter 5 concludes the project with both a closing and an opening. It draws to a conclusion by proposing a central rhetorical feminist tactic emerging from living in paradoxical spaces that appear on first glance to create Gordian knots of immobility. Rather than resign themselves to that complexity or retreat into their bubbles of privilege, project participants pursued a different form of agency that leveraged their (in)visibility and was feasible considering their power(lessness). That tactic is dubbed micro*praxis*, as the reparative inverse of microaggression, and is the practice of finding small, often invisible ways of acting within overlapping constraints. Much more than "random acts of kindness," micropraxis is a rhetorical feminist tactic because it directly resists or subverts the unjust systems that create social and economic disparity. One person's act of justice may be small, but the power of micropraxis is in its aggregate form, as it spreads through feminist alliances and potentially grows from a molehill into a mountain.

# Introduction

> We tell ourselves stories in order to live. . . . We inter-
> pret what we see, select the most workable of the multiple
> choices. We live entirely, especially if we are writers, by the
> imposition of a narrative line upon disparate images, by
> the "ideas" with which we have learned to freeze the shift-
> ing phantasmagoria which is our actual experience. . . .
>
> Or at least we do for a while. I am talking here about a
> time when I began to doubt the premises of all the stories
> I had ever told myself, a common condition but one I
> found troubling.
>
> —Joan Didion

We are made of stories. Woven together, they construct our
lifeworlds. Therefore, the rhetorical impact and consequences of our storytelling cannot be underestimated. Individual stories—sometimes fully formed and sometimes incomplete,
mere hints at happenings—circulate within communities, and through
their energy, we are enveloped and implicated in the rhetoric of that
community. Through individual stories and their emergent narratives,
we are socialized into shared values, norms, and attitudes converging
to create the "common sense" practices of the community. We belong
to the community because we use the strategies and tactics accepted
by the community and learned through its storytelling. Usually, our
assimilation is unconscious, particularly if we stay in the communities
where we were raised or if we relocate to places with rather similar
narratives and standards. In contrast, relocating into highly unfamiliar spaces can disrupt our previous sensemaking, a process sometimes
called "culture shock." What was natural or common sensical for us as

insiders becomes odd, distorted, or confusing when we are outsiders. Our old narratives fail us, requiring us to develop new narratives out of the stories of our new location. Changes in our rhetorical scenes, while potentially discombobulating, offer rich opportunity for learning to (re)evaluate and adapt as rhetors.

The beginning of Joan Didion's epigraph is used often to argue the importance of narrative and storytelling, but most of the time, those quoting her do not continue on to her revelation that sensemaking had become uncertainty. Reflecting over the USAmerican social landscape, Didion's old stories failed her during the turbulence of the 1960s and 1970s. Shifting contexts, their consequential disruption of individual and group positionings, and failing stories can indeed be troubling. But they can be productive as well, as the women's and civil rights movements of Didion's time were and still aim to be. Most of our daily habits avoid the discomforting upheaval of change. We shield ourselves in our social, media, and social media bubbles. Our webs of relations, including family, friends, and colleagues, soothe our very human need to belong, to be insiders to sets of overlapping and usually complementary circles. Estrangement and displacement are scary and painful, so we avoid them. Even the opportunity and excitement associated with something as mundane as a new job is accompanied by anxiety over fitting in, finding like minds, and adjusting to new norms.

However, a small subset of USAmericans purposefully and sometimes repeatedly makes the choice of uprooting themselves for life outside of their national homelands. Theirs is a voluntary upheaval. These "expatriates" are not exiled although they may come to feel estranged. They do not experience the dangerous precarity of asylum seekers or the potential political and legal backlash against immigrants, yet the expatriate's acceptance in her host country is not assured either. Expatriates have the privilege of moving across borders to live and work as a means of professional and/or financial opportunity and of learning about the world, but opportunity comes with the risk of growing apart from extended family and home friend groups. Expatriates must learn to adapt quickly to new cultures and situations, and must develop their own set of border-spanning rhetorical strategies for communicating across difference.

In 2010, I became one of these expatriates as I moved with my partner and our three children to the tiny Arab-Islamic nation of Qatar.

Similar to Didion's experience, the premises of many of my previous understandings about being a woman at work and in the world began to dissolve. It felt quite like the literal ground shifting under my feet. As I bumbled through my first year in new scenes, making all sorts of intercultural gaffs and marveling at the generous grace of most everyone around me, I developed new forms—some conscious, some unconscious—of agency or ways of being a rhetor, of recognizing new possibilities (and being confronted by glaring systems of privilege), and of getting things done at work and in general public spaces. As I listened to other expatriate women tell stories about their own experiences and growth, I realized they were sharing implicit lessons in perspective, adaptability, persistence, and unlearning. These valuable lessons, when considered through a feminist lens, offer savvy tactics for rhetorical agency.

Intrigued by this combination of my own learning curve as well as by the storytelling vehicle for forming our communities, my research project emerged, circling around this central question: What do expat women's stories reveal about living as white USAmerican women in complex transnational spaces? The short and easy answer was that they learned new rhetorical feminist tactics for existence and resistance. This project's purpose, therefore, is to demonstrate that living in paradox and moving among perspectives generates new feminist sensemaking and new feminist strategies. Being voluntarily displaced is a privileged as well as compelling source of unlearning and new learning.

The deeper and more nuanced answer is woven from dozens of stories into a narrative that unfolds through this book. Viewed from thirty-five thousand feet, that narrative is an argument made up of these claims: Our worlds are rhetorically constructed of sites, actors, and actions. The scene in which my expat stories were set was a paradox-laden sub*stance* shaping everything else. Within that scene, we actors simultaneously appeared and disappeared. Identities both internally and externally ascribed to us as agents—white, USAmerican, woman, expatriate—defined how we could and could not act. The layered paradoxes created by the scene and by the agents' identities were sources of transformative rethinking resulting directly out of being certain bodies in certain spaces. As we rethought our scenes and identities, movement or mobility emerged as a primary form of individual agency. However, learning where we were free to move or risked being restrained amplified that we were simultaneously powerful and powerless. As we experienced being entangled in a web of paradoxical dead ends, we became willful, creative, and subversive. We leveraged our positioning between home/host and between being free/restrained, visible/invisible, and here/there to develop feminist rhetorical tactics for constrained spaces. What the stories and emergent narrative of expatriate women's lives taught us—and what I hope I can pass on to you, as the reader—was how to spot, design, engage, and critique small, less visible but aggregable and hopeful acts that can defy the systems constraining us and others, a process I call *micropraxis*.

In the remainder of this chapter, I establish the footing for the project by grounding it in rhetorical feminist concepts. The chapter closes with a description of my data-gathering and analytical methods, as well as with a brief introduction to micropraxis.

## EXPATRIATE WOMEN AS PROVOCATIVE RHETORICAL AGENTS

Although defining *rhetoric* remains the uncompleted project of many theorists, my attempt amalgamates those of Kenneth Burke and Lloyd Bitzer. For Burke, rhetoric is a system of symbols for making meaning and persuading via identification, and for Bitzer, it is "a mode of altering reality . . . the creation of discourse which changes reality through the mediation of thought and action" (4). Locating myself at the intersection of relational consubstantiation and mediation of reality, I define rhetoric as the symbols and tools through which we constantly and collaboratively (re)create "reality." Far beyond Quintilian's "good [hu]man speaking well" and much more complicated than Aristotle's "available means of persuasion" applicable "to a particular case," rhetoric conditions when and how we interact, when and how we develop a sense of belonging, and when and how we together create (and alter) reality. Burke's dramatistic method provided a starting framework for this project because the stories and narratives informing my work are first-hand accounts of scenes and actions shared by agents. His pentad—as described in *A Rhetoric of Motives, A Grammar of Motives*, and *Attitudes Toward History*—was useful in pulling apart interrelated aspects of rhetorical activity. Listening to these stories as perspectives on scene, agent, and agency revealed a layered process of sensemaking: scene provided the substance from which transnational activities proceeded, agents' tactics for functioning within that scene were shaped by their ascribed identities, and movement-as-agency emerged as a central feature of transnational life, even as it was marked by paradoxical positioning. Although Burkean concepts were useful for organizing the analysis, they were not sufficient. A feminist rhetorical lens facilitated deeper examination of how power, positionality, and privilege entangled with outsider vulnerability and resulted in creative tactics for living in uncertainty. This feminist rhetorical undergirding is established shortly, but first, I address the particular category of agents at work.

To identify the rhetorical agents in the transnational scene, the term *expatriate* was purposefully chosen as the label for my participants and for me. As a subcategory of migrant workers, expatriates often are assumed to be white collar, male professionals who relocate from home across a border to work in a foreign or host country for an extended period of time. An expatriate is not an immigrant, however, because the expatriate has no inclination and/or no power to transfer citizenship. Although no standard exists for the minimum length of time working abroad, for the purposes of my project, it was a minimum of one year. An expatriate assignment can be self-initiated or appointed by the employer. Multiple factors affect the experience of moving abroad, including the reasons for going, cultural training prior to departure, the language(s) of the host community, the cultural norms of the host community, and the availability of cultural mentors. Although expatriate is a common term for professionals who work abroad, it is also contested because of its associations with power and privilege. In light of this association and of the increasing complexity in migratory work, recent scholarship offers other terms to describe border-crossing employees: international workers, global managers, transnational (knowledge) workers, multi-national workers, diasporics, cosmopolitans, mobile professionals, mobile knowledge workers, sojourners, international assignees, internationally mobile families, and global nomads. Many of these also are contested.

Expatriate also is used here intentionally because expatriates occupy a provocative space of the "outsider-within." In *Black Feminist Thought: Knowledge, Consciousness, and the Politics of Empowerment*, Patricia Hill Collins postulates the outsider-within as a location from which to identify and leverage tensions in systems of domination. This positioning and knowledge-making resulted from the presence of

Black domestic workers laboring in white homes and developing insider knowledge of "perspectives largely obscured from Black men" (Collins 13). Being outsiders-within allowed "racist ideology [to be] demystified" even as Black women domestic workers existed in contradictory and oscillating positions: they paradoxically remained oppressed and exploited even as they were able to generate new "distinctively Black and female forms of resistance" (13). Expatriates in this study were also outsiders-within in the sense that found "insider relationship(s)" useful, yet they also knew that "they could never belong" to the host culture (13). Contrapuntal to Collins's outsiders-within fighting their own oppression, however, expatriates in Qatar came to recognize *their own implicated roles* in the oppression of others. In the face of acknowledging their roles, some retreated into insulating bubbles of privilege, while others became more aware of and sensitive to injustice.

Women are relative newcomers to being expatriate professionals (in contrast to being expatriate stay-at-home wives) and so are less frequently studied.[1] Consequently, the gendered nature of their experiences abroad is erased when they are lumped in with studies of men. What can we learn from the stories of expatriate women in particular? To begin, they offer thought-provoking insights into one kind of gendered world created through globalization. Historical accounts of women in transnational spaces are often told in the contexts of colonization, for example, stories about expatriate wives as influencing their empire-building menfolk. In contrast, contemporary expatriate women are moving into workplaces rather than staying at home. Their presence, even in organizations structured according to gender-inclusive rules, reveals the influence of patriarchal flows. Moving outside

---

1. Nancy Adler is a foundational voice regarding perceptions of and opportunities for women as international managers, and while Yochanan Altman and Sue Shortland take stock of how women's international career opportunities have changed (or not) over the past twenty-five years, their survey is limited to the concerns of human resource management. A body of research—small considering that it is thirty years old—focuses on women, agency, and international management (examples include work by Adler; Caligiuri and Cascio; Fechter; Fischlmayr; Fitzgerald and Howe-Walsh; Hartl; Insch et al.; Janssens et al.). Only a few concern Western female expatriates in the Middle East (Figenshou, Harrison and Michailova, Metcalfe, Schwedler, and Stalker and Maven), only a fraction focus on international education (Richardson and McKenna, Saudelli), and only an occasional article (e.g., Daskalaki) reflects on the shifting perspectives inherent in transnational life.

the workplace into the everyday social spaces—the grocery store, traffic, etc.—unveils additional rhetorical tactics they must use to simply exist in public places and how they must address the tensions over being highly visible yet often erased. Finally, expatriate women's experiences reveal alternative perspectives on power and privilege. They are highly valued professionals often recruited to the host country because of their special expertise; however, their status as visitors can be precarious. Expatriates must navigate systems that make them both powerful and powerless, a process that challenges them to develop rhetorical tactics that can function in those complex flows. Male expatriates also face this challenge, but because of gender discrimination, female expatriates must approach it with more purpose and care.

As Ahmed writes, "We need to tell other feminist stories" (*Living* 4). Because experiences of expatriate women are not centered in previous scholarship, we miss lessons they can teach us from their uniquely positioned locations. Those lessons have a lot to offer in terms of rhetorical complexity.

## Paradoxical Positioning and Sensemaking as Rhetorical Feminist Praxes

Expatriates in transnational spaces are compelling rhetorical agents because they live in paradoxical conditions.[2] Paradox, from the Greek παράδοξο (*para* as "distinct from" and *doxa* as "opinion" or "common sense"), is the presence of two beliefs or conclusions that are, each alone, reasonable but taken together appear contradictory.[3] As word

---

2. As I was puzzling through my stories and analysis, I read Joyce Osland and Asbjorn Osland's "Expatriate Paradoxes and Cultural Involvement." While their work did not direct my analysis, it informed and strengthened certain aspects of it. For example, being freed and constrained, as well as functioning within the competing demands of multiple employers, were common themes where their work reinforced my confidence in my own analysis. Other themes from their article (e.g., "self-identity paradoxes") were not as clearly evident, perhaps because expatriates in Qatar did not have much access into the host spaces.

3. Throughout this project, I use the terms *paradox, contradiction*, and *contradictory states* interchangeably as well as variations of the word *simultaneous* to cue readers to paradoxical situations. Margaret Cuonzo's *Paradox* provides a useful, multidisciplinary survey of paradox as contradictory states and con-

puzzles and objects of philosophical study, interest in and use of paradox (also referred to as *antinomy*) dates back to the earliest surviving records of rational thought, and includes contradictions of logic, math, decision theory, physics, biology, chemistry, linguistics, perception, and politics. Economics has identified a large number of disciplinary paradoxes, including the "paradox of thrift," wherein the more people save money, the less is circulated in the economy, meaning the more a community's financial stability is at risk. Some paradoxes, such the "grain of millet" (in which one falling grain makes no sound but thousands of falling grains make a loud sound—therefore, a thousand silences become a roar), date back to Zeno of Elea (ca. 490—430 BC), a pre-Socratic Greek philosopher who is cited by Aristotle in *Physics*. A resonant modern paradox is the "paradox of tolerance," formulated by Karl Popper in *The Open Society and Its Enemies: Vol. 1 The Age of Plato*. It states that "Unlimited tolerance must lead to a disappearance of tolerance" (226n7). In other words, although tolerance is conceived of as a full openness to the spectrum of ideas, that spectrum can include evils such as white supremacy. In order to combat evils and create a tolerant society, a community must be intolerant of ideologies that constrain tolerance. Paradox is rooted in uncertainty. "Conflicting intuitions" cue cognitive dissonance and trigger making (new) sense of the situation.

Rather than being expressed through logic puzzles or word play, expatriate paradox is a result of an *embodied* repositioning and thus re-viewing of the self (and communities to which the self relates) in new or alternative terms. Rather than seek resolution to living in contradictory states, sustained and conscious positioning *in* paradoxical tensions can be productively leveraged as a site of rhetorical feminist practice. Paradox offers opportunity to engage in Spivak's unlearning or in Didion's doubting. For example, being white USAmerican women in Qatar meant we were paradoxically advantaged/powerful as white Westerners while also disadvantaged/powerless as women. My participants and I could not resolve the paradox because the forces that created it were outside of our control, so our sustained living in that situation and our willingness to remain sensitive to it motivated us to re-evaluate the nature of our privilege and find creative ways to address disadvantages. Paradoxical positioning pushed us to engage in

---

siders how thinking in and through paradoxical puzzles can be a generative source of critical problem solving.

the feminist practice of "standing under" other discourses (Ratcliffe, *Rhetorical Listening* 28) and to experience the "double recognition" of "unlearning our privilege as our loss" (Landry and MacLean 4). We experienced the life of "las nepantleras," finding ourselves and our agencies in "the cracks between worlds" (Anzaldúa, *Light in the Dark* 79). In short, the organized narrative—or logos—within which we had previously (as USAmericans) functioned was disrupted and demanded a new sensemaking.

A singular, authoritative (i.e., masculinist) attitude would have had us choose one perspective and dismiss the other, thus resolving the paradox. Put more bluntly, a masculinist approach would respond with something like this: "Yes, I am powerful and deserved my stature of being a valuable professional that exemplifies USAmerican intelligence and ideals. The fact that I am sometimes disregarded is other people's shortcoming and ultimately meaningless to me." In contrast, a feminist reaction to paradoxical positioning generates reassessment of our assumptions regarding relational positioning, community values, and who "deserves" to be powerful. Rather than a dismissal, a feminist response evokes reflexive re-examination of our Western cultural logics and how other cultural logics also are at work in the transnational space. The jarring disruption of paradox-as-feminist-positioning summons reflection over our accountability to systems that persistently favor certain national and racial/ethnic groups over others. It also motivates new feminist rhetorical tactics for living within (and resisting) similar situations.

As a form of rhetorical feminist critical imagination, inhabiting a paradoxical positioning inspires re-viewing from a liminal location and is a source of inventive, generative thinking and potential new rhetorical feminist tactics. Re-viewing does not require living overseas; we all experience contradictory tensions when moving between locations and identities. For example, a young adult returning home after living independently—working or attending a university—would exist in a paradoxical and liminal space of being simultaneously independent and dependent (as well as adult and child). Upon return from another living situation, home might not still seem like home at all. Women inhabit liminal and paradoxical spaces, for example, working in traditionally male dominated fields. Tensions generated by living and working in a both/and situation can cause Didion-style doubting of the stories we tell ourselves, of the narratives we use to structure and predict our worlds. What do we do when our narratives are disrupted? This brings me to another through-line of feminist and rhetorical grounding in my project: sensemaking.

Sensemaking is a rhetorical theory of social construction, the process by which groups review the bits and pieces—often individual stories—of an event or set of events and rationalize those bits into a narrative framework of "what happened."[4] It is the way we communally express our experiences then use them to predict future situations and know what to do. We make "the unexpected expectable through stories" (Weick 127) via the reciprocal telling and listening.[5] Because it is collaborative, sensemaking implicates us with each other: "Through narrative you formulate your identities by unconsciously locating yourself in social narratives not of your own making" (Anzaldúa, *Light in the Dark* 6). Knowing what to expect and what to do is a process and product of assimilating into a community. Sensemaking is rhetorical because it is based on social symbolic patterns and results in a persuasive argument for what happened (and, therefore, what is likely to happen in the future). For feminists, then, sensemaking evokes the critically reflexive questioning of our assumptions about our roles in what happened, what *really* happened, as well as what it means for us as agents seeking better ways of being, acting, and relating to others in the world.

Feminism itself is a "sense-making process of becoming feminist and navigating a way through a world" (Ahmed, *Living* 20). Reassessing, resisting, and dismantling oppressive narratives and making new sense where old unjust sensibilities exist are the goals of the feminist enterprise. Feminist critique grows out of the cognitive dissonance that comes with awareness of inequality and a drive to interrogate the status

---

4. Sensemaking differs from interpretation, because the latter is understood to be simply a translation of a text for an audience. By comparison, sensemaking is social: it is about "how the text is constructed as well as how it is read. Sensemaking is about authoring as well as reading" (Weick 6–7). Whereas interpretation involves discovery of a meaning believed to be already present, sensemaking is an inventive activity growing out of cognitive dissonance—feelings of uncertainty and discomfort—during which "authoring and interpretation are interwoven" (13).

5. Russell Kirkscey's "From *Homo Narrans* to *Homo Attendens*: A Revision of the Narrative Paradigm" extends Walter Fisher's "Narrative Paradigm" by elevating the role of listener to co-meaning-maker.

quo. Similar to Weick's "parliament of selves" (264), feminists leverage strategically essentialized personas to allow them access to scenes and acts from which they may otherwise be excluded, and sense-re-making is at the center of our work. As Glenn defines rhetorical feminism, it is a process of re-casting how we frame our power as speakers, listeners, and actors through a reclaiming and re-making of what counts as worthy subjects and spaces, of how rhetorical appeals are framed, and of the fundamental goal of rhetoric itself (as collaborative rather than agonistic). As a feminist rhetorical practice, sensemaking engages tacking-in and tacking-out through the oscillation between close/personal and broader/contextual factors. It also is a process and project of circling through time, engaging the *then-that-is-now* (Ratcliffe, *Rhetorical Listening* 107) in order to re-examine our logics. Although sensemaking in its original terms is limited to what is *experienced* rather than contemplated from a stance of what might be (Royster and Kirsch's "strategic contemplation"), feminist sensemaking engages our "critical imagination" as a means of brainstorming—and locating hope in—strategies and tactics for combating inequality. Finally, sensemaking is feminist in its collaborative nature. One authoritative rhetor does not design and deliver the narrative; instead, sense is made through collectively remembering and re-membering what was.

## METHODOLOGY AND METHODS

Jacqueline Jones Royster and Gesa Kirsch's *Feminist Rhetorical Practices* served as my grounding and guiding methodology, by which I mean that their work formed the philosophical and theoretical basis within which the study was designed and proceeded. To enact their "critical imagination," I centered all my inquiry activities in deep listening and open-minded observation, both of myself and others. I also embraced the critical or reflexive stance of Royster and Kirsch's work by persistently reflecting over my own positionality as a white USAmerican woman and as an educator in an international branch campus. The *critical* in my critical imagination practice included the analytical work of weaving together women's stories into narratives, then examining those narratives with a particular eye towards power and privilege. Royster and Kirsch's "strategic contemplation" influenced my processes of meditating on the intersections of Burkean dramatism and feminist theories. Pausing to work in these intersections, rather than adopting a singular theoretical framework and applying it without question, resists the simplicity of a monological perspective and instead embraces feminist multiplicity and complexity.

My project examines "social circulation" of women's narratives less through time, as described in Royster and Kirsch's original work, and more through a process of collaboratively building a "narrative lifeworld" (see A. Gross). Two central questions in my conversational interviews asked participants about stories they *heard* from other expatriate women and what stories they *told* current and potential expatriate women about what it's like to live and work in Qatar. Through the interview process, I tapped into the web and substance of social circulation, and through analysis revealed "how such performances ebb, flow, travel, gain substance and integrity, acquire traction, and not" (23). Finally, this project addresses Royster and Kirsch's "globalizing point of view" that calls for broadening our "locally defined assumptions, values, and expectations regarding how rhetorical performance is constituted and valued" (112). My study is set in transnational spaces through which forces of globalization shape rhetorical situations and agency. But beyond that direct connection to a broadening perspective, I argue that transnational spaces by their very nature open up new ways of thinking about rhetorical performance.

By valuing the experiences of everyday women in international and multicultural settings, we can (re)evaluate how paradoxical positioning and shared sensemaking reveal new rhetorical feminist tactics for consideration. That said, every transnational space and the groups of women operating in it are ultimately unique. Identities, histories, locations, times, and other contexts mean the outcomes of a study like mine cannot be precisely replicated. My hope is that other scholars, after reading about my project, will inquire into the lived experiences of women of different identities in different locations and over different contexts. The great value—again, a function of social circulation—is in becoming attuned to commonalities as well as differences in women's (and humans') experiences.

In my pursuit of a methodology grounded in the deep listening and pondering of feminist rhetorical practices, in the value of storytelling and story sharing, and in the critical consideration of how our daily lives are a process of co-constructing community identity, I engaged three data collection tools or methods: ethnographic observations, auto-ethnographic reflections, and conversational interviews.[6]

## (Auto)Ethnographic Foundations

Ethnographic observations throughout my study were based on six years living and working in Qatar. Therefore, innumerable conversations with students, colleagues, neighbors, shopkeepers, domestic workers, and other Doha residents informed my understandings, contextualization, and rich description for the project. I spent substantive time engaged in Krista Ratcliffe's rhetorical listening within this context. I also wrote in a variety of forms throughout the study, particularly I wrote a private family blog and shorter papers for graduate courses during my PhD coursework. These, and other less formal note-taking and journaling, were sources as I made my observations and as I was immersed in the analytical and interpretive iterations of the project. As an ongoing means of being attuned to my own biases, the points and narratives reported in the analysis chapters were iteratively discussed with participants, colleagues, and acquaintances. Our ongoing discourse persistently tested and triangulated the shared themes and narrative emerging through the interviews and observations.

Because of my own identity—informed in part by being white, cisgender/female, USAmerican, and academic—this project is undoubtedly autoethnographic. Autoethnography, as first-hand observations of the situated participant-researcher, helps address the ethically questionable intrusion and participant vulnerability of intimate ethnography. As a method, autoethnography is reciprocal because it reveals richer detail about the researcher's own positioning, both as a complement to the researcher's more detached reporting on others and as an acknowledgement of the social construction inherent in knowledge-making. Autoethnographic work emerges in here when the interviewees cease to be "they" or "them" and instead become "we" and "us." Although my emphasis is on stories told by the interview participants, I occasionally include events or reflections from my own experiences.

---

6. The duration of the ethnographic work was 2010–2016 but the interviews were completed in mid-2013.

## Interview Participants and Technique

My twelve interview participants and I formed a purposefully homogenized group in external identity: USAmerican, cis-female, white, and "white collar" or "knowledge worker." As a homogenized group, we represent contemporary border-crossing professionals but from a particular positionality. I chose to stop with twelve because clear themes had emerged—I had reached a point of data saturation. Twelve was also a point at which I could still imagine having all their voices present in the manuscript without overwhelming the reader. The resulting narrow participant pool foregrounded how individual and group identity affected expatriate experiences, and my project reveals how our "small stories," the bits and pieces we share informally, coalesced to form a greater narrative lifeworld with implications generally left unexamined amid the rush and priorities of daily life.

All participants were employed within the same USAmerican university branch campus and were recruited via purposeful sampling in light of the gender, national, and racialized identities I sought. I also chose women who worked outside the home because doing so put them in daily interaction with a variety of host-country citizens and foreign nationals. Articles such as Anne-Mieke Fechter's "Gender, Empire, Global Capitalism: Colonial and Corporate Expatriate Wives" and Ann Coles and Katie Walsh's "From 'Trucial State' to 'Postcolonial' City? The Imaginative Geographies of British Expatriates in Dubai" as well as my own experience chatting with stay-at-home expatriate women in Qatar indicated that their experiences differed in terms of scenic influences and sources of agency. Staying within the walls of only one of the branch campuses controlled for complexity regarding institutional policies. For example, learning the nuanced scenic factors of multiple branch campuses would have made the inquiry even more complicated to explain (see discussion of the agreement under "Meeting Home and Host Demands" in chapter 1).

Within my branch campus, however, I was careful to recruit participants who had varied job roles: upper administration, finance, marketing, building operations, technology services, academic support services, student activities, and research administration. Their ages ranged from mid-twenties to early sixties. All but one interviewee grew up and lived in the USAmerican south or southwest before expatriating. Only four had previous experience living outside of the USA: for three, it was as children in military families and for one, it was a multi-month study abroad. Some participants had traveled extensively but others had not. At the time of their interviews, they had lived in Qatar from two to ten years. Six out of twelve were married when they arrived. Five were unmarried, and one arrived single, went back to the US to marry then returned to Qatar. Four of the twelve had children living with them in Qatar, while the others either had grown children or no children.

Across all of the interviews, feminism was only brought up twice, and those two interviewees were indifferent about it. Susan's quotation captures their consensus:

> *I'm not a feminist type person who says women rule because we're women. I've never been like that. Some of my friends are. They'll say they can't wait to have a woman president. I don't care as long as we have a good president. I don't care if they're purple, black, blue, male. I don't care! (laughing) Just do the job. I've never been the type of person that says "because I'm woman, hear me roar."—Susan*

This quotation is representative of the attitude towards feminism in general. If any of the interviewees adopted a feminist mantle, they did not mention it. I purposefully chose women with whom I had not discussed these topics previously, and in fact, had no more than the briefest acquaintance with most of them at the time of the data gathering. Because I worked as a faculty member and had frequent conversations with other faculty members, their voices are represented in the ethnographic threads of the work.

Aligned with my central research question ("What do expat women's stories reveal about living as white USAmerican women in complex transnational spaces?"), my interviews focused on gathering stories. Between May and October 2013, eleven semi-structured discursive interviews were recorded, ranging from fifty-one to ninety-five minutes.[7] I began with the same set of interview questions (see Appendix) but followed the lead of the interviewee when focusing on particular experiences. Conversations were transcribed into 121 single-spaced pages of text. Responses to the twelfth interview were written,

---

7. Approved by the Protection of Human Subjects Committee at Texas Tech University on March 18, 2013, as study #503847 "Experiences and Perceptions of American Women Living and Working in the Arabian Gulf Region."

at the participant's request, but based on the same set of questions as the in-person version.

## Interpretive Processes

Because of my interest in group sensemaking at a broader macro-thematic level, I did not analyze the micro-linguistic level of the interviews. During and after the transcription process, I removed pauses, repetitions, and utterances such as "um." Beyond this general smoothing, none of the wording was changed. I left in a notation of "(laughing)" to clarify general tone; identifying information was deleted and names replaced with pseudonyms. Participants were invited to review and comment on their interview transcripts; seven out of eleven did so, and one suggested a substantive change to protect her anonymity. My own stories are told in first person and are presented as my own.

Transcripts were uploaded into NVivo, and open coding was applied at the thematic level. To identify sensemaking moves, I relied on David Boje's theory of antenarrative, or the *story* preceding any *narrative* was the initial focus: "Story is an account of incidents or events, but narrative comes after and adds 'plot' and 'coherence' to the story line" (1). Therefore, each participant told stories, but reading across participants, a broad narrative of expatriate life became evident. The initial code passes resulted in thirty-four nodes, eighteen of which included commentary by all twelve interviewees. Secondary and tertiary passes resulted in cross-coding where comments related to more than one of the nodes and foregrounded the fully formed stories, tales of incidents that could stand apart from their surrounding commentary and still be coherent. These stories were coded separately using key themes emerging from the transcripts. Five colleagues—four female and one male, all white USAmericans—crosschecked codes. This group included two of the interviewees. I did not seek a particular statistic of cross-coding reliability but instead used others' interpretations reflectively to consider alternative perspectives on the stories' functions and meanings.

One limitation of weaving these stories and other commentary into a narrative is that doing so "stops storytelling in its tracks; it arrests it" (Boje 125), or as Didion says, it "freeze[s] the shifting phantasmagoria which is our actual experience" (11). In other words, vibrant and dynamic lifeworlds inherently lose some of their rich variety by being transformed into a narrative. Like most qualitative research, my project can be reconstructed but not replicated. Asking these same questions of a similar population in Qatar now would yield different answers because the location continues to evolve. For example, the *kafala* system described in Chapter 3 has continued to change. As I noted in the Preface, my study does not pretend to speak for Qatari women or other folks in the country. Asking these same questions to USAmerican Women of Color, to women from other countries, or to people who work in other transnational spaces would yield different stories. Rather than generalizable, this project foregrounds the specificity—and thus the rhetorical complexity—of how scenes and contexts shape rhetorical tactics and agency. Although few readers will have the chance to experience expatriation, transnational education, or life in Gulf Arabia, the patterns of sensemaking in my study can inspire new ways of thinking about how rhetorical feminism and feminist rhetorical practices support movement among complex spaces.

## MICROPRAXIS AS ACTIONABLE EMERGING OUTCOME

As my white USAmerican expatriate women interviewees and I learned to navigate a setting at once both familiar and unfamiliar, as the scope of our international privilege looked us back in the face, and as we came to keenly feel the simultaneous power and vulnerability of our positioning—both literal and symbolic—we developed tactics for existing in paradoxical uncertainty. The process was gradual, happening over the course of months or even years, and a sort of first-hand grounded-theory experience. Mundane daily interactions, as well as the occasional jarring situation, culminated in a shared sensemaking. That shared sensemaking then generated a potentially powerful rhetorical tool for action amid the constraints of paradoxical positioning. That rhetorical feminist tactic is micropraxis. I introduce it briefly here so its development can be traced through the chapters that follow.

Interwoven as a gradually more present thread in the upcoming storytelling and narratives, micro*praxis* materializes as a rhetorical feminist tactic performed through purposeful small acts of respect, relationality, and reciprocity designed to in/visibly acknowledge, re-sist, and/or subvert injustices and narratives of oppression targeted at marginalized people(s). I intend it as a complement to the theory of microaggressions developed by Derald Wing Sue and his associates in psychology and education. Micro*aggressions* are "the brief and commonplace daily verbal, behavioral, and environmental indignities, whether intentional or unintentional, that communicate hostile, derogatory, or negative racial, gender, sexual-orientation, and religious slights and insults to the target person or group" (Sue et al. 271). Similar to the "micro" in microaggressions, the "micro" in micropraxis occurs in brief, commonplace, and daily ways. However, instead of reinforcing injustice and marginalization, micropraxis is concerned with addressing them. In contrast to the often-unintentional nature of microaggressions, micropraxis is mindful and decided, even as it negotiates the actor's own blend of privileged and precarious positioning.

Although its presence was found in the threads of storytelling, micropraxis binds together other motivating elements of this project. It is a tactic related to paradoxical positioning, where agents felt trapped—but learned to resist feeling trapped—in conflicting statuses. Rather than freezing in the complicated spaces of hypervisibility/invisibility, freedom/restraint, belonging/estranging, power/vulnerability, certainty/uncertainty, and more, my participants sought out small-scale agency. As discussion of these small outlets emerged, it became part of our community sensemaking about lives abroad and in complex spaces. Acts of micropraxis were possible because of white USAmerican women's identity and positioning, their privileged outsider-within status and techniques for navigating their vulnerability. Micropraxis is a rhetorical feminist tactic as it grows out of a theoretical stance concerned with systems of inequity, responsively reassesses daily situations, and is a form of willfulness in the face of restraint. Finally, micropraxis is a feminist rhetorical practice because it engages critical imagination on the fly and can become more habitual through the social circulation of community storytelling.

This short introduction to micropraxis is a spoiler intended to mark our landing point even before we take off. By having a bit of insight into our route, you might notice details in the upcoming stories that point to factors leading to its emergence as well as reinforce, contradict, and further complicate the practice. Chapter 5 fully explores and troubles this tactic, ultimately proposing it—call-to-action style—as an addition to our rhetorical feminist toolkits. But to get to that destination, we must begin by expatriating to new spaces and places of familiarity and dislocation. The next chapter takes us there.

# 1 Traditional and Modern

*Working for two masters has its stresses. —Patricia*

Imagine yourself in a job interview. After years of working at the flagship campus of a large public university, you've flown nine time zones away from home for an on-site visit to its international branch location. The idea of moving across the globe is exciting, but you're a bit discombobulated by the jet lag and the unexpected mix of newness and sameness of your surroundings. Your ears buzz as they are filled with many languages you've never heard, yet English is common enough that you don't need a translator. You've toured the beautiful state-of-the-art campus building (much nicer than your 1970s moldy concrete block at the flagship!), seen departments and job titles echoing those of your home campus, and met an incredibly diverse staff and faculty.[1] Now you're at lunch with a group of USAmerican expatriate women who have

---

1. At the time of this study, our international branch campus (IBC) employed approximately four hundred employees, including approximately ninety faculty and administrators, 130 researcher and graduate research assistants, and 170 staff members. Except for a few Qatari nationals employed by the branch, all employees were sponsored by Qatar Foundation as temporary residents. According to our human resources office, the most common countries represented by our IBC's faculty, staff, and researchers were the USA, India, Egypt, Pakistan, and China; however, the branch was more diverse than that. On a daily basis, I worked with folks from New Zealand, the Philippines, Kenya, Nepal, the United Arab Emirates, Saudi Arabia, Iran, Iraq, Syria, Lebanon, Jordan, Palestine, Yemen, Oman, and of course, Qatar. Many of my colleagues were of blended or multiple national and/or ethnic identities (e.g., Iranian-American, Jordanian-Palestinian, Lebanese-Canadian, Emirati-Qatari). Gender ratios varied according to role. Only about twenty percent of the faculty were women, disproportionately represented in the liberal arts and in teach-

worked at the branch campus for a while. The obvious unspoken goal of this meal is to determine if you're a good fit for the opening and if the opening is a good fit for you. They ask what you'd like to know about the branch and your potential role there, and you ask them to tell you what it's like to work at an international location of your USAmerican university.

Susan kicks off the conversation by saying, "You don't just do one thing here. You wear all hats at times. Extra duties get assigned to you that you don't expect." You ask Susan if those extra duties are a good or bad aspect of the work, and she replies that it's a mixed bag. There's the stress of the extra work and pressure but also opportunity to grow your skills and qualifications.

Melissa chimes in: "I think the difference is that you're not working over here the same way you worked before at the home campus in the USA. So you're not only doing different things but you're also having to figure out ways to get things done in a system that isn't used to just normal business practices."

In response, Lisa laughs, commenting that the campus has been built on adaptation. Compared to the heavy and rigid bureaucracy of the US campus, "normal business practices" were out the window at the branch. She reflects on her early years in Qatar, recalling "back then, we were flying by the seat of our pants in a lot of situations. There was no precedent for things, so you would just make it up." Others around the table chuckle knowingly.

Emily sighs with a smile. She is pragmatic and wants you to make the right decision about whether or not to take the job: "If you're very strict and want things done a certain way, then I don't recommend you come here. The first thing to understand is that things here happen when they happen. People you work with may or may not have the things you want when you want them, and people may or may not understand what you're saying."

A look of concern passes over Susan's face—the two of you have hit it off in prior sections of the interview, and she doesn't want you to be dissuaded from seriously considering a likely job offer. She adds in a positive tone, "All of the sudden you have a problem you've never seen and you have to think outside the box and get it done."

---

ing—as opposed to research—positions. By comparison, about forty percent of the staff were female.

You press Susan for an example, and she continues, "One of the first big problems I inherited here was with the sewer backing up into the building's basement, to the point of being three inches deep every time we had a rain event. Little things like that you would just never see, and all the sudden out of the blue you're dealing with something like that or with people detained at the airport [immigration desk] or whatever the issues are. Whether it's an individual's personality or a problem. I just can't imagine being in the United States and back in that working world, that there's anything that's going to come up that I haven't seen here."

Noting the look of surprise on your face as you ponder sewage back-ups and airport detentions, Susan quickly adds, "I think that as women who juggle careers and being a mom and being a wife, we're really good at that problem solving anyway. Sometimes we just don't see how good we are at it until we're put into a position like this and it's outside of the norm."

The composite conversation constructed above begins to reveal the complexities of working in a hybrid scene of institutional cultures and practices. [2, 3] It was "not normal" even for seasoned professionals, required consistent adaptation, and meant daily struggles regarding cross-cultural communication and misunderstandings. While the conversation regards employment at the branch campus, it was further complicated by being set in the state of Qatar and its only metropolitan area (Doha) during the 2010–2016 time period. Qatar itself was rapidly developing during my study, so its social and political sands were shifting. Within that larger context, the international branch campus was a contested space respon sive to these shifts, too. I joined the branch just as it was celebrating its tenth anniversary, so it was somewhat established but still tumultuous as it continued its institutional maturing. Stories about what it's like to live

---

2. The conversation approach used here is inspired by Aja Martinez's "counterstory" and further informed by Rebecca Willis's article on composite narratives. All the quoted comments in this constructed conversation (a rhetorical act of Royster and Kirsch's "critical imagination") are verbatim utterances from my participants. Although they are taken out of their particular interview contexts, I carefully used the quotations in a way that sustains their original intentions and meanings.

3. Throughout this chapter, scenic terms—including scene as "substance" and "container"—hearken back to Burkean theory. See *A Grammar of Motives* and *A Rhetoric of Motives*.

and work in those fluid scenes reveal them to be chaotic and frustrating even as they satisfyingly create opportunity for transformative growth.

*Transnationalism* I define as the movement of people, relationships, and communication across borders.[4] It is an aspect of globalization or international economic systems of trade, investment, and consumption across geographical and political borders. Globalization is about laws, international agreements, and the importing/exporting of goods and services, while transnationalism is about movements of people. Transnational, although often set in terms of bounded geospatial locations (nations), broadly refers to flows of knowing, being, and acting (Fernandez 104–105). Here, I refer not only to the hybridity occurring where multiple cultures and practices overlap but also to movement within and through those spaces as a constant circulation. For example, my nascent awareness of my positioning within the branch campus as well as within the larger Qatar location emerged *not* just as a function of my time in Qatar but as a product of me leaving and returning to Qatar, of me circulating between and among scenes. Movement triggered realizations about how I functioned and was perceived within those varying scenes and positionalities. In short, the revelatory value of transnational existence is found in these inter-scenic movements themselves and the realities they reveal.[5] Stories and comments featuring oscillation—a both/

---

4. Transnationalism focuses on human implications of globalization. M. Jacqui Alexander and Chandra Talpade Mohanty consider these terms in more depth and from a perspective of feminist praxis in their chapter, "Cartographies of Knowledge and Power: Transnational Feminisms as Radical Praxis."

5. Although a (Western) feminist study set in transnational spaces, my project does not make claims to being grounded in "transnational feminism" itself due to the potentially colonial overtones of the international branch campus project that brought my colleagues and me to Doha. Transnational feminism critiques the hegemonic capitalism of globalization along with the imperialist and white supremacist implications entangled with it. Transnational feminism also proceeds from an intersectional methodology, which I acknowledge cannot be a central source of critique here. That said, I do circle around issues cogent to transnational feminism, including positionality, gender, power, contemporary colonialism, and the impacts of globalized context. Putting my expat stories in conversation with other transnational feminist perspectives would yield additional fertile ground for analysis and (un)learning. For a concise yet comprehensive definition of transnational feminism, see Anneeth Kaur Hundle, Ioana Szeman, and Joanna Pares Hoare's "What Is the Transnational in Transnational Feminist Research?" in *Feminist Review*.

and perspective or lenticularity (see especially chapter 4)—grow out of the transnational setting, as do the very paradoxes featured in this and the following chapters.

Navigated via a feminist mindset, the adaptation and innovation demanded by our liminal, transnational scenes generated development of rhetorical feminist tactics. This chapter describes the paradoxical national and local contexts within which expatriate women's experiences unfolded, beginning in the macro-scene of Qatar then moving into the micro-scene of the branch campus.

## A Paradoxical State of Conservative Traditionalism and Progressive Modernism

> *When you fly into the airport and you drive down the corniche and you see all the big buildings and you think, "It's really modern! It's really cool!" and then you start peeling away a little bit and you see the conservative side of it. . . . You pick away at things and you start to see how the society is. I mean, I truly believe this, that it's two steps forward and one step back. They're fighting for who they want to be, and that's going to take probably twenty years to figure out, that next generation, right? But right now, a lot of this is going on internally for them, and the growth here. So as many things, it's shiny and pretty on the outside but you know you get inside and it's like that pretty apple. You bite into it, and sometimes it's really good over here and a little bit of a bruise over there. But it's not all good or all bad. It just is. —Susan*

As Susan's metaphoric apple illustrates, Qatar was a wonderfully contradictory place and space where tribal heritage[6] and modern vision converged and co-existed. Bordered by Saudi Arabia to the southwest and otherwise surrounded on the other sides by the Arabian Gulf, it is tiny in size but significant in resources. During the time of my study, its leadership aggressively pursued a balance between holding onto the customs of an indigenous community identity even as it modernized its economic,

---

6. Sultan Al-Qassemi's "Tribalism in the Arabian Peninsula: It Is a Family Affair" provides a thought-provoking commentary of the limits of modernizing while maintaining tribal-based approaches to the public sphere. Qassemi is an Emirati and so is writing from an insider perspective to an audience that includes other Gulf citizens.

educational, and institutional systems. The reasons for a carefully negotiated approach to its own identity were multiple, but two primary drivers
were its relatively short history of being completely independent and its
recent emergence of significant wealth. History, collective memory, and
contemporary resources are primary aggregates in a scenic foundation.

Established on a desert landscape sparsely populated by traders and
Bedouin tribes, Qatar's economy originally depended on fishing, pearl-
ing, and livestock (camels and goats). However, after emerging from
under British protection and becoming fully independent in 1971,
Qatar's situation was changed dramatically by two crucial events: discovery of petroleum reserves and a change of leadership.[7] Oil and gas
exports began in the mid-twentieth century, but the income off those
reserves was not managed well and so did little to change the lives of
average Qatari citizens.[8] In 1995, however, Sheikh Hamad bin Khalifa
Al-Thani, took over the government in a bloodless coup. From 1995 to
2013, Sheikh Hamad and one of his three wives, Sheikha Moza bint
Nasser (hereafter, Sheikha Moza), led the country's rapid modernization
movement. Expatriate feelings regarding Sheikh Hamad and Sheikha
Moza were persistently positive. Patricia, who had been in the country
a decade, said she tried to explain to her family back in the USA that
Qatar's "Emir is a benevolent dictator. That he is forward-thinking, and
reasonable. That he has at the forefront of his mind, the best interest of
the citizens and expats in his country. That he is not a greedy, uncaring,
thug." Patricia described Sheikha Moza as "a dominating force with real
power and vision" and my closest faculty friends at the branch campus—
who were declared feminists—agreed. What was viewed from the US as
a rather conservative country was, experienced from the inside, surprisingly progressive.

Fueled by income from Qatar's massive petroleum reserves, the state
experienced an astounding transformation from the late twentieth century into current times. Qatar's capital city Doha (*ad-Dawha*) and its
surrounding municipalities were the location of approximately ninety
percent of the country's population. In the fifteen years between Sheikh

7. For fuller studies of Qatar, some book-length works include book-length
works include Allen J. Fromherz's *Qatar: A Modern History*, Matthew *Gray's
Qatar: Politics and the Challenges of Development*, and Mehran Kamrava's *Qatar: Small State, Big Politics.*

8. See Andrew Rathmell and Kirsten Schulze, "Political Reforms in the Gulf:
The Case of Qatar."

Hamad's ascension and our arrival, a dense downtown, composed of a fascinating array of architectural styles and skyscrapers (Fig. 1), had emerged from the sandy shores of the Gulf. In the face of that growth, however, Qatar's leadership continued to emphasize its commitment to preserving local traditions. The *Qatar National Vision 2030* anchored its dynamic, comprehensive development in religious and national identity: "Despite rapid economic and social gains, as well as political change, Qatar has maintained its cultural and traditional values as an Arab and Islamic nation that considers the family to be the main pillar of society" (1). Emphasis on family was woven into the local social fabric. For example, a patriarchal structure at all levels—national to neighborhood—centered the public sphere in the male-only *majlis* or meeting place.[9] Marriages were still family-arranged, so a Qatari woman's public performance was constantly under scrutiny as a potential mate and/or as a representative of her family. Women and men still adopted local dress styles (see chapter 2), and some public spaces, especially restaurants, still offered gender segregated seating so women who wore veils could remove them to eat but remain unseen by men outside the immediate family.

Figure 1. The West Bay or downtown area of Doha, photographed in 2014 around the time of this study. Thirty years prior, the only multi-story building on this land was the pyramid-shaped hotel on the far right. The traditional dhow boat in the foreground contrasts with the modern high rises of the city. "Doha Skyline" by Francisco Anzola is licensed under Creative Commons 2.0 (creativecommons.org/licenses/by/2.0/), cropped from original.

---

9. In *Deconstructing Global Citizenship: Political, Cultural, and Ethical Perspectives,* my chapter on "Qatar's Globalized Citizenry and the Majlis Culture: Insights from Habermas's Theory of the Development of a Public Sphere" provides a fuller explanation and analysis of majlis culture.

Signs of progressive cultural growth included commitment to a variety of economic and educational opportunities, as well as concerted efforts to attract national attention through sporting events and tourism. However, the modernization of Qatar was not the Westernization of Qatar. The host population sought to hold on to their identity through formal policies as well as everyday practices. As established in the first article of the Qatar Constitution (overwhelmingly approved by popular vote in 2003), Islam is the state religion, Shar'ia the legal system, and Arabic the official state language. Access to pork and alcohol were strictly controlled through a licensing system, and opinion was mixed regarding women's roles in public capacities. For example, in summer 2010, controversy erupted over a photograph published in local papers featuring Sheikha Moza shaking hands with a religious leader, Sheikh Yusuf al-Qaradhawi. She not only challenged norms of cross-gender interaction, but also was in a public space with the clear approval of her husband, the Emir, who sat in the center of the frame smiling.[10] For everyday residents, social change was visible in even small gestures. When we moved to Qatar, my partner and I were warned that any cross-gender display of affection, even a married couple holding hands, was frowned upon. In my last year there, however, I frequently saw young married Qatari couples in public with their hands affectionately intertwined. From educational opportunities to daily interactions, evolution of cultural norms was undertaken cautiously because it could be interpreted by the Qatari public as "an outright betrayal of indigenous cultural and societal values and standards."[11] Neither leaders nor citizens wanted the state to be thought of as "another Dubai," a reference to material excess and its associated loose ethics and morals.[12]

---

10. John Lockerbie's website provides more detail, specifically referring to this controversy on his webpage titled "Society 01," under the heading "Marriage" and the subheading "Interaction." Al-Qaradhawi himself discussed the reasoning and scripture behind the belief that women and men should not shake hands in public, and a citation to his interpretation is in my bibliography.

11. Magdalena Rostron, "Liberal Arts Education in Qatar: Intercultural Perspectives," 221.

12. For a fascinating and unusually public discussion of GCC perceptions of Dubai, see the Doha Debates, "This House Believes Dubai Is a Bad Idea," originally broadcast December 14, 2009. Although the motion was rejected, participants air some significant Qatari and GCC concerns about the financial and moral health of their UAE neighbor.

Although Westerners were welcomed in Qatar, especially as long as they conformed to local norms, that tolerance was tempered with skepticism about what opening the country to outside influences might mean. Sheikha Moza directly addressed the Islam/West dichotomy as a divisive trap, distracting from the celebration of cooperation and shared values.[13] However, she also cautioned against aimless progress and called for design thinking or deliberative inquiry as a means of blending the best of Western social progressivism and democracy with the heritage and cultural foundations of the Arab world. Qatar was not easily labeled as a borderland, as postcolonial, or as neocolonial.[14] As their *National Vision 2030* acknowledges, "Qatar is at a crossroads. The country's abundant wealth creates previously undreamt-of opportunities and formidable challenges" (1–2). To differentiate, however, did not mean to relinquish. It meant negotiating among goals and paths. It meant, as Susan's story above emphasizes, biting into an apple of mixed and perhaps

---

13. See bint Nasser, "Remarks of Her Highness Sheikha Moza bint Nasser Al Missned" and "From Illusions to Clashes to An Awakening of Alliances: Constructing Understanding Between 'Islam' and the 'West.'"

14. Qatar is a borderland, but not. Its only bordering neighbor is Saudi Arabia, and although the family histories of the tribes that helped settle Qatar extend across state borders, the result is not an intersection of two cultures. Rather, Qatar is a multi-national meeting point, not reducible to a binary of "host" and "visitor or neighbor."

Qatar is (post)colonial, but not. Prior to establishing its full independence in 1971, Qatar had been a British Trucial State, an agreement framed as a mutually beneficial agreement that Britain could use the area for trade purposes while also providing military protection. British presence influenced the country's infrastructure, including the constitutional monarchy design, government system of ministries, and the educational system. Forced British colonialism is not part of Qatar's history; however, a troubled "protection" is. The post-colonial lens also disregards the role of the other Gulf States and risks erasing the Ottoman Empire's lingering influences.

Qatar is neo-colonial, but not. Neo-colonialism is defined as "first world" control over a "third world" nation, directly through military intervention or indirectly via political and/or economic means. Qatar has close economic ties and is currently politically compatible with Western nations, and its oil and natural gas reserves grant it financial power. However, Qatar also has been criticized for purchasing high profile assets in the UK and Western Europe. An argument could be made that this situation is sort of reverse neo-colonialization, as Qatar—originally protected as part of the Great Britain's East India Trading Company—now invests in England to diversify its own economic portfolio.

clashing textures. Living in a rapidly evolving location was exhausting but also engaging. As Sarah commented, "the beautiful part about being in Doha is that the complexity is always shifting." That shifting scene contributes to tensions over gender, visibility, movement, and justice in future chapters.

## PARADOXES OF THE IBC

In the epigraph to this chapter, Patricia describes being a branch campus employee as "working for two masters." She refers to serving both the home campus back in the USA and the local students and community in Qatar. In reality, our stakeholders were more layered and complicated than her comment reveals. At the time of my study, six USAmerican international branch campuses[15] (IBCs) made up the heart of the 6,200-acre Education City in Doha.[16] Each university represented a college: Carnegie Mellon for business and computer information systems, Georgetown University School of Foreign Service for diplomacy and international relations, Northwestern University for journalism and media studies, Texas A&M University for engineering, Virginia Commonwealth University for fashion and design, and Weill Cornell Medical College.[17] Qatar Foundation (QF), a non-profit government-owned organization invited these universities to participate in the Education

---

15. One study in 2009 catalogued fifty-seven university-level transnational education efforts in the Middle East region alone (Miller-Idriss and Hanauer). Of those, thirty-four were "international branch campuses" (IBCs), which import a specific disciplinary area of a USAmerican university into a foreign host space. IBCs are long-term investments, as they require facilities, development of a faculty and staff, and recruitment of students both from the host country and its surrounding region.

16. Neha Vora's *Teach for Arabia: American Universities, Liberalism, and Transnational Qatar* provides a broader view of the project.

17. Additional facilities included a K–12 school, Qatar University of Islamic Studies, and a research and technology park. University College London and Hautes Études Commerciales de Paris offered master's degrees in museum studies and international business, respectively. More recently, the development of curriculum and faculty for the Hamad Bin Khalifa Univeristy (HBKU) had been focusing on interdisciplinary programs interweaving courses from combinations of the main Education City schools in order to offer additional degree options.

City project in the early 2000s as a means of providing wealthy Qatari citizens and residents the opportunity to earn a USAmerican degree without leaving the country. Costs for the project were difficult to calculate. However, extrapolating figures published for Cornell's medical IBC, an estimate is that Education City costs QF—and thus costs the state—at least $4.5 billion per decade.[18]

Considered from a bird's-eye view, each IBC sat at a bewildering intersection of bureaucratic oversights. Although by no means exhaustive, the following list begins to illustrate the complexity of governments and agencies to whom my specific IBC was accountable:

- Host country's government (Qatar's Supreme Education Council)[19]
- Host country's sponsoring organization (Qatar Foundation)
- Physical and/or virtual site(s) (Education City)
- Local research funding agencies (Qatar National Research Fund)
- Home campus administration in the USA
- Owners/regulators of the home campus (e.g., a US state)
- Disciplinary accrediting agency
- USAmerican university accrediting agency
- Home national government regulating the home campus (US Department of Education)[20]

---

18. Total costs to date for the project are unavailable, but reportedly, Qatar Foundation pledged $750 million over eleven years to Weill Cornell Medical College alone (Lewin). Multiplying that number by six to account for the primary programs puts the cost of just the Western universities at approximately $4.5 billion per decade.

19. During the study, the governing body for schools in Qatar was the Supreme Education Council. Since then, the agency has been restructured into Qatar's Ministry of Education. I've kept the agency name consistent with the context within which this project is situated.

20. This list does not include additional bureaucracies affecting life as an expatriate (for example the USA's Internal Revenue Service). My IBC's situation was likely to differ from the others in Education City, particularly as a state institution. Other IBCs could have had more or less local administrative control and could have been managed more or less by main campus administrations located back in the US. Some IBC regulators were likely more hands-on

The two primary controlling organizations for the IBC were QF and the home campus in the USA, but the other stakeholders could exert influence at any given—and typically unexpected—moment.

Details regarding the campuses were described in secret legal agreements between each separate IBC and QF. Employees at our branch were not allowed to see the agreements even as they were often cited as the reasons for budgetary and structural changes in the IBC. Only the highest-level administrators were privy to their contents, a situation made even more disconcerting considering we were a branch of a *public* university in the US, meaning we were accustomed to major documentation about our university being public knowledge. When substantive administrative decisions were made and the faculty and staff asked for the rationale for the change, we were told "this change is due to the agreement with QF, but we will neither show you that agreement nor cite the specifics of the agreement motivating this change." In other words, the foundational documents of our professional lives were not visible to us—analogous to being a citizen in the USA but not having access to the US Constitution. Because our personal lives—most notably where we were allowed to live—were affected by the agreement, it loomed over our whole existence. The mystery of the secret agreement's influence was a persistent source of uncertainty, anxiety, and frustration.

In late 2016, however, Nick Anderson, a reporter for the *Washington Post* filed a Freedom of Information Act request forcing my IBC to release its secret agreement and publishing it as part of his journalistic writings. According to the 2013 ten-year agreement (and presumably the original 2003–2013 agreement that preceded it), my IBC functioned as a direct extension of the home campus in the USA that maintained control over admissions, curriculum design, and faculty and staff hiring (*Agreement* 2). The goal was to import a full USAmerican experience to Education City.[21] The replication of the US institution located within a foreign country with its own distinct local values and culture made the IBC scene fundamentally hybrid. In other words, the IBC was constructed as a transnational scene through the negotiated back-and-forth

---

than others. Because they are complex organizations, comparisons across IBCs were difficult.

21. For a description of how the branch was shaped to replicate the home campus, including the struggles that the process introduced, see Cynthia Howman Wood's "Institutional Ethos: Replicating the Student Experience."

between the flagship in the USA and Qatar Foundation over the terms and ongoing operations of its existence.

For example, the 2013 ten-year agreement between Qatar Foundation and our home campus reaffirmed the rights of faculty to make curricular decisions (section 2.2.1.2), but later in the agreement, section "11.10 Local Laws and Customs" indicated that all affiliated with the IBC "shall respect the cultural religious and social customs of the State of Qatar" (*Agreement* 30). In this case, a faculty member's decision to include controversial content in her course was aligned with home campus policy but potentially in conflict with the host location's social customs. Considering that both policies were expressed in the same legal document, a faculty member's decision paradoxically could be both supported and denied by the agreement. In fact, if a faculty member taught something so controversial as to cause offense to a high-powered Qatari family, she could be fired and deported.

The paradoxical tolerance and intolerance we felt was real and tangible, as well as circulated through stories shared. Patricia, who had been at the branch since its beginning, related the following about how a male IBC student threatened consequences for perceived violations of local cultural norms:

> *During the first semester of classes at our branch campus, one of the Qatari students called a meeting of all twenty-nine students. He told the students that the faculty and staff were trying to run this school like a Western university, but this school was in Qatar, and the students would follow the local cultural norms (separation of male and female students, etc.) or face consequences. He also said that if any of the infidel faculty or staff members needed to be fired, just to let him know, and his family would take care of it. The powers-that-be at the university dealt with the situation handily, but this illustrates the animosity that some of our new students feel towards the Western faculty and staff. —Patricia*

While this display smacks of posturing and machismo, experienced expatriates knew that the threat was real and that the IBC's status as both local *and* USAmerican was tricky ground. My colleagues and I all knew of specific instances where people had been fired and deported over an individual Qatari's accusation of cultural offense. Chapter 2, under the section "Veiled, Unveiled, and Surveilled," contains one story and chapter 3, under "Negotiating Justice," contains another.

Even as it was well funded and heading towards completion of its second decade, Education City as a whole was not without controversy within the Qatari community. All the academic units were co-educational, and gender mixing was still frowned upon by more conservative segments of the local society. Because of these concerns, Education City was sometimes referred to as "Sin City," a reflection of ongoing tensions created by self-modernizing while also striving to hold on to traditional gender-segregating norms. Some of my Qatari female students told me stories of having to argue with their families to be allowed to even apply to our IBC because our academic focus was still "too masculine" for female students and because families did not want to put their daughters at risk of their behavior being socially judged as inappropriate (e.g., interacting with males). Although my classrooms contained generally balanced numbers of Qatari males and females, they would self-segregate and sit on opposite sides of the room. Although they would work in gender-mixed teams when I asked them to do so, many would be nervous and uncomfortable. When I asked Qatari female students about their hesitation, they said that if they were to say something "dumb" in class, the male students would make fun of them and they did not want their reputations to be marked by being judged as "stupid" or "silly." These female students' struggles were evidence of how gender norms within the IBC—and as a greater reflection of gender norms within Qatar—were trapped between the traditional and the modern.

The branch campus was structured as liminal space between the here and there of the US and Qatar, and was constructed via a formal agreement attempting to align overlapping and competing territories simultaneously claimed or colonized by two powers. Feminist geographer Gillian Rose writes of this masculinist territorial view, "Everything in that space is known" and is identified as the "Same" or consubstantial with the conquerors. Everything outside that space is then labeled as "Other" (149). Sameness and Otherness become the premises of *topoi* or commonplaces—grounds for common *senses*. They dictate what that group considers acceptable, questionable, and/or offensive. In other words, perceptions of Sameness and Otherness underpin "territorial logics." In retrospect, language in the contract establishing and maintaining operation of the branch campus seemed to codify a relatively clear rationale, a set of *topoi* and system of *logos* under which to operate. However, daily practices and the ongoing inter-scenic swirl of influences produced uncertainty over which territorial power occupied the center and, therefore, controlled decision-making and which power (or powers) were relegated to marginal sites of contention.

Because of tensions created through simultaneously maintaining tradition while also self-modernizing, Qatar as a rhetorical scene vacillated between being predictable and chaotic, and as a result, working in the IBC was a persistent existence between certainty and uncertainty. Employees who came from the home US campus (a site of Rose's Sameness or center) felt some certainty about the curriculum, policies, and procedures that were the norm on the home campus, yet being in a simultaneously claimed territory of QF and other Qatari agencies created uncertainty regarding how to work at a complicated and sometimes contradictory intersection. What was acceptable in one moment risked being unacceptable in the next, and vice-versa. As expatriate employees in various roles—faculty, staff, administration—my participants and I experienced these competing territorial constraints as paradoxical positioning. We were neither here nor there, located within the Same or the Other—in a US institution or in a Qatari social context. We were in both and felt the daily tensions and consequences of friction between the two.

Having described the general sense of the instability created by the paradoxical conservativism and modernization of the country and the competing identities of the branch campus, we move further into the stories of working and living in that complex transnational space. Because of competing commonplaces, it was the site of paradoxical demands (home and host) and positioning (ideal and real), as well as a space where divisions between public and private dissolved. In response, my participants and I reacted by adapting. Weaving together our stories into a narrative of our choices as actors reveals a shared set of rhetorical feminist tactics at work.

## Meeting Home and Host Demands

Scenic forces—here defined as the IBC's workplace demands—are the priorities and requirements established through an organization's mission, goals, policies, procedures, and management practices. Agreement over what matters, how work is completed, and what standards are met ideally creates a scene grounded in shared values and expectations of what counts as good or successful work. In turn, those commonplaces shape everything from employee evaluations ("are you meeting our standards?") to the broad organization's local cultural logic. Commonplace expectations are the rationale by which the organization establishes itself as orderly, ethical, and accountable to its stakeholders: "based on our values and standards, here is how we do things." When people agree on policies and use procedures in similar ways, a workplace seems cohesive and efficient; when disagreements or different approaches lead to a multiplicity of views and practices, a workplace can seem chaotic, capricious, and even unjust. For organizations set in the liminal spaces among multiple claiming agencies, establishing an orderly and positive work environment can be a daunting challenge. For the IBC, competing demands of home (USAmerican university) and host (QF) locations sometimes introduced substantial confusion.

Participants in my study had been at the IBC for varying lengths of time—some from its inception—and their metaphor-driven interpretations of the complex scene varied. Sarah saw her job as coming to a "blank canvas," emphasizing the lack of standard practices. Rather than a scene riddled with a confusion of competing rules and regulations, she framed the space as not yet fully encoded through local policy and therefore a potential site of creativity. However, Sarah also was strategic about institutional decision-making in order to balance promoting "the values of both the [home university] institution and [Qatar's] national vision." She understood the campus to sit in a borderland of sometimes dovetailing and sometimes competing values. Similarly, Patricia talked about needing to "craft policy that didn't run contrary to main campus but addressed local issues" even as she had "no precedent to follow." Although she had the power to draft policy to structure the scene, she was conscientious about finding liminal spaces where both host and home needs could be met and divisions transcended. Patricia's lack of precedent hints at anxiety about striking a home/host balance in the absence of successful models.

Patricia's concerns over lack of precedent were merited, as our IBC's adoption of home policies generated conflict. For example, at the time of my study, our home campus did not grant paid maternity leave to its employees. Sick leave and the US Family and Medical Leave Act were the only benefits and were contingent upon length of employment. By comparison, Qatari law granted Qatari women a mandatory two months paid maternity leave, which could be extended in special situations. Confusion and frustration arose because the IBC was under the policy regulations of home location in the USA but had employees who were citizens of the host country. Echoing back to the 2013 ten-year agreement mandate to "respect the cultural religious and social customs of the State of Qatar," which policy held? Emily shared her memory of a similar conflict: "When I first got here, local employees used to get six weeks extra paid vacation given to them because they're local. Paid vacation. Six weeks. Because they're local, and the American workers didn't get that. That was a huge problem for our morale." Qatari labor policy granted its citizens an automatic entitlement to paid vacation upon being hired; however, the university policy back in the USA required employees to earn vacation hours by accruing them each month. Expatriates, as non-citizen residents, had to abide by less generous university policy while Qatari citizens did not. To accrue the equivalent of six weeks paid vacation took about two and a half years under home campus policy. For a branch campus situated at the intersection of two territories, which leave system was centered? As expatriate workers viewed the system transnationally, as a back-and-forth between policies in the USA as compared to policies at the IBC, inconsistencies were perceived as unfair treatment within the IBC.

Because QF was required to cover all funding of the IBC, cost became a complex political issue. If a policy at the branch campus provided benefits not available to the US home campus employees, then controversy ensued ("Why do the branch employees get this benefit but we don't? We're all technically part of the 'same university' and so should be subject to the same regulations"). Our home campus provost frequently used a rationale of "if we can't do this for all university employees [in both the US and Qatar], then you can't have it either" as a basis for revoking IBC resources and for changing IBC policies. In these instances of territorial (re)clamation, employees of the IBC felt a total loss of agency, a response made worse by the perception that each side used the other as its out. If we complained to QF, QF would tell us to talk to our main campus leadership. When we complained to main campus leadership, they would blame policy changes on QF. Because we existed in a transnational space of liminality, this back-and-forth blame game could work. As Patricia commented, "at any given time, someone somewhere in the university is changing the rules. It's hard to keep up. It's hard to be constantly adapting." The scene and who claimed it as their administrative territory shifted, and because the terms establishing the scene itself were kept secret, only a few high-level leaders controlled how the situation was explained (or not).

The IBC territory was marked not only by competing bureaucratic systems but also by the local logics or scenic premises of the multiple cultures working it. Susan's story illustrates where those created a literal and metaphorical gap:

> *What we do here [at the IBC] in a lot of instances is foreign for many of the people who work here. We have lab safety and federal requirements in the United States, and as US employees, we're obligated to follow these requirements here at this campus whether they make sense or not. And about this, I had someone say to me once, "You know what's the problem with you Americans? When you see a hole in the ground, you put a fence around the hole. You put a sign on the fence that says, 'This is a hole.' And then you train everybody that it's a hole and how to avoid the hole. In my country, we just don't walk into the hole." And I was like, "Can I move to your country?" (laughing) But it's true! We're a very lawsuit happy society, and litigation makes the world go 'round in the United States . . . so you've got the clash of two extreme worlds coming together, and you have people looking at me like I've sprouted something out of my head. —Susan*

Her story reflects the competing commonplaces of a safe work environment. What was understood by USAmerican expatriates to be rational—where safety standards created a scene and attendant logic within which actors and acts are contained—was seen by a non-USAmerican person as illogical, even silly as those safety standards highlighted nothing more than common sense. Susan's reaction indicates that she shared her interlocutor's disapproval but saw the safety standards as symptoms of a larger USAmerican legal context she was powerless to affect. As an IBC employee and USAmerican expatriate, Susan's views of what made sense oscillated between the safety as personal responsibility versus organizational liability. But that liminal space was *not* one where she felt she could engage agency. She centered her decision-making on the US-American safety procedures and served as a conduit, justifying policies across her coworkers' cultural perspectives.

Although expatriates might arrive on a local scene expecting to "show them how USAmericans get things done," experience in transnational spaces and with diverse colleagues and subordinates typically revealed a choice: adapt or be miserable. Michelle had worked for a local business in Doha before moving to the IBC. She said that when she moved out of the Qatari workplace and into the IBC, she "thought 'Great! Now I can get back to doing business the way that I'm used to in the West.'" However, that wasn't her experience. She reasoned it was "because we work in this kind of hybrid space. . . . I think the institution itself struggles with responsibilities and procedures that it has to support and then trying to meet duties, responsibilities, and procedures the way they should be managed locally." Michelle found the IBC tensions between home and host demands made her job more difficult. At her previous local workplace, she had not faced the same level of organizational split. More generally, she missed feeling supported by her international co-workers. Beyond being helpful colleagues, they had served as cultural mentors by introducing her to the local customs and religious celebrations, including how to navigate the challenges of overly aggressive traffic. While Michelle felt equally welcomed by her IBC colleagues, she did not feel the same level of care and creative possibility as she had in her local workplace. The difference was due to the IBC's confusing liminality. Her Qatari workplace had positioned her as an outsider in need of mentoring, support she found incredibly valuable. In contrast, the hybridity of the USAmerican branch campus created confusion between the centered cultural insiders and the marginalized cultural outsiders, and therefore, less conducive to cross-cultural mentoring.

A colleague and I similarly fell into our own cross-cultural gap as faculty members at the crossroads of USAmerican organizational policy and IBC student culture.[22] We knew the branch was having a significant struggle with the university honor code imported from the home campus, as the number of infractions each year was high relative to our student population. Some infractions were also rather egregious. For example, one student hacked into a professor's computer and another used a key code logger to steal professors' usernames and passwords then used that information to access exams and grade books. After conducting a pre-study literature review, gathering data from our honor council coordinator, and receiving Institutional Review Board approval, my colleague and I set out to unpack the local notion of honor and to under-

---

22. Our student population hovered around fifty percent Qatari and fifty percent "international" (Indian, Pakistani, Egyptian, Omani, Emirati, Saudi Arabian, Lebanese, Palestinian). Most of the international students had actually grown up in Qatar. Of the Qatari students, around fifty percent were men and fifty percent women. The overall gender split was forty percent women and sixty percent men, a high number of women for our disciplinary focus.

stand why systematic cheating was rampant at our IBC even though personal integrity was a prominent part of many students' home cultures. Through essays and a focus group, we asked students to share their own definitions honor and to discuss why the imported honor code was not effective in the local context. Essay responses were cliché references to family and religious values, as students seemed to avoid or actively resist the discussion.

As we reflected over the ineffective design of our project, we realized how our own Western notions of honor, especially in an academic setting, grew out of an assumption that our honor was a shared common honor for everyone. The implication of our questions was that students did not *understand* honor or did not *have* honor (as if it were a thing to be possessed by the individual), when in reality, they very much functioned within their own codes of local community honor that they were not willing to expose to our colonialist "hunting and gathering" (Smith 99). Our efforts to deeply understand—through our students' eyes—the divide between our home institution's formal academic integrity policy ("code" or home institution logic and standards) generally failed.[23] In this situation, the competing educational and social ideals between home and host forced us to face our hubris and naïveté as well as challenged us to rethink our roles and assumptions. Indeed, it pushed us to rethink our purpose for being at the IBC and whether we were doing more harm than good.

In transnational spaces, status as insider-outsider can change agency within a given scene based on where along that identity continuum you fall. Our students were willing to talk to us because we had shared insider status with them as teachers in their classrooms, but ultimately, we remained far enough on the outsider end of the spectrum to be denied access to more sensitive or controversial conversations. LeeAnn Mysti Rudd's article, "'It Makes Us Even Angrier than We Already Are': Listening Rhetorically to Students' Responses to an Honor Code Imported to a Transnational University in the Middle East" provides an in-depth reflection on how she struggled to confront our colonialist assumptions and how she continued to work on making her classroom and the IBC into more cross-culturally just locations.

---

23. I have critiqued this through the faculty perspective in my chapter "Risking Our Foundations: Honor, Codes, and Authoritarian Spaces," in *Western Higher Education in Asia and the Middle East: Politics, Economics, and Pedagogy.*

Expatriates across the spectrum of national identities (not just US-Americans) who had been at the IBC for longer durations complained that the organization's policies were slowly constricting, cutting off benefits and freedoms previously allowed. As the IBC stakeholders competed for control over the branch, employees perceived themselves to be increasingly squeezed in the middle. Multiple factors contributed to the ongoing sense of constriction, including revision of "bad" policy and closing of loopholes as the organization matured, changes in leadership and leadership styles at the branch and home campuses, and fluctuations in economic situations both in the home US state and Qatar. Although fluctuations in the home state economy should not have affected the IBC (because the home state did not fund any branch activities), the US and state home economies did affect the *home* campus, and as home campus policies were often forced out to the branch, results were felt without their attendant causes. In other words, we experienced the effects of the home state scene without being located *in* the home state scene.

A prime example was the move of the home campus faculty to nine-month appointments. Faculty at the IBC had been on twelve-month appointments because housing and residency requirements lasted all year long. Expatriates could not re-locate back to their home countries just for the summer months. To complete the twelve-month contract, the IBC faculty taught a summer course or attended to research duties paid out of a separate budget pool. When the US-located campus began the process of forcing its faculty to nine-month contracts, the policy extended to the branch and meant a three-month loss of pay. When IBC faculty complained, the provost told us that the change was written in the ten-year agreement with QF. In fact, it *was* included in the agreement (section 6.5), but at the time, the agreement was confidential between the IBC and QF, so faculty and staff were not allowed to see it. As a result, the IBC faculty felt they were being deceived, and the IBC leadership's efforts to justify the change were ineffective, in large part due to the mystery of the secret agreement. Towards the end of my time at the IBC, a sagging petrochemical market led QF to reduce funding to the branch, too, resulting in additional organizational and policy changes. Regardless of economies, intentions, and communication failures, the IBC scene was set within the larger influential contexts of multiple state economies and stakeholders. What may have been seen as a liminal space of creative potential for transnational projects was also perceived as an unjust multi-layered bureaucratic maze of mystery and deceit.

Although the picture painted of the IBC may have appeared bleak, being a small yet complex organization meant it offered unusual opportunities for its employees. As Melissa said in a tone both optimistic and exhausted, "there is no team B" during stressful times. Another way of framing Melissa's remark is that she existed *both* as a member of "team A" that had a set of expected job duties *and* "team B" that took on new tasks as they were needed. Being both team A and team B was stressful, as she remarked, "I don't think I've ever worked as hard as I do here, ever in my career, and I've had demanding jobs." In a small branch working to replicate a full USAmerican educational experience, employees were asked to take on projects typically assigned to others in larger organizations. "No team B" foregrounds the challenge of taking on tasks that would have been beyond participants' hierarchical location on the home campus.

For example, as the senior member of the *instructional* faculty "on loan" from main campus, I led an international search for two new tenure-track style *research* faculty. On the home campus, I never would have been asked (or allowed) to take that leadership role. Being asked to run that search was both an unanticipated labor burden and an unusual opportunity to have big influence in shaping our department through writing the job ads, choosing the hiring committee, leading the interviews, and being part of the hiring decisions. My study participants and I learned to judge these unique opportunities in terms of how they would help us build our qualifications in anticipation of leaving the IBC for a better job. We knew that our status as expatriates was permanently temporary. None of us would retire in Qatar, so we became savvy about choosing to take on extra assignments "beyond our paygrades" as a means of qualifying ourselves for a future job. A basic Burkean scene is assumed to have all of the actors that it requires, but such is not always the case. Because the IBC scene contained only limited actors, what was possible within that scene afforded unusual opportunities, and the stress of meeting additional and sometimes unusually complex demands as an IBC employee could be concurrently exhilarating and exhausting.

The paradoxical positioning—simultaneously existing as both home/USAmerican and host/Qatari IBC sites—created frustrating complexity in how we as rhetorical agents understood and expressed our scenic realities. Faculty and staff continually shifted between home views and host views of how the organization should run, navigating the competing internal logics that had created the culture of the IBC. Burke writes that "the curtain rises to disclose the stage-set, this stage-set contains, simultaneously, implicitly, all that the narrative is to draw out as a sequence explicitly" (*Grammar* 7), but that is not necessarily true. The mystery of working under an IBC agreement that guided so much of our daily work yet was kept secret from us meant that our shared narratives, or how we understood the logics within which we were working, were based on scenic directions invisibly inscribed the IBC actors' scripts. Patricia's quotation at the top of this chapter, "Working for two masters has its stresses," was an apt metaphor because it framed the "masters" as equals meaning she had double the demands. Her stresses grew out of having to adapt to seeing both home and host as claimants to the territory on which she worked.

## Living the Ideal and the Real

While previous discussion of home and host demands reveals confusion due to conflicting IBC territories, the following tacks out to examine the paradox of the "ideal" versus the "real" transnational workplace in broader terms of intercultural relationships and communication.[24] The stories begin at work, but, reflecting the liminality of the IBC, expand to dissolve the public/private or work/home divide.

Whether contextualizing or delimiting a space, marking a *kairotic* moment, or prompting an exigence, *chronos* shapes our rhetorical construction of scene. For USAmerican expatriates transitioning to the IBC, having to adjust to varied notions of time was a common experience and source of frustration. In the USA, time is framed in economic terms: we value it, spend it, invest it, and run out of it. Despite our awareness of the IBC being a hybrid transnational space and despite acknowledging the diversity of our colleagues and stakeholders, talk of time typically was in stereotyped terms of us (Western) versus them (Arab). "Home" treatment of time was centered as normal, and "Arab time" often was viewed as deficient by comparison. Amy observed "Americans, we live by the

---

24. Osland and Osland found a similar paradox in their study of thirty-five expatriates, set approximately two decades prior to mine. Their participants were overwhelmingly male (thirty-three of thirty-five) and were not in educational professions. Most "(63 percent) had been assigned to Europe, but there were also postings in Africa, Asia, and Latin America" (97). Consistencies between our studies' outcomes—which vary in setting, time, participant identity, and disciplinary analysis—point to the power of transnational work in creating disruptive liminal spaces.

clock . . . there's American time and there's Arab time [for which] the clock is not as powerful a force." My partner said some of his contacts in industry differentiated how their meetings were scheduled based on the nationalities in attendance. A Western/American meeting time started punctually and ended as scheduled, while an Arab/local meeting might start anywhere from thirty minutes to several hours late and might go well beyond its indicated duration.

Learning to live in both USAmerican and Arab time, to differentiate between perspectives, and to adapt based on audience were important adjustments for expats. Lisa said, "I had to learn that people are not going to be on time," and Ashley explained "it's not so rush-rush but is more relationship oriented." Emily called the two cultures "almost opposites when it comes to how things work" but said she had learned "it's okay for people to do their jobs in different ways," and being in Qatar taught her to relax her expectations concerning time management and her previously narrower (USAmerican) perceptions of work ethic: "It may be a different approach from mine, but that's okay as long as they get it done by the deadline that I need." Although Lisa, Ashley, and Emily acknowledged that time may have functioned differently in the multicultural workplace, the tone and content of their comments point to a deficiency model[25] of comparing how others (do not) value time. USAmericans and other Westerners used frustrations over schedules as one means of defining themselves as insiders centered in a more "efficient" system and their Qatari or other international colleagues as outsiders marginalized by that system. Emily said it directly: "It may be a different approach from mine, but that's okay *as long as they get it done by the deadline that I need.*" For Emily, variation was acceptable but only within the confines of American limits.[26]

---

25. See LuMing Mao's "Reflective Encounters: Illustrating Comparative Rhetoric" for a critique of the deficiency model of cross-cultural scholarship.

26. These tensions reinforce Edward Hall's theory in *The Hidden Dimension* regarding monochromic and polychromic orientations to time, where the US-American view and Arab views reinforce the sides of the binary. The time difference also might be considered from several of the proposed continuums in Hofstede's *Cultures Consequences*: individualism/collectivism, power distance, and short-term/long-term orientations. However, relying on these systems of classification is risky because it invites over-generalization or "sophisticated stereotyping" (Osland and Bird 66). The original research supporting these cultural taxonomies—which are applied as premises underpinning cultural

# Traditional and Modern 43

Meetings were scenes where study participants foregrounded differences between home/US-like spaces as "ideal" and host/Qatari spaces as "real." Although stories such as Susan's about safety standards were set in the competing bureaucracies of the IBC, other transformative moments were set in places where my interviewees were the visitors. Here, Ashley describes a discombobulating experience trying to bridge the gap between Western (British/American) and local norms for holding a business meeting. Ashley took her expatriate assignment from the USA through the IBC but ended up spending a significant part of her early life in the country working in a Qatari educational location (not the IBC). The space still involved multiple cultures working towards a shared goal, but the scene was more strongly and monologically Qatari or Gulf Arab, making Ashley an outsider/Other to their insider/Same territory:

> I was in a meeting, feeling like I was floating above the meeting table, looking down, thinking "Who is this? What is this?" because it was just so foreign. I had a translator, they had translators. It was a zoo, honestly. And I had hired supervisors to do some work on evaluating a program, and these supervisors were British and American ladies. I started becoming good friends with them and am still good friends with them to this day. But I was embarrassed to have them to meetings because it was a zoo . . . The local ladies would constantly be on their phones in the middle of the meetings . . . They would walk in and out. They would call their maids to come in and refill their teacups. I mean, it was like we were on different planets. I had these objectives for the meeting and the local ladies didn't have any objectives, and so trying to get things to work . . . and the evaluators coming from the West expecting to get things accomplished. They just sat there with their eyes really big because it was just bizarre . . . It was a tough time, but it was also a really

---

logics—is now significantly outdated or limited. For example, Hofstede's labeling of Arabic cultures as collectivist, uncertainty avoiders is based on scant and problematic data drawn from only 141 respondents located in only seven countries and collected in 1969 and 1972 (52). Comparing the United Arab Emirates (or UAE, one of Hofstede's collection sites) of 1972 to the UAE of 2017, the change—both physically and culturally—is astonishing, shaped by globalization, immigration, the Internet, and other factors. The hybridity of both Qatar and the region challenge the enduring "truths" of these labels and comparisons. For additional critique of cultural taxonomies, see Holliday, McSweeney, or Witte.

> *great time because I got put into the local culture faster than I ever thought I would. —Ashley*

Ashley's story frames her existence in simultaneously familiar and unfamiliar scenes. She began with a Western commonplace of what an ideal business meeting scene should be: highly organized, driven by objectives, and focused on outcomes. However, participants in this gathering shared a different starting point, one that reflected multiple ongoing priorities (phone calls, leaving to attend to other requirements). As Ashley remembered this moment through her storytelling, it seemed to be originally a site of Anzaldúan "grating and bleeding" (*Borderlands* 25) as the observable purposes of the "local ladies" were either incomprehensible or at odds with the purposes of Ashley and her British and American supervisors. Her disconnect was embodied as she was "floating above" and observing their locations on "different planets." Tension arose because specific tasks or institutional demands (Ashley's "objectives") were at stake if the meeting or immediate scene were not brought under Western-style control. Although her experience was set in a local place, Ashley's description of the meeting was not unique. In my own classes at the IBC, students wandered in and out and answered texts or calls despite my policy against it, and in our annual graduation ceremony, family and friends of the graduates did not sit quietly and patiently as they do in the USA. Instead, the audience milled around the seating area in a constant dull roar of conversation. As the honored speakers reminded graduates to keep their feet on the ground as they reached for the stars, the audience engaged in their own simultaneous yet separate reception or party in the auditorium seating area.

A masculinist and Western-centric interpretation of Ashley's meeting, my classes, and our graduation ceremony would conclude that they were failures because they did not conform to their scenic genres: the expected narrative, a clear locus of rhetorical control (one or more speakers or leaders), and monochromatic notions of time. Yet my interviewees and I learned to adjust, accepting the tension of competing territorial logics as our co-existing reality. This adjustment was not the same thing as assimilation, for we did not adopt our host culture's practices. Instead, we observed them as a means of rethinking and reflecting over our home practices. Do meetings always have to be so uniformly and hierarchically structured? Do graduation ceremonies have to be so quiet and passive? Even as Ashley was "embarrassed" in the moment, she reflected over and later recognized the rewards of these extra-planetary experiences: "It was a tough time, but it was also a really great time because I got put into the local culture faster than I ever thought I would." As her other story-telling would reveal, Ashley made the rhetorical feminist move of rede-fining the *logos* of her location based on the relationships she built with her Qatari colleagues rather than by the ways it conformed (or did not conform to) the rationality of Western workplace norms. When Ashley's daily work location then moved into the IBC, she carried these transfor-mative lessons with her and as a result was better able to adapt to IBC relationships and situations based on an appreciation of Otherness and multiplicity rather than an expectation of Sameness and singularity.

Other interviewee stories about being managed also reveal a grating of leadership and workplace values in the transnational scene. Most of my participants were supervised by Western men. Our dean and assis-tant/associate deans at the time of this study were all white, USAmerican men. My program chair was a white, USAmerican male, too. Their styles of management were typically masculinist (linear rather than iterative, singular or limited rather than collaborative) and so went unnoticed as "normal" or the Same under the auspices of being a branch of a US-American university that was also patriarchal in structure and masculin-ist in style. In contrast, Michelle, who had spent a short time working outside of the IBC when she first relocated to Qatar, and Patricia—who worked in a more diverse IBC unit—both commented on what they identified as culturally based management styles. Patricia summed it up by saying, "most local supervisors think that the most effective way to motivate their team is to yell and berate." As an illustration, Michelle offered this story about a client managing the team at her locally run, non-IBC agency:

> *My agency had a local client, and that client's local business had their own in-house group that my agency worked with. Their in-house group was incompetent, so my agency ended up doing a lot of extra things, which was fine. They were incompetent by Western standards, to be fair. They may have been doing enough by their own standards. Anyway, we had an ongoing problem and fortu-nately for me, my client realized his problem was in-house, within his own group. It wasn't our agency. He had us all [his own in-house group and my agency] in for a meeting, but I didn't know he had realized [the source of the incompetency]. So there's me and two of his own guys and my boss, my country manager in the room. And*

*he lays into us all equally: "awful, unacceptable, I should fire you, terrible." I mean, it was awful.*

*In the Western world, you would have been like "The problem is this." And you would have laid it out and that person would have defended themselves, right? And I took it; something in me said "Don't. Just let this go. Take it." And so we all took it. The moment I stepped back into my office, my phone rang, and I picked it up. It was my client, and he said, "I just need to tell you, since you're an American, you may not know. That is not directed to you. That is directed towards my team, but you know how we have to do things. Everyone gets [the berating]."*

*It showed this incredible understanding on his part that he still had to do business the way they do business, but he knew I probably didn't know that. And so he called to tell me, "That was not for you, just so you know. We love the work you do." And that was just one of the most sit-down things where I just learned a great lesson, you know? Even though I just got yelled at for half an hour. –Michelle*

Similar to Ashley's story, Michelle's illustrates the potentially chaotic and confusing nature of transnational scenes. Although she approached workplace management from a Western perspective, Michelle intuitively adapted in the moment. Her decision to give into the pressure of the scene, to "Just let this go. Take it," was both a use of rhetorical silence (Glenn *Unspoken*) and a pause of non-identification based on an intuition (Ratcliffe *Rhetorical Listening*). She chose to "stand under" the situation. Michelle remarked that being berated for something she did not do was "a great lesson" that caused her to significantly reflect ("just one of the most sit-down things"). In other words, the originally confusing scene allowed her to recognize conflicting territorial logics at play in both expectations regarding work standards (the in-house group versus Western), and expectations regarding ethical and beneficial management methods (dominating versus interactive). Rather than reject the client's verbally abusive style, Michelle praised him as demonstrating "incredible understanding" for recognizing cultural differences and for backchanneling to explain his approach afterwards. Although she existed in a paradoxical space of here/Western and there/local that shared different centers and margins, she turned to silence, listening, and observation as her rhetorical feminist tactics, even if the situation required her to experience the "awful" situation passively rather than resisting by talking back. As Anzaldúa writes, "At some point, on our way to a new consciousness, we will have to leave the opposite bank . . . so that we are on both shores at once and, at once, see through serpent and eagle eyes" (*Borderlands* 100–01). Ashley's floating above and Michelle's pausing before reacting reveal them to be expatriate agents learning to consider perspectives of *both* home *and* host, to make sense of how two seemingly oppositional views can be focused towards similar goals.

Stories and comments in this section so far have ended in some acceptance of the hybridity of the transnational workplace and some adjustment to a diversity of workplace values and behaviors. My interviewees demonstrated a willful resistance to reacting and instead engage Glenn's "alternative delivery systems" (*Rhetorical Feminism* 4) allowing them to reassess their scenes as set in complex transnational scenes. Amy sums up her approach as "I try to listen more than I talk." As Susan commented, "You can't bully your way through all of this stuff. You have to pick and choose how you're going to do things based on the individual, whether it's something that you recognize as a cultural difference, a male-female difference, whatever it is. You just find a way around it, and you really learn to do that quickly here. It makes you a better person all the way around." Collectively, these stories foreground the *ideal* of learning to navigate or "find your way" through difference *and* the *reality* of how potentially troubling and frustrating transnational scenes can be. Behaviors labeled as unacceptable and even abusive in typical Western workplaces presented themselves as opportunities for intercultural reflection and learning. Of course, the danger is in rationalizing and accepting abusive treatment as the *logos* of the workplace: Michelle did not celebrate or adopt that aggressive approach, but it did open her eyes to the notion that Western styles of management were not to be taken as the norm, and as she commented later in our conversation, it encouraged her to be open-minded about finding different ways to support and encourage (*not* through yelling or berating) her own diverse staff.

In addition to these specific moments of transformation, working in diverse transnational spaces made expatriate women more conscientious about their general rhetorical strategies. Despite an absence of formal training in cross-cultural communication, all participants reported attentiveness to what working in a culturally hybrid environment meant for their daily practice. Amanda put it this way: "I have found myself explaining what I needed to one of my coworkers who I knew would understand me better because they know me. I would explain what I was trying to communicate to them then ask, 'If you were going to say this to [the rest of the staff], how would you say it?' And it's usually different than how I would say it." By seeking out informal mentoring and developing her collaborative communication strategies, she learned to function more inclusively.

Awareness of differences in perspectives is fundamental to creating a productive scene in any multicultural institution, and all participants talked about ways they sought to function effectively in hybridity. Melissa mentioned avoiding or carefully choosing jargon and colloquialisms as well as being culturally sensitive, while Amanda reflected over differences in her reader responses, saying "I'll get comments from US expats saying 'Wow, your emails are so detailed.' And then I get comments from the other cultures, that 'I didn't understand this at all.'" Lisa talked about tailoring her interactions to different cultural backgrounds, specifically acknowledging the good works of Egyptian subordinates in more subtle ways because they did not seem to react positively in direct praise. Jessica acknowledged sussing out "trigger points" when working with faculty of different cultural identities. She and Amanda separately had worked out situationally sensitive strategies of interacting with people and described specific ways they bridged the USAmerican bureaucracies and their international audiences.

In these broader terms, participants endeavored to frame their strategies by foregrounding Western norms or non-Western deficiencies. Their collective tone tended toward pragmatism, not judgment, as they were all concerned with fulfilling their job duties. The spirit of their comments was one of shared survival amidst the fluctuating but persistent confusion of the complex and conflicting demands of the IBC. In sum, the reality of the hybrid scene clashed with notions of an ideal workplace, causing them to reassess. But rather than striving to shift the workplace to align with their (USAmerican-influenced) ideals, they developed tactics for existing between the two.

## Revising the Private as Public

This last scenic paradox is where my study shifted. Although designed to stay situated within the workplace, my participants' stories persistently crept out into their broader lifeworlds. By this, I mean that interviewees whom I did not know on a personal level and who were being asked questions about their work at the IBC, all spontaneously shared stories about their individual lives outside of work. I attribute this transfer to a foundational aspect of the branch campus: its very design broke down most barriers between our private and public lives, even if that break-down was not by our own choosing and even as it seemed at odds with local standards. Rather than being able to draw our own boundaries as individual agents, the IBC and expatriate scenes resituated our private lives into more public spaces, and we had to reposition ourselves to live in the awkward liminal space in between.

Qatari norms prioritized the sanctity of privacy, sometimes in the workplace where men and women might function in segregated spaces but specifically in terms of the gendered domestic sphere. As described in chapter 2, living compounds and villas were surrounded by walls to block outside views, and many had security gates to control access. Restaurants had private family sections where women could eat without their veils. Inside Education City (also surrounded by walls), identification badges were required for entry into any of the campuses, reinforcing institutional privacy and insider/outsider designations. Even cubicles in the library had chest-height walls rather than the open configurations common in the USA. Local social norms clearly impacted if, when, and how personal matters were discussed. If a man and woman engaged in polite conversation, social norms dictated he should not ask about her children, especially her girl-children because information about them was private. (A woman, however, could ask a man about his children.) When my literature students and I read a book with a mild sex scene in it, they explained to me that sinfulness of extramarital sex was not their concern (the nature and consequences of that sin were between the individuals and Allah), but that writing about it as part of a memoir—*publishing* it for the world to see—was not acceptable. The transgression should have stayed private.

Despite the local commitment to dividing the public from the private, working in an IBC as an expat demanded dissolving that separation in multiple ways, one of the biggest through the housing system. In Qatar, non-citizens could not buy property, and the rental market was expensive and competitive. Sponsors were required to provide their employees—from executives to laborers—with either a place to live or an allowance to apply towards rent,[27] and the IBC employees could choose to live in one of several walled compounds or in high-rise apartment buildings. During the time I worked for the IBC, the university con-

---

27. One way that unethical sponsors abused laborers was by providing substandard housing. One "camp" was adjacent to our compound, and it was no better than a series of shanties with no running water.

tracted with property owners or managers to secure the best monthly rates by reserving large numbers of villas for its employees (bulk buying), and having employees in a limited number of compounds or apartment buildings ensured we could all be located in case of emergency. Housing offers were based on a combination of job title and family size. Many compounds had their own corner stores with basic household supplies; many had pools, playgrounds, and workout facilities; and some even had restaurants, salons, and other amenities. One had a tiny shop stuffed with groceries and emblazoned with a hand-painted sign that read "Wallmart." The compound where my family and I lived had approximately 140 villas, a store, restaurant, pool, workout facilities with daily classes, a playground, tennis and basketball courts, large-screen TV room, pool tables, and a dry cleaner. In other words, leaving the compound was not necessary for daily life except for major grocery store trips and going to school or work. As a result, we lived in a relatively small and privately enclosed community. A guarded front gate restricted who could enter and exit.

Because public social spaces (e.g., malls) were often crowded and because the climate in Qatar was harsh, many IBC faculty and staff spent substantive time in the shared spaces of their compounds or apartment buildings. Therefore, employees at the IBC lived and worked within the same small circles. My neighbor on one side was a professor and on the other side was the director of our writing center. Sometimes, I would see them in the IBC hallways, and other times, they would see me disheveled in my pajamas taking out the garbage on Saturday mornings. My colleague Mary described it as living in a "small town," but compounds also functioned as "golden ghettos" (Gannon and Pillai 20) segregating white collar expats as a privileged population. Other metaphors my interviewees used to describe what it's like to live as an expatriate IBC employee also emphasized simultaneous privilege and constraint: Michelle referred to Education City as a "gilded cage." Several of my participants called expat life a metaphoric "bubble." Another reference was to the "comfort zone of the American sub-community." Participants were aware of the privileged implications of their language, which will be further explored as the book proceeds.

Living next door to your co-workers, supervisors, and supervisees meant that private life became public. It reconfigured the relationships of work in positive and negative ways. Lisa explained that you could "depend on your friends as your family." Indeed, holiday and birthday celebrations, weekend brunches, and other leisure activities (including 3:00 am football-watching parties) happened with people from the IBC, and co-workers helped newly arriving colleagues make the transition to their new living and working environments. I remember asking my co-workers where to buy good quality chicken breasts and if it was possible to find the blue box mac and cheese. Over-the-counter medicines such as pain relievers were unfamiliar, so even knowing what to do to relieve a headache or sinus infection meant asking for advice. Amanda explained, "I don't think I could have been here without a particular co-worker/ friend that first year . . . there seems to be a network of the expats that tend to home in on making sure people are okay." Co-workers jumped to assist if someone needed to go to the doctor or had to deal with a family emergency.

Experiences of adjustment and community, however, differed for expatriate women who were single versus married, and for those living in compound villas (which functioned as neighborhoods) versus high-rises. Ashley and Jessica, both single, talked about significant struggles with isolation. When Ashley's initial appointment had her physically located in a Qatari organization, she experienced "overwhelming" bouts of loneliness until she eventually found ways to connect with other USAmerican expatriates. Jessica described a lack of shared interests with other single American expatriates, who in her observation, socialized mainly in the few hotel restaurants and bars where alcohol was served. Amanda explained single expatriates functioned in groups—the "party group," the "movie group," etc., and "it's hard to go back and forth between groups." You had to invite yourself to the group's social activities, and "if you're not part of it from the get-go, it's hard [to feel accepted]." The struggle to find spaces of belonging did not seem to be a result of other IBC expats' intentional exclusion[28] but rather had to do with in-groups forming their own habits and inside jokes. Expatriate bonding happened quickly, so being a "late comer" even by a few months could feel awkward.

Social networks and help adjusting to a new job and/or location are not unusual, but where the hybridity of the IBC scene did vary was in the blurring of lines between public and private. Melissa described her personal and work lives as "all intertwined . . . [The two] just can't

28. Bonding in home spaces provided the comfort of a network of other expatriates, but close social relationships can also complicate dynamics in the workplace. See Jakob Lauring and Jan Selmer's "Expatriate Compound Living: An Ethnographic Field Study."

be separated. And so that complicates things." Two of the most obvious concerns where the overlap became evident were (1) knowing what topics were appropriate for social conversation, and (2) knowing what personal information should be shared as a function of being employed that would not normally be shared between friends. Regarding the first overlap—topics of conversation—living in the same spaces as colleagues meant a breakdown in boundaries for talking about work. Going out to dinner on a weekend or watching a football game together likely included discussions of IBC-related issues. Escaping work seemed impossible. Experienced expatriates commonly declared "this is a no-business zone" to openly and immediately set limits, and lack of respect for these limits affected the feasibility of the social relationship. If you tended to talk about work, you might not be invited to the next gathering. Easy access to personal information (e.g., salaries and benefits packages and annual review information) further complicated friendships. Because we served on sensitive committees, such as those designated to choose award recipients and those assigned to investigate workplace ethics and civil rights violations, we sometimes knew too much about each other and/or had too much complicated influence over each other's professional lives.

The dissolution of public/private boundary is what Susan called "a blended life," one she did not find healthy: "My biggest stressor is that the people I report to are also people that are my really good friends." Melissa describes it as a challenge of "work-life balance," saying "It's compounded here and all intertwined because we have, as a university, to be responsible for where we live and many of the things that are associated with daily life. It just can't be separated, so that complicates things." Michelle, who initially worked for a local organization, indicated the overlap was particularly strong at the IBC. She said "compared to my working with the other (non-IBC) agency, working with this university, my social life and my work life are very homogenous and you have to be really careful." One of my personal stories illustrates the awkwardness of the intertwining: one spring weekend, I put on my swim suit, gathered up my kids, mixed up a large gin and tonic,[29] and walked to our

---

29. With a license—only granted once you provided a letter from your employer stating your monthly income, confirmed you were not Muslim, and paid a sizable security deposit—you could purchase alcohol and pork in the one store that sold them (the "Qatar Distribution Center"). Possessing alcohol and pork in the store was legal, and possessing it in your own villa was legal, but everywhere else, it was illegal and could result in fines, jail time, and deportation. For example, if I had alcohol and/or pork in my car and got in an accident,

compound pool to escape the persistent heat. As I sat down to relax, I noticed the director of our student services unit was having a party—including a dozen students, some of which were currently enrolled in my classes—two tables away. Not wanting to be seen by my students in a bathing suit with questionable beverages, I awkwardly packed up and retreated to my villa.

Similar to those in the IBC transnational workspace, home spaces and social spaces were scenes of confusion that revealed the ideals and privileges of the golden ghetto scene, but at the same time, reflected the reality that the expatriate community was so small that it created inherent constraints as well. Our advantages were also our restrictions. An odd dissonance of scenic constraints was created by the local government and the local culture as it prioritized privacy and protected the personal sphere, and by the IBC that was designed to breach the barriers between the public/work and the private/home/personal. The territorial claims of the IBC stretched beyond the workplace walls. The only real solution was to accept the reality of a blended life within the ideals of the privileged golden ghetto.

## A RHETORICAL FEMINIST LENS ON
## AGENCY IN PARADOXICAL SCENES

As participants in this study experienced and told stories about their lives at the IBC and in Qatar, what emerged were a series of paradoxical positionings rooted in the oscillation of the transnational scene. For USAmerican women working at the IBC, contradictions were based on competing commonplaces: what worked and what didn't work could be defined in radically different ways depending on which here (home campus? branch campus?) was in the foreground and which there (home campus? branch campus?) was in the background. Persistent awareness of *both* home and host campuses generated the transnational oscillation here-and-there between the two. USAmerican expatriate women working at the branch could not rely on the expectations of "normal" university business from the home campus or completely adapt to the particular expectations of the local stakeholders. Instead, they had to

---

I could have been arrested. For this reason, products were packaged in solid boxes or black bags, stowed out of sight, and driven directly to one's villa after purchase. So, is taking an unmarked cup of gin and tonic to the pool in my compound a public (illegal) or private (legal) act?

work within the paradoxical both/and of serving multiple bosses and systems, even when that service was accountable to secret agreements beyond their access. Although the IBC was designed as an idealized, highly rational border-spanning space established on a specific shared territory collaboratively structured by multicultural policies and procedures, its reality was rather different. It was a space of ongoing negotiation—the oscillation of transnational movements—simultaneously stabilized by replication of the one-hundred-forty-year-old flagship campus while also destabilized by ongoing social, economic, and other influences *both* on the home campus and in the self-modernizing/tradition-maintaining state of Qatar.

If feminist resistance to patriarchy is refusal to acquiesce to masculinist leadership practices and male-centric norms, then employees at the IBC had to confront competing patriarchies, primarily those of the IBC and Qatar (with QF and other governmental agencies as its mouthpiece). Masculinist IBC policies and procedures emphasized hierarchy and gatekeeping, even as the hybrid nature of the branch created confusion over whose values and logics held the keys. Add on top of that the multicultural nature of the workplace, and the result was a confusion of competing value systems emerging through everyday activities and mundane communication. Outside of work, local norms assigned expatriates to specific spaces and threatened deportation if we caused offense by transgressing those spaces. Within these scenes, it seemed "patriarchal reasoning [went] all the way down to the letter, to the bone" (Ahmed, *Living* 4).

How does an actor respond to a terrain that is a site of competing centers and margins, one that is plurilocal,[30] polylogical, and in a persistent state of change? As Burke writes: "terrain determines tactics" (*Grammar* 12). A masculinist approach would be to plant a flag, establish a singular guiding rationale to which everyone will adhere, and to encode the policies and procedures that will authoritatively guide action. Indeed, that is what the IBC set out to do, to replicate the directive, hierarchical structure of the masculinist home campus in the USA. Analysis of my interviewees' storytelling, however, reveals they reassessed the effects of their paradoxical positioning as "moments of beginning again" (Ahmed, *Living* 6). They acknowledged the complexity of and sought to learn from the shifting scene of "serving two masters," viewing it as a liminal site that required accepting complexity, seeking out mentorship, and observ-

---

30. Rose uses the term *plurilocal* but credits Peggy Kamuf for its origin (151).

ing (but not necessarily adopting) alternative perspectives and methods. In a rhetorical feminist move, they leveraged feeling *dis*-placed from our "normal" US scene as a chance to re-evaluate assumed premises.

A stubbornly persistent openness to learning from and living in liminality, as well as sensemaking based on pausing, listening, and prioritizing inclusivity emerged as rhetorical feminist tactics. Reflection prompted, for example, reconsideration of *kairos* not merely as constructed through calendars and meeting times but also nurtured through relationships and interactions that transcended them. It opened spaces for rethinking the common senses structuring our workplaces and how different people conceive of notions such as safety and honor. Despite the risks and stresses, we also often took on new challenges emerging from the IBC scene ("no team B") that allowed us to expand our professional qualifications in anticipation of pursuing better positions in the future. We learned to navigate the gratifying yet ethically and socially tricky "blended life" where the public and the private overlapped.

Viewed through a feminist lens, expatriate women's strategies of re-assessment, openness, and creative problem solving proved stressful yet were a source of Burkean "alchemic moments" (*Grammar* 24) through which the complexity of our scene (external) transformed us (internally). The overarching strategy was a form of Anzaldúa's *mestiza* consciousness: the IBC and Qatar were re-conceived of as spaces of experimentation or re-positioning, a revision from Western logics to more adaptive thinking: "The borders and walls that are supposed to keep the undesirable ideas out are entrenched habits and patterns of behavior; these habits and patterns are the enemy within. Rigidity means death" whereas "tolerance for contradictions" is a sustainable path (*Borderlands* 101). When my interviewees and I reassessed the priority of a Western/home mindset, we chose to "let it go," and to view our paradoxical positioning as moments of reflection or "sit-down things." Through learning to resist imposing our Western-centric practices on our transnational spaces, we believed ourselves transformed into better communicators and colleagues.

Particularly in light of the hostile policies, immigration raids, border walls, and detention camps along the southern USA at the time of this writing, I must amplify here that the "death" to which Anzaldúa refers is much more real and dangerous than a "death" that white USAmerican expatriate women risked in Qatar. For expatriates in Qatar, death could mean imprisonment, but most typically would translate to loss of a middle-class job and quick deportation. While those would have been traumatic, they are not the same as the potential dangers of the death to which Anzaldúa refers. The choice and ability to "let it go" and sit with our paradoxical positioning reflected our privileged status as white people with USAmerican passports. Our knapsacks of privilege are addressed more fully in the next chapter.

Recognizing multiple and shifting positionalities within a scene affirms an actor's fluid relations to power, oscillations between centers/Sameness and margins/Otherness. As Rose describes, women have learned to inhabit both the center and the margin by nature of being female agents within patriarchal systems. Simultaneous center/margin positioning invites a feminist "strategy of oscillation" or "the occupation of two positions at once," what Rose identifies as a "spatial paradox" of feminist localities (152). As USAmerican expatriate women at the IBC learned to live within the contradictory space, they began to develop this kind of oscillating perspective, an ability to recognize and consider the different territorial logics at work. As they grew more aware of the transnational scene's conflicts and complexities, they were able to both inhabit and critique it at the same time (151). Rather than shutting down the possibilities of multiple perspectives, my participants and I chose to "respond, reassess, and self-correct" (Glenn, *Rhetorical Feminism* 4) by accepting paradoxical hybridity and multiplicity as our new normal and devising rhetorical approaches for getting things done.

By being positioned in both the here-and-there, simultaneously in the center and at the margins, expatriate women recognized both the weight of their privilege and the reality of their vulnerabilities. Existing in this outsider-within space was both transformative and persistently troubling, and as this project continues to unfold, an oscillating perspective and growing critical awareness will lead further, to the possibilities of micropraxis for resistance and "strategies of subversion" (Rose 154–55) in part *because* of the shifting grounds on which our experiences were set. The transnational space of the IBC was generative because it created a shared soil—a Burkean consubstantiation—from which micropraxis could emerge. The ongoing tensions and confusion of the IBC taught us to recognize that small spaces for creative agency exist even amidst competing and formidable systems.

The paradox-laden scene, now established as the substance of our narrative lifeworlds, impacts everything else that occurs in our storytelling. The scene and our storytelling set the stage for micropraxis to emerge (previewed in the introduction, "Micropraxis as Actionable Outcome" and explored more fully in chapter 5). Micropraxis—as intentionally small, purposeful actions resisting socio-economic oppression—required creative problem solving, shifting positionalities, and awareness. As a practice, it emerged because white USAmerican expatriate women themselves felt the presence of contradictory and sometimes inaccessible (hidden, secretive) systems that disempowered them. The scene's alchemic moments pushed my participants and me to seek out small "moments of beginning again" (Ahmed, *Living* 6) through micropraxis.

The next chapter moves out of the IBC and into the public lives of my interviewees as gendered agents, telling stories of simultaneous hypervisibility and invisibility, of both privilege and vulnerability. The transformative impact of the transnational scene upon these agents is that it inspired some expat women to become more aware of and to rethink their responses to being white Western women in public places.

# 2 Invisible and Hypervisible

*I was never really self-conscious about being a white woman until I came here. —Michelle*

As feminist rhetoricians create, claim, and share space, the nature of the agent—as an actor with skills, strategies, and tactics—is centered. Rhetorical feminist practices should, as Glenn reminds us, "make a difference in the world" (*Rhetorical Feminism* 4). An actor or agent is defined by both her personal properties and her positioning relative to her co-agents and counter-agents (Burke, *Grammar* xix–xx). In other words, an actor's identity is relational. Any actor in a scene is always implicated in her web of contextualizations: she is not an agent unto herself but is an agent in relation to other agents and factors in the scene. Burke's paradigm is not as clear in accounting for the effects of how *other actors* define the agent and how externally applied labels of gender, race/ethnicity, age, socio-economics, etc., impact power relations and agency. Especially in places like Qatar, where language differences and social norms separated people, others' expectations about an agent were based on visible cues. In "Face, Skins, and the Identity Politics of Rereading Race," Ellen Cushman describes how we read each other's phenotypical features—primarily through faces—in order to determine then make assumptions regarding identity. Beyond being positioned within systems of control, being read by other actors in the scene further frees or constrains an agent's strategies and tactics. In sum, the agent's identity in the scene is a complicated and ongoing function of her own identifications, ascriptions made *about* her by other agents (with their own histories and identifications), and broader contextual factors that bring her into presence in the scene.[1]

---

1. Fernandez critiques the limitations of transnational feminism as grounded in "regimes of visibility" limited by tropes of materiality (102–05). (In)visibilities

Stories in this chapter provide an emergent narrative of ways white USAmerican expatriate women in Qatar adapted and responded to the paradoxical positioning associated with them as relational rhetorical agents. They were simultaneously hypervisible and visible, moral and immoral, privileged and vulnerable. As Michelle comments above, being in Qatar made expatriate women hyper-aware of their status as white, as women, and as white women. After exploring those identities as paradoxical sites of privilege and vulnerability, the chapter proposes that using principles of rhetorical listening to reframe our interpretation of and reaction to some forms of the gaze might open new spaces for cross-cultural curiosity and intersubjective connections. In doing so, it argues for a rhetorical reconsideration of in/visibility as a generative liminal space, an opportunity for self-reflexive examination of white privilege.

## WHITENESS IN A TRANSNATIONAL SCENE

The implications of whiteness are (re)invented upon arrival in other spaces. As Sarah commented, "White looks different across the world and what that means in America is very different than in other places." For example, even fair-skinned Arabs—in the Gulf and elsewhere—may or may not identify with the troped associations of whiteness.[2] Sarah's next story relates a conversation that happened on a service trip she took with a group of international branch campus (IBC) students, where her visibility as a white person and the troped nature of whiteness were foregrounded:

> In Uganda, mzungu *is the word for white person or foreigner. So clearly, I, pale and of Anglo-Saxon descent, am a white person . . . they call me* mzungu. *But the students would also get called that and they would just lose it. They were variant shades of darker than me but not as dark as the native Ugandans. And the students would say "I'm not white! Stop calling me white! No!" and I'm like,*

---

emerging in this chapter and my common grounding in the nation-state (e.g., branch campus as nation-state meeting point, national borders as navigable spaces) throughout the project demonstrate that commonplaces are the foundations of transnational study. They are a starting point, but as Fernandez points out, cannot be our ending point.

2. See Kristin Arjouch, "Gender, Race, and Symbolic Boundaries: Contested Spaces of Identity among Arab American Adolescents."

> *"No, you're* mzungu*" (laughing) and the students just lose it. It was*
> *very interesting that they couldn't deal with just being the Other.*
> *But also that they didn't want to be labeled the same as me. They*
> *didn't want to be the same Other as a white person. They were like,*
> *"*mzungu *is you, not me." —Sarah*

Sarah's situation finds multiple agents assigning identities to their co-agents in the scene. Sarah accepted her external designation as "white" and "foreigner" because it aligned with her own internal identifications as "Anglo-Saxon" and "pale," but the IBC students of varying national and ethnic identities disavowed this affiliation. To be *mzungu*/white was to be the Other, but not just any Other. To be *mzungu*/white was to have access to the wealth and privilege of the West. In East African countries including Kenya, Tanzania, and Uganda, "white Western women are socially constructed as 'Others' with access, or foreign and non-normative avenues by which black East African men can access the wealth, mobility, and status of an idealised Western lifestyle" (Z. Gross 2). Sarah's students' insistent rejection was not of being Other to Ugandans but of being white like her as a USAmerican/Westerner. Whiteness, although still generally a privilege, carried additional connotations regarding identity in international and transnational spaces with which her students disidentified. Because connotations varied according to situation, neither my participants nor I felt we could consistently predict what they entailed. Our white knapsacks (McIntosh) were visible, yet we had to guess what they contained.

Colorism, or the valuing of lighter over darker complexions, is a world-wide export of Western whiteness-driven discrimination. The beauty aisles of grocery stores all over Doha were stocked with lightening creams. Patricia experienced first-hand the value assigned to fair skin: "I remember being shown a photo of a student's mother. The student said her mother was very beautiful. I thought her features were not at all attractive. The student said that you couldn't really tell by this photograph, but her mother was very light-skinned. In her mind, this was the most important factor in her mother's beauty." I was traveling in Sri Lanka, sitting in a tuk-tuk as my partner went into a shop, and a man approached me from the street. His only purpose was to show me a photo. He removed the picture from his wallet with great care, and the age of the photo hinted that this girl was now a grown woman. He pointed to my face, rubbed his own dark cheek, then pointed to the girl in the photo, saying "white like you . . . pretty like you." As Krista Ratcliffe argues, whiteness itself is a paradoxical concept, simultaneously proven false or deniable as biological identity while persistently reinforced as true or undeniable through our global cultural systems (*Rhetorical Listening* 16). Stories like Patricia's and mine illustrate how we were confronted with the supremacy of beauty standards privileging light skin.

As a trope, whiteness in Qatar was tied to national identity and at the foreground of the local cultural logic. White was conflated with being Western, as originating from the UK, the USA,[3] and Western Europe. Globally, the Western/white trope is associated with economic, military, and political strength, and with social advantage. The "first world" is the Western/white world.[4] Therefore, the economic and social progress promised by globalization are defined by and reflect the values of the West, of whiteness. For example, Standard English, the language of corporate, capitalist, global culture, is white. Capitalism and the Western values associated with it drive globalization, so globalization is built on a cultural logic of whiteness and white supremacist beliefs (see Ratcliffe, *Rhetorical Listening* 14–15).

Demographics reinforced the conflation of being Western with being white as well as the locally privileged status it implied. While I lived there, Qatar's population passed the 2.2 million mark, with approximately ninety percent of people living in the Doha metropolitan area. Of the nation's inhabitants, only about twelve percent were Qatari nationals; seventy-eight percent of people were expatriates from Southeast Asia, mostly India, Nepal, Bangladesh, and the Philippines. Brits accounted for one percent and USAmericans for 0.43% (approximately eleven thousand) of the population (Snoj).[5] The country's overall popu-

---

3. Although celebrated through melting pot and salad bowl metaphors, the USA's media, government, entertainment, education, and fashion/beauty standards—broadcast to many parts of the world—are still dominated by fair-skinned faces, thus constantly reaffirming the convergence of USAmerican and white identities (Twine and Gallagher 10).

4. Japan is included in this "first world" category although it is not technically Western. However, the power of the first world trope and the multi-world narrative is so strong and so associated with the USA, the UK (including Australia as part of the Commonwealth), and Western Europe that the geographic distinction is often erased.

5. Most USAmerican were soldiers assigned to Al Udeid Air Base. Although the base does not release official figures, the number of military personnel was estimated to be ten thousand. Therefore, the number of civilian or non-military

lation also was heavily male. A large population of construction laborers was building the city; therefore, they were visible everywhere, while most expatriate and local women remained in domestic spaces. The estimated gender ratio in public was twenty men for every one woman,[6] meaning populated areas often seemed to be a "sea of [brown] bachelors."[7] In other words, white people were a tiny minority and white women a rarity in public. In relation or contrast to the high number of laborers, white women and men were in positions of elite economic and social privilege.

Whiteness intersected with other cultural categories, particularly national identity, to create a local caste system of who mattered more, a judgement affecting everything from who had to wait longest in a line

---

US expatriates in Qatar was small, around one thousand. Specific information on the gender and racial or ethnic identities of these USAmerican expatriates was not available. Outside of Education City, USAmerican expatriates in Qatar would have primarily been in white collar petrochemical jobs.

6. During the time of my study, Qatar's total population (including Qataris and expatriates) age fifteen and above had a gender ratio of one woman to every five men. Focusing only on the workforce, gender divisions were severe: the percentage of employed women to men was approximately one to ten. Within the Qatari population, the employment ratio was one woman to three men, so the differential was not due to local restrictions on women working but instead was a function of the sheer number of male expatriates in the country. See Qatar's Ministry of Development Planning and Statistics, "Labor Force Survey: The Second Quarter (April–June) 2013." Of non-Qatari women, approximately fifty percent toiled as nannies and maids in private homes. Domestic help came from a wide range of countries, but most common seemed to be the Philippines, India, and Sri Lanka. Out of every one hundred expatriate workers, only ten were women, and of those, only five (out of every one hundred expatriates total) worked in non-domestic spaces. That meant the effective representation of expatriate women in the public workforce was approximately one in twenty.

7. Expatriate laborers were recruited to build Doha's rapidly expanding infrastructure (for a study of their experiences, see Sheshan). Men—I never saw a woman working in a labor situation outside of the home—working in construction jobs were not offered the privilege of bringing their wives and families to Qatar. As a result, they were colloquially called "bachelors" even though many were married and had children in their home countries. The presence of so many seemingly "unattached" men, was a source of anxiety for some in the Qatari community. For example, a high-ranking official in the Gulf Cooperation Council (GCC) said that the expatriate male laborers in the region "represent a danger worse than an atomic bomb" (Janardhan).

to who had more influence in IBC or national decision making. Qataris were at the top of the hierarchy as the wealthy territorial owners and gatekeepers.[8] They controlled who could visit, who could be sponsored as an expatriate worker, the terms and conditions of our temporary residencies, if and how we might participate in Qatari society and culture, how we would be dealt with in the legal system, and when we could be dismissed from our jobs and deported. Through the employer sponsorship system, Qataris held enormous power over the other eighty-eight percent of the population, and sometimes assumed an entitled right to demanding priority in public situations (e.g., traffic, lines at the grocery, etc.). Following the Qataris in the local hierarchy, according to this lore structuring the expat community, were other Gulf Arabs (Emiratis, Kuwaitis, Saudis), then the British and the USAmericans. The great middle of the caste system included those from the broader Arab/Middle Eastern region and Western Europeans, with southeast Asians and Africans coming next. Although service jobs in hospitality and high-tech jobs gave some southeast Asian and African expatriates a higher individual status, overlap between social value and perceived worker role based on racial, ethnic, and presumed national identity seemed to be a defining factor in the overall ranking of how people were regarded. In other words, people who were seen as white were expected to have higher value—aside from Qataris and other Gulf Arab elites—in the nation's development and, therefore, were more privileged in daily life.

At the bottom of the caste system were domestic helpers and construction laborers. Women hired as maids and nannies worked long days, frequently with little time off. Although domestic laborers went on household errands, they were usually accompanied by their families or other household staff (e.g., a driver). Confined primarily to their villas and compounds, these women were generally kept silent and invisible. In contrast, construction laborers were a very visible presence as they worked long hours outside in brutal environmental conditions, including temperatures that could soar above 120 degrees Fahrenheit. In contrast to well-paid Qataris and Westerners, construction laborers were paid as little as 1,000 QR (~$274 USD) per month for working twelve

---

8. For Qatari nationals employed in the state, the gross national income per person in 2014 was estimated at over $120,000 USD. The country consistently has ranked in the top three richest countries in the world, and poverty has been considered non-existent among Qatar nationals (United States, Central Intelligence Agency).

hours per day, six days per week. Labor unions were illegal in Qatar, and the low pay and poor treatment of these expatriates led to the situation being called out as modern "slave labor."[9] Our privilege was defined in direct relation to their injustices, as the sheer size and depth of the systemic inequities were publicly apparent—and expressed via their exhausted brown bodies and tired stares—at all times.

The frankness with which I lay out this system reflects the stark nature of its presence in the country. It was everywhere and irrefutable. Evidenced by my participants' comments, my own experience, and innumerable conversations I had with other USAmericans in Qatar as well as while traveling abroad, white USAmericans knew we were externally identified through our faces, bodies, dress, body language, and accents, and that we synecdochically represented the USA or the West. Therefore, we were aware of being always in a process of reifying, complicating, and/or disrupting the stereotype of the loud, uncouth USAmerican and/or the economically and culturally empowered white person. Ethics, conscience, reason, and self-expression are features that define the identity of the agent (Burke, *Grammar* 171); by extension, an agent's acts define—and confirm, confuse, or contradict—the broader populations they represent.[10]

Beyond whiteness being a trope implicating people into a system of transnational stereotypes, the valuing of some national/racial/ethnic identities over others was a discriminatory commonplace, a shared as-

9. Unethical recruiting and illegal employment practices—including confiscation of expatriate passports, failure to provide reasonable living facilities, and late or non-existent salary payments—created concern over basic human rights (see reporting by Ames or by Pattisson). The situation drew the attention of Amnesty International ("Qatar: Migrant Workers Still at Risk of Abuse Despite Reforms") as well as Human Rights Watch ("World Report 2013: Qatar").

10. Nira Yuval-Davis writes that "(Hetero) women/mothers are, indeed, often constructed as embodiments of the homeland" (94). "However, it is not the figures of the women/mothers alone that symbolize the homeland, but rather the imaginary social relations networks of belonging in which they are embedded" (95). So USAmerican women are not simply synechdochal extensions of the USA as a nation. Instead, USAmerican (white) women represent the greater systems and opportunities of the USAmerican mythos. As Raka Shome argues in *Diana and Beyond: White Femininity, National Identity, and Contemporary Media Culture*—a deep examination and critique of white femininity—the media, and national identity, "white femininity is a mechanism for the distribution of national hope" (26).

sumption from which daily life proceeded in small but significant ways. As an example, I had a Nigerian friend who had lived in the USA, a woman with a dark complexion and a mildly Texan accent. She and I discussed the nature of how whiteness indicated status in Qatar, and she told me the story of needing to take her young daughter into an open K–12 school to use the restroom. As they approached the door, the security guards denied her entry, but when she opened her mouth to speak and they heard her USAmerican accent, their refusal immediately transformed into an apology and a gracious welcome. Although her skin color marked her as undesirable, her presumed national identity flipped her status to respected. Amy's comment reinforces that discrimination is based on ethnic or racial identity more than perceived economic status:

> *We have friends, she is Scottish and he is American. He was born and raised in the Midwest somewhere but he is African American, and I casually brought up in a conversation one day something about how interesting it is here how it's more a separation of class rather than a separation of skin color . . . And he was like "I beg your pardon?" He was like "I've lived and worked in this region ten years and I'm constantly being handed empty coffee cups." I was like whoa, okay, it is kind of alive and well even though I didn't perceive it that way before. And so for me, I think about my skin color and, whether it's here in Doha or it's in the region in general or even as we travel, I'm more aware of it even than I was back in the States. —Amy*

Other intersections with whiteness further categorize agent identity, particularly through establishing *ethos*. As will be discussed later, a white woman was assumed to be some combination of moral and immoral, trustworthy and dangerous. A white woman *professional* was a curiosity, assumed to be unusual in her intelligence or abilities if she had been chosen for a job over a man. Being in a white body meant being treated with unearned deference and respect. Being in a white *woman's* body meant being *both* patriarchally protected as an assumed possession of white men *and* erased, ignored, or resisted.

Exposing whiteness as a trope reveals it as a fallacy driving scenic logics and determining a scenic commonplace; however, despite—or perhaps because of—its fallacious nature, it created another paradoxical positioning. Being white women made us both hypervisible and invisible. Whiteness also made the scale of our privilege undeniable and became a primary force shaping how we framed ourselves as agents and related to other agents within the scene. Krista Ratcliffe writes that "if we associate discursive agency with tropes . . . what emerges is . . . a question of how the agencies of different sites converge to effect moments of rhetorical usage" (*Rhetorical Listening* 121). What emerged in this study is how transnational scenes and white privilege converged to awaken or disrupt white USAmerican women's awareness of their racial advantages as well as their en-gendered inequality.

The focus here is on agent visibility/invisibility or presence/absence within the scene, because seeing and being seen were primary modes of intercultural interaction, particularly as our transnational space was shaped by differences in language or social norms (e.g., keeping people separated due to gender and economic class). Because these divisions prevented other forms of interaction, visual communication was sometimes the only option. Visibility occurred in many layered ways: the state watched its residents, the organization watched its employees, the compound watched its inhabitants, and people in public places watched each other. The challenge of how to act in response to the gaze invited a rhetorical feminist rethinking of the relations across expatriate caste systems and the options we had for bridging those terrible gaps.

## Veiled, Unveiled, and Surveilled

During my time in Doha, *all* expatriates received mixed messages about gazing across cultures in public spaces. Local norms emphasized privacy or respect for invisibility. Architectural styles favored walls around all individual houses (called villas) and around groups of houses of any size (compounds). For local families, privacy within and surrounding domestic spaces was paramount.[11] Walls were typically beyond head height and many entrances were covered by solid metal gates. Courtyards or parks in larger compounds were generally at the center, and exercise equipment, recreation areas, and swimming pools were behind internal walls of their own. Facilities and parks had "family days" or "ladies' days" to allow women to participate in activities out of the view of men.

---

11. For a detailed description, including illustrations, of Gulf domestic architecture, see Lockerbie's website, catnaps.org. The page "Gulf Architecture 01" considers the role of privacy in particular. His "Expatriate Housing Study" page describes how villas were adapted for families of middle- and upper-level managers from the West (Britain) and northern Arab states.

As a part of cultural Islamic practice, keeping women away from the male gaze was purported to maintain female respectability and to shield men from temptation.

Beyond allowing for women to be out of public view in buildings or other facilities, Qatar's local dress norms created another standard of "invisibility" in the name of modesty for women. One ubiquitous way Qatari nationals marked their identities and affiliations was through dress. Qatari men commonly wore white *thobes* (robes) and either white or red-checked *guhtras* (head covering), and Qatari women wore the traditional full-length black *abaya* (women's over-garment) and black *shayla* (scarf). Some women wore the full-face veil (*niqab*) and gloves to be completely covered. Older local women often wore the traditional *batoola* or gold-colored mask to cover their faces. None of these traditional garments was required by law, but local customs—bolstered by familial pressure—led to a vast majority of Qatari men and women wearing the garments daily.[12] For women, the *abaya* and *shayla* were public performances of Muslim modesty intended to draw attention away from sexuality.

A good example of tensions over modernizing while maintaining tradition was discussion of visitor dress codes. Typically focused on women, it concerned communication and enforcement of social rules. Non-Muslim women and men (people who otherwise do not subscribe to Islamic dress code) were instructed to wear clothing that covered from their shoulders down to their knees. In the weeks leading up to the holy month of Ramadan, norms grew more conservative, and experienced expatriate women made sure to cover at least to elbows and mid-calf, if not fully to wrists and ankles. Other expatriates either consciously or unconsciously pushed these boundaries—it was somewhat common to see white women in the mall or the grocery wearing spaghetti straps or shorts. Figure 2 is one of several posters that were part of a "Reflect Your Respect" campaign, published and distributed by the Twitter account @ oneofus_qa in 2012, with slight variations re-released in 2013 and 2014.

---

12. Fromherz hypothesizes that Qatar has been able to maintain its stability in the shifting regional sands by reasserting (he would say inventing) its cultural identity via national dress and the construction of a strategic national and Islamic historical narratives in local museums. He says that this process is intended to reify definitions of insiders and outsiders, further stabilizing local tribal identity.

According to the Twitter account, the purpose of the campaign was "to make Qatar a modest and peaceful place for everyone."[13]

IF YOU ARE IN QATAR, YOU ARE **ONE OF US..**

HELP US PRESERVE QATAR'S CULTURE AND VALUES, **PLEASE DRESS MODESTLY\* IN PUBLIC PLACES**

**\*BY COVERING FROM SHOULDERS TO KNEES**

FOLLOW US @ONEOFUS_QA

Figure 2. In the weeks leading up to Ramadan each year, local social norms become more conservative, in anticipation of the holy month. During this time, handouts and posters such as this one from 2012 are distributed in malls and other places expatriates frequent. Modesty Poster by @oneofus_qa, published via Twitter.

---

13. See D'Mello and Scott, "Campaign for 'Modest Dress' Relaunches in Malls and Public Spaces," published on *Doha News* on June 21, 2014.

The "Reflect Your Respect" poster emphasized women's bodies and dress as three of the four figures appear to be feminine. The X underneath each figure indicates the types of inappropriate clothing: no short dresses or exposed shoulders, no tight-fitting clothing or short pants, and no exposed midriffs. The fourth figure is male and indicates no exposed shoulders, no exposed chests, and no shorts. Although the signs came in other colors, making the bodies purple in this example marks them as generic or un-raced. They are every-bodies. Wording on the sign is in all capitals and uses liberal bolded font to highlight the main messages. The effect of the bold all capitals was one of authority, the tone of which could be interpreted as accusatory. The writer could be yelling.

All the posters I saw in malls and online were written in English, implying they were aimed at Western audiences or at least audiences that have been educated in Western-influenced styles. The sign's language is inclusive, stating boldly "If you are in Qatar, you are one of us." Telling an expatriate that she is "one of us" was ironic, because we knew that although we were valued as invited guests, we would never be "one of" the Qatari citizenry. In fact, we also knew that being accused of "culturally offensive" behavior (I put that in quotation marks to indicate that offense is often in the eye of the beholder) could get us deported within forty-eight hours. Despite that obvious mismatch between the ideal (tolerance for Western dress norms) and the real (intolerance of Western dress norms), my interviewees and I—indeed most in the expat community—respected the local norms and abided by them. An asterisk on the flyer further defines what the sign means by "please dress modestly" as "covering from shoulders to knees." It also specifies that this modesty campaign was concerned with "public places." The host country's differentiation between public and private was consistent and clear, which made the IBC blending of public into private (discussed in chapter 1) feel even more paradoxical. Expat spaces for IBC employees were *both* public *or* private and public *and* private.

Disobeying local systems of privacy and modest invisibility could be met with swift and serious consequences. For example, a visiting research assistant, newly arrived at the IBC, heard music from his villa one evening and saw decorative lights draped over the house next door. He went up to his roof to see what was going on—it was a woman's wedding. In Doha, women's wedding parties were held separately from the men's so attendees could remove their *abayas* and *shaylas* to enjoy their social time together. Phones and cameras usually were banned to uphold local standards of privacy. According to what I was told from multiple sources, the visiting researcher could see the beautifully dressed (and uncovered) women from his rooftop and took a picture of them. Less than an hour later, the Qatari police came to his villa and arrested him. He was deported within days—and that deportation was the result of negotiation with the IBC. The family of the woman hosting the party had wanted him imprisoned.

While privacy and elected invisibility were part of local scenes, expatriates were expected to respect them yet not assimilate into them. The most common first question friends, family, and future colleagues asked me before coming to Qatar is "do you have to cover?" Covering can mean anything from the basic *hijab* headscarf to the *niqab* or *burqa* (full covering). The short answer was no, we were not asked to cover. Once someone spent any time in Qatar and got to know Muslim women through work and social life, the various coverings became normal. As Amanda told it, "My mom will ask silly questions, like 'Is it intimidating when you're with people who cover?' And I'm like, 'No. Is it intimidating to you when you walk into church and someone is wearing a dress?'" In this project, I do not address the politics or perceived oppression of the veil for two primary reasons: (1) most of my interviewees did not bring it up, and (2) the Western obsession with the Islamic veil is an enormous topic on its own.[14] The veil has become its own Orientalizing trope, an assumed source of oppression and frustration for women who wear it. But the actual story is both more complex and persistently oversimplified. Mohja Kahf, in her chapter "The Pity Committee and the Careful Reader," describes how the Western media portrays women in Middle East—marked by the visibility of Islamic coverings—as either helpless victims or heroic escapees of Islam.

In contrast to the local emphasis on personal privacy and elected invisibility, a sense of being watched, of being visible, was also strong for expatriates. Government surveillance was high. At the heart of expatriate sponsorship was the controversial *kafala* system. To work in Qatar for any reason and in any job required a sponsor and qualifying for a

---

14. See Fatima Mernissi's *The Veil and the Male Elite: A Feminist Interpretation of Women's Rights in Islam* and Rabab Abdulhadi, Evenlyn Alsultany, and Nadine Naber's *Arab and Arab American Feminisms: Gender, Violence, and Belonging.* For additional perspectives see Margot Badran, "Understanding Islam, Islamism, and Islamic Feminism" as well as "Between Secular and Islamic Feminisms: Reflections on the Middle East and Beyond."

residency permit. Sponsors were Qatari employers, although a spouse (almost always male) could in turn sponsor his wife and family. Homosexuality was considered a sin, so the only relationships recognized as legitimate in Qatar were heterosexual. Sponsors controlled the expatriate's rights to leave (and re-enter) the country, get bank loans, and buy alcohol and pork. Sponsorships and permits were renewed annually but could be terminated at any point by the employer or state. *Kafala* sponsors received immigration notifications each time an expat passed in or out of the country. My partner, as the male head of our family, was my sponsor, and he received a text message the instant my entry or exit was affirmed at the airport kiosk. For our first year in Doha, he also received a text notification from the bank with the location and amount every time I used my debit card.[15] Security guards—generally unarmed—observed our comings and goings at most compound gates, the Education City gates, the IBC parking garage gates, and most building entrances, even in public spaces including malls and major grocery stores. Inside Education City university buildings, an identification card tracked every room an employee entered. Traffic cameras monitored all major intersections and highly traveled roads.

A public service campaign appeared—seemingly overnight—enigmatically reminding all Doha residents, "We all see you. You are not alone" (Figure 3). The message was written in both English and Arabic, with the English font again being in bold all capital letters similar to the modesty campaign sign. The bright yellow background was reminiscent of a warning sign. The shadowy figure's proportions and hair seem to indicate it is a child and so may be relatively innocent; however, the figure's lurking and peering implied a creepier public surveillance and disruption of local privacy norms. The lack of additional information—all we knew was that we were being watched—created confusion when the signs appeared. Not surprisingly, the campaign's initial effect for expatriates was to increase paranoia. A few weeks later, more new billboards clarified the public service message aimed at reducing litter and public spitting, but the "We all see you" tagline remained the same.

---

15. The *kafala* system kept tight control over all expatriates in Qatar and other states in the region, but was applied in the most troubling ways to labor and domestic workers. Some sponsors used it as an excuse to confiscate passports and, even when workers were not being paid, refuse them the right to leave the country. Due to these and other abuses, stories of expatriates fleeing to the protection of their home country's consulates were common.

Figure 3. In 2014, public service billboards such as this one appeared through-out Doha. Expatriates were confused and concerned over the message that they were being surveilled, but the campaign turned out to be about public cleanli-ness (e.g., spitting, littering). Image from the author's personal archives.

Surveillance of all Qatar citizens and residents extended to online ac-tivity, too. At the time, Qatar's Internet access was through one state-owned provider that monitored traffic and blocked sites identified as pornographic, anti-Islamic, or critical of the government.[16] Figure 4 is the censorship screen a user received if she tried to access a site deemed inappropriate. The silly characters, their surprised expressions, and the

16. Although Qatar's page on The OpenNet Initiative is out of date, it explains the general surveillance capabilities.

helpful, informative tone of the page is non-accusatory, indicating a gentle redirection for the user. However, expatriates knew that their Internet activities were being surveilled, so many used VPNs (virtual private networks) to shield themselves and avoid the censorship net altogether.

Figure 4. Websites considered pornographic or antithetical to local morals were blocked, and users trying to access prohibited material were taken to this screen from Qtel, Qatar's sole telecommunications provider. "Qatar Filtering Message" by JadIJadI Is licensed under Creative Commons 3.0 (creativecommons. org/licenses/by/3.0/deed.en).

Individuals could censor each other online as well, reporting to police remarks or actions they deemed culturally offensive. These accusations were not without consequences. Qatar's 2014 Cybercrime Prevent Law specifically assigned a fine and a prison term of up to three years to anyone who "violates social values or principles, publishes news, photos or video or audio recordings related to the sanctity of people's private or family life, even if the same is true, or insults or slanders others" (Kovessy). The threat of imprisonment over critical commentary—regarding the government, a Qatari organization, or a Qatari individual—being deemed an insult halted online discussion over the realities of living in Qatar (e.g., harsh inequalities of the local labor system). Keeping the complex local reality invisible was important to the nation's reputation and so meant keeping the reality of the country's struggles silent or only within private quarters. Visibility in both real and virtual spaces was managed to ensure expatriates stayed within the legal and moral constraints of the host nation.

Being surveilled—and knowing that you were being watched—revealed the power of the state as an agent within the scene. In Qatar, state agency was a means of controlling everyone but particularly the expatriate population as invited guests who could be uninvited at the hosts' pleasure. Being in the privileged Western or white class did not exempt one from being surveilled and caught up in the local legal system, but when an IBC employee faced a legal situation, she had the privilege of asking for help from the IBC. For example, when I was in a minor traffic accident, an IBC employee who was fluent in Arabic and versed in the local systems helped to make sure my situation was resolved fairly. The picture-taking research assistant above also avoided jail time because the IBC intervened on his behalf. Therefore, the local power and influence of our Western/white employers provided an advantage that could help us navigate the complicated justice system. We also had a well-staffed, responsive, and visibly engaged US embassy in Doha.

Despite knowing they were being surveilled in numerous identifiable ways, my interviewees did not seem sensitive or resistant to the government's eye. When I asked several white female faculty colleagues about this lack of concern, they theorized it could be because Qatar was generally considered to be a safe place with very little crime, and expatriates likely attributed feelings of safety, in part, to pervasive surveillance and the social control it reinforced. Because we felt safe in our daily routines, we accepted surveillance as the trade-off. Although none mentioned concerns regarding this visibility, knowing it existed as part of the scene amplified anxiety over other troubling forms of being seen. Although we felt somewhat protected—less visible—because of our Western/white ascribed identity, we felt hypervisible because of it, too.

## Paradoxical Hypervisibility and Invisibility

Because so many women in Qatar (certainly not all, but a vast majority) did cover their hair, the lack of covering unveiled us as non-Muslims and having a light skin color further identified us as white Western-ers.[17] In other words, the primary impact of the *shayla* or Islamic veil

---

17. I recognize I'm engaging reductive binaries here: Western/non-Western, veiled/unveiled, Muslim/non-Muslim (which for white/Westerners was as-

for USAmerican expatriate women is that we *lacked* it. By embodying the externally assigned [Western] woman trope and the internally as-signed USAmerican woman trope, we represented not only the USA as a national imaginary but also the morality of USAmerican women. Summarizing Peter Stallybrass, Glenn writes, "For the past twenty-five hundred years in Western culture, the ideal woman has been disciplined by cultural codes that require a closed mouth (silence), a closed body (chastity), and an enclosed life (domestic confinement)" (*Rhetoric Retold* 1). Yet the trope of Western feminine modesty was at odds with our be-ing in public spaces that required speaking and interacting. The presence of our bodies—not "closed" off by *abayas* or *shaylas*—further marked us as potentially immodest no matter what we wore. Our heightened visibility often was read by others (particularly non-Western men) as an invitation to gaze. Because we were not participating in the local cultural performance of modesty, we must have been inviting attention. At the very least, we sent and received mixed messages.

A faculty colleague told me about a classroom exercise confirming this view. She had designed a transnational collaborative project between students at the IBC and students in the US. In preparation, she discussed stereotyping with her IBC class so her Arab and international students would be sensitive to assumptions embedded in online interactions. As part of the discussion, she asked her students to tell her their stereotyped perceptions of USAmerican men and women. USAmerican men were seen as hard working, excessive consumers of alcohol, and sports lovers. *Female* IBC students said USAmerican women were well educated and ambitious, but *male* students said USAmerican women were known to be blond-haired and loud, scantily-dressed cheerleaders and "sluts." My colleague did not know if the female students characterized women as well educated and ambitious as a way of defending her honor as their in-structor, if the female students were seeing things their male colleagues refused to acknowledge, or if some other gendered perspective dynamic was at play. Another colleague who had lived for years in other areas of the broader Middle Eastern region verified to me that USAmerican women, even in places labeled more "cosmopolitan" such as Cairo and Beirut, were commonly assumed to have loose morals. Knowledge of

---

sumed to be Christian), etc. Because of the linguistic and social barriers that prevented more frequent communication across different national, gender, and economic identities, these binaries and their associated stereotypes were often the primary tools for people's daily intercultural sensemaking.

these stereotypes shaped how we knew we were perceived by others and would influence how we reacted to being aware of our visibility.

If being identified as white in Qatar made an agent visible and if being identified as a woman made an agent visible, then being a white woman made her *hyper*visible. Her knapsack of privilege[18] was also visible, to others not like her but sometimes to her as well. As Michelle's epigraph states, "I was never really self-conscious about being a white woman until I came here." Our self-consciousness was a result of an oscillating positioning where we reflected over being embodied at home in the US as well as in the host space of Qatar. When on US soil, I was an *in*visible middle-aged woman, which made the feeling of being looked at in Qatar particularly unsettling, something I did not know how to react to. Even in Qatar, however, our positioning was paradoxical, both hypervisible and invisible. Expatriate storytelling reveals this paradoxical positioning was a source of both power and vulnerability.

## In/Visibility as Privilege

All twelve interviewees responded with an immediate "yes" when asked if living in Qatar had changed their perceptions of themselves as white people. Nine out of twelve agreed their experiences had changed their perceptions of themselves as women, mostly in terms of confidence, assertiveness, and the ability to move in and across different spaces. All twelve associated their hypervisibility with privileged social status. Emily said, "With my own blond hair and blue eyes, it's very easy for me to get special treatment here. Whenever I had to get my car inspected, I went up to the female only area, and they let me go first, before the other women there. There were other Arab women, but they let me go first and I know it's probably because of my appearance." Ashley said others told her of difficulties getting attention or service in the city, and when she told them she has not experienced that struggle, they replied,

18. In the spirit of McIntosh's list of conditions in "White Privilege and Male Privilege," I offer a few of the assumed conditions I experienced as "white expatriate privileges in Qatar": I could trust my employer to pay me on time and according to the terms of my contract. I could expect the terms of my individual contract to be stated clearly, ethically, and in my primary language. I could expect to be able to enter and leave my host country as many times as I wished as long as I remained in good standing with my employer and the law. I could expect to be able to gain entry (a visa) to most nations in the world, many visas upon arrival rather than through prior application.

"that's because you're blue eyed and blonde." Sarah offered the following specific example of when she and two female friends went to a crowded sporting event:

> *We went to a soccer game, and leaving the game, out of fourteen gates only seven are open, and everyone is being redirected towards those. It's mass chaos and a sea of men and they're pushing all up against us . . . Other people's sweat is on my body, which is disgusting. If a [a famous] team had not been playing, I probably would have turned around and gone home. So finally, the guards see us and say "You three!" and they pull us to the front of the sea of seemingly sub-continental men, which made me feel really guilty. I knew they were only doing this because I'm a white woman, but I felt uncomfortable and possibly unsafe, so I took the chance to get out of the chaos [and skip to the front]. I've spent some time thinking about the privilege that comes with that. —Sarah*

Emily's and Ashley's reflections as well as Sarah's story focus on the power associated with being identified as white women. What Sarah describes as the "mass chaos and a sea of men" centers the gender imbalance in some public spaces. The phrase "seemingly sub-continental" highlights the men's brown skin in contrast to Sarah's and her friends' white skin. Being unveiled, unrobed white female bodies in a "sea" of brown men heightened the women's visibility. Sarah recalls feeling "uncomfortable and possible unsafe" because of the crowd's size and sheer force of being masculine. Although they did not ask for special treatment, their visible existence led the guards to pull them to the front, granting them the privilege of quicker access to the exit.

Patricia's story considers hypervisibility from a different perspective:

> *Women in this culture are taught to walk very slowly so as not to make anything jiggle. Once, I had left my office heading to the ladies' room. I was thinking of the million things I needed to do, looking at the floor as I charged down the hall. I don't think I was jiggling, but I was definitely in a great hurry. Out of the corner of my eye I saw two young custodians—who, together, didn't weigh as much as me. They were terrified as they fell all over themselves and each other trying to escape from an infidel Western woman. I didn't slow down, but I did hug the opposite wall so they would know they were safe. It was all I could do not to laugh. But I did feel sorry for them. —Patricia*

Here, Patricia is concerned with the custodians being terrorized by her being an "infidel Western woman" as she "charged" authoritatively to the restroom. She remembered being amused, yet Patricia also had become aware of her body as a trope of white domination, identified in relational opposition to local women. Calling herself an infidel was a self-effacing and humorous way of saying that she knew the men in the hallway saw her as a potentially dangerous Other. That danger emanated out of the hierarchy that extended her advantage or power over them both as employees inside the IBC and as expatriates in a system that valued white skin and Western affiliations over others. As she remembered the power dynamic that sent the custodians falling "all over themselves and each other trying to escape" her sudden presence, Patricia simultaneously referred to the immodesty of a woman's body jiggling as a potential visibility that worked to her disadvantage. Her story highlights both the power and vulnerability of the embodied presence of the white expatriate woman.

These embodied experiences inspired both Sarah and Patricia to reflect over what Ahmed calls "sweaty concepts," ideas that cannot "be fully comprehended in the present" (*Living* 12) and so "throw up a life as a question" (195). Sweaty concepts can be tied to specific experiences, like Sarah's situation "that comes to demand a response" (13) not in the moment that she and her friends are leaving the soccer game but in the ways she subsequently related to others through her whiteness and her female identity. A sweaty concept emerges out of "a critical, problematic, or striking set of circumstances" (13) like Patricia being jolted out of contemplating the million things she had to do and into the power-riddled scene she inhabited. A sweaty concept inspires the reassessment and self-correction of being a rhetorical feminist (Glenn, *Rhetorical Feminism* 4). In other words, a sweaty concept invites feminist sense(re)making.

Just as a conversation moved Ashley to realize her ease in getting attention was related to being white (as well as blond-haired and blue-eyed), Sarah "spent some time thinking about the privilege" she experienced at the soccer stadium. The power of being white women in relation to non-white others (of all gender identities) was the source of privilege in some situations. Krista Ratcliffe establishes that in the USA, "performing whiteness is often a very visible practice for non-white people" (*Rhetorical Listening* 112) while "performing whiteness is often an invisible practice for white people" (113). Patricia lacked awareness as she moved down the hallway contemplating her job duties, enmeshed in the

Sameness of the white IBC system. In that moment, her performance as a Western professional busy at her job was not visible to her until she was confronted by her own hypervisible Otherness in the eyes of the custodians. Across the city of Doha, the sheer number of expatriate laborers—embodied as "subcontinental bachelors," a.k.a. scores of brown men—makes whiteness and its advantages highly visible. Rather than reinforcing a USAmerican assertion of colorblindness or "denial of race as an issue" (116), experiences such as Sarah's and Patricia's amplified awareness of racial differences and associated systems of bias. My interviewees' reassessment and self-correction, a repositioning that amplified rather than denied whiteness, was a rhetorical feminist tactic that shaped their stories about what it's like to live in the country. Their experiences also joggled them into reflection over their roles in the local systems and their privileged status at home and abroad.

While previous stories have described privilege set in public spaces, Michelle told a story of how being a white woman elevated her status and *ethos* at her job:

> *When I worked for the non-IBC agency here in Qatar, it was during a global financial crisis. And lots of Western media were very interested in Doha and how it was so successful [in the midst of the crisis]. So since I was obviously the Westerner, I was the "perfect fit" (sarcasm) to talk to these people even though I have no idea about [the financial sector]. So the media was talking with a major Qatari business leader, and I was brought in to chitchat with him about the interview prior to it taking place. And he was absolutely knowledgeable about the financial industry in general and [about local practices] specifically. I told him, "Here's what they're going to be asking you: 'With the global financial crisis, business is failing, banks are failing, and real estate is history. How is [your sector] posting recording profits and rewarding their stakeholders record benefits?'" And he said, "Well, we just won't answer that because the government is propping up [this sector] but we can't say that to the media." And I said, "Well, you can't just tell the media you're not going to talk about it." And he said, "Yes, I can." And I said, "No, sir, you cannot." I said, "You can say it, but here's what will happen: you saying that will make even more of a story." And so it was me, discussing with [this powerful local leader] how he may or may not speak to the media. And he was actually listening to me.*

> *As a professional [at my level], that would never happen anywhere else. — Michelle*

Michelle said occasions as that one made her feel like a "superstar" but at the same time "very humble because you're working in this environment" in which "you hope people are supportive" because ultimately you know that "you don't understand the social fabric."

Michelle's story illustrates opportunity created via agent visibility, through being *gaijin* and "third sex." The exotic[19] nature of being present as an outsider female agent can work to a white Western woman's advantage. Human resource management scholar Nancy Adler describes "*gaijin* syndrome" as the tendency of host nationals to see foreigners as outsiders first, regardless of gender ("Pacific Basin Managers" 187). In the workplace, being *gaijin* grants foreign women a higher level of access than male expatriates because being *gaijin* is complemented by a "curiosity factor"[20] or what Adler calls a "halo effect" where local stakeholders assume female expatriate professionals are even *more* qualified than their male counterparts. The sentiment goes like this: "if the company sent a foreign *woman*, then she must be the best of the best." In Qatar, white women's visibility functioned in relation to the more modest and moderated visibility of local women, making expatriate women's visibility even more evident compared to local norms. A final feature of being *gaijin* is that a foreigner woman is not expected to act like a local woman[21] and is

---

19. This term is used purposefully to echo and invert Edward Said's foundational work in Orientalism on the fetishizing of the exotic Other in representations of the Middle and Far East.

20. See Nancy Napier and Sully Taylor's "Experiences of Women Professionals Abroad: Comparisons across Japan, China, and Turkey."

21. The most conservative, Shari'a-based social norms—adopted by some but not all Qatari families—could prevent women from any dealings with men outside of their immediate families, could mark the choice of work over motherhood shameful, and could place men in the role of primary earners (Bahry and Marr 109) yet still effectively bar Arab women from fully entering the public sphere (Metcalfe, "Gender and Human Resource Management" and "Women, Management, and Globalization"). Expat women in the workplace were not in direct tension with traditional Islamic law or practice, but expat women made visible the controversial presence of any women in public spaces and lingering arguments over what spaces women can inhabit. As a result, the presence of women in public spaces fed tensions in the state's traditional/self-modernizing approach.

not expected to be a standard bearer for local morality. Political scientist Jillian Schwedler writes about conducting field research across the Middle East, where she witnessed Western female scholars calling themselves the "third sex" (425) because they could speak to both Arab men and Arab women in the workplace without facing local gender constraints.[22] The ability to recognize and negotiate this form of agency-via-identity may offer expatriate women access, but being a source of curiosity has risky implications for other ways foreign women are perceived. Women of other identities and men may resent their access, and being the object of this sort of amusement may mean their work as professionals is not taken seriously.

Tacking back to Michelle's story, a halo effect was assigned to her because of her gender and foreignness. As a result, she was granted access to local leadership "that would never happen anywhere else," particularly because she "had no idea" about the financial sector situation on which she was asked to advise. As a *gaijin* foreigner and third sex woman, risks regarding gender norms (e.g., speaking to an unrelated male in private, directing a high-powered government authority) were mitigated. Assumptions of exceptionalism, paired with curiosity regarding her as outsider, granted her discursive agency and authorial *ethos* (Ratcliffe, *Rhetorical Listening* 121–126). Despite her relatively lower rank within her organization Michelle advised the high-ranking Qatari official, and he listened to, respected, and followed her instructions, even though she contradicted his original rhetorical strategies of avoidance. Being a woman in *gaijin*/third-sex situations is paradoxical because in those spaces, gender is both a source of limitation—a reduction to an exotic, extra-moral Other—and a source of opportunity.

Along with the power of their visibility, expatriate women recognized power associated with purposeful *in*visibility. Michelle, who had felt like a "superstar" due to her enhanced opportunities as a foreign woman, told another interesting story of purposefully reducing her visibility at work. When she arrived at her job with the local agency, she requested to hire a male, Arab counterpart to appear or act as the lead in specific situations. She made this request because she knew "some local clients would not want to deal with a woman." She explained that she would accompany her male employee to meetings but would remain quiet and let him take

---

22. Also see Tine Ustad Figenschou's "Young, Female, Western Researcher vs. Senior, Male, Al Jazeera Officials: Critical Reflections on Accessing and Interviewing Media Elites in Authoritarian Societies" (973).

the visible lead. Hers was, in Glenn's terms, a rhetorical self-silencing: it was active, predictive of interrupting contextual gender issues, and supportive of a specific discursive scene and purpose (*Unspoken*). Intentionally stepping back from view, Michelle nevertheless maintained her status as primary or controlling agent in the scene by hiring and managing her male employee, and by choosing when to foreground him in client interactions. Through her knowledge of local contexts, she was able to subvert the gender hierarchy by reducing her own visibility in it. As a rhetorical feminist tactic, choosing silence as a form of agency allowed her to listen to the clients and empowered Michelle to think purposefully and critically about their needs. Hers was a savvy adaptive agency. Ahmed writes about women and the feminine: "To become accommodating, we take up less space" (*Living* 25). While that diminishing is usually to a woman's disadvantage, Michelle flipped the script and used it as a means of disrupting the patriarchal status quo.

## In/Visibility as Vulnerability

Although powerful in their in/visiblity, USAmerican expatriate women also experienced vulnerability tied to their externally ascribed agent identities.[23] Being the object of the male gaze was generally associated with negative implications. Sarah said she felt men "ogle" her and "heap extra criticism" on her because of her identity, and Amy commented she "didn't know being a female was a disadvantage" before becoming an expat and finding herself either stared at or ignored. In conversation, "dyadic visibility" is established as dialogue partners make eye contact. However, social and cultural norms prescribe when, how, and how much eye contact to make. Multiple interview participants mentioned receiving specific advice about avoiding eye contact with Gulf Arab men. For

---

23. Continuing in the spirit of McIntosh's list of privileges, here are conditions that I could not depend upon. Sponsorship and gender were the root issues—many rights were granted through sponsor permission. However, because my husband technically was my sponsor—even though I was employed by the IBC—he was in control of my situation. Almost all sponsorships in Qatar were through the male head of a family. Although single women could be sponsored by their employers, a wife sponsoring her husband was unusual. Because I was an expatriate in Qatar, I could not assume that I could leave the country with or without my children unless I had my sponsor/husband's permission. I could not get a phone or a bank account without my sponsor/husband's permission. I could not buy alcohol or pork products without my sponsor/husband's permission.

example, Melissa said, "I was told, you know, because of the segregation of genders in Qatari culture, to never look a man in the eye. So I automatically was just freaked out about that." I was told the same in the hour-long "cultural sensitivity training" I received at the home campus prior to relocating to the IBC.[24] The effect of the warning was awkward, especially considering that in USAmerican culture, eye contact in conversation typically indicates attention, turn-taking, and integrity.

Avoiding dyadic gaze led to frustration and a sense of invisibility. For example, Lisa said, "the most interaction you have with Qatari men is in the mall, and there, I feel like I'm invisible. They never look at me in the eye." The IBC was staffed mainly by expatriates, so for staff who did not teach local students, interactions with Qataris were limited to the kinds of informal moments that occur in public spaces. In conversations with Gulf Arab men, most of them college aged and in my capacity as a faculty member, I noticed eye contact was brief. In the next chapter, I describe my experience getting my Qatar driver's license, involving a long quest of trying to find the *one* person in the country who could sign a form converting a USAmerican license into a Qatari license. On four separate trips, a branch campus liaison escorted me to different traffic offices, where groups of men would talk about me in Arabic. As I stood to the side awkwardly, they discussed my request in terms I could not understand. No one would look at me or signal formal awareness of my existence, and certainly no one spoke to me. I was invisible and the status of my license to drive was at their disposal. A similar public erasure happened at restaurants, where a friendly male waitperson would have extensive conversations—in English—with the men at the table, but would avoid eye contact with me, even when taking my order.

I discussed eye contact differences over multiple semesters with many classrooms of IBC students, and the conversations unfolded in a remarkably consistent way: when I talked about being told to "never look a Gulf

---

24. I was also told that the local culture understood blue eyes to symbolize jealousy or greed, so when a blue eye settled on someone or something, a local person might perceive it as a curse. Having blue eyes myself, I did not know what to do with that information. Should I wear sunglasses all the time? Always look away from other people? Such tactics would be ridiculous. As students explained to me later, it was not just looking through a blue eye but the way anyone—of any eye color—looked at material goods and how their body language might impart a sense of jealousy. Although I gradually made a better sense out of my visibility in my host culture, the comment in the pre-departure training was a source of stress for months.

Arab man in the eye," the male students would laugh and shake their heads, "No," they would say, "that's fine for you as a non-Arab woman [*gaijin*], to look men in the eye." However, the Arab female students would eventually speak up and correct the men, explaining that yes, a "lady"[25] must be careful about eye contact. They told me it is more serious between Gulf Arab men and women—that eye contact perceived as flirting can give the Qatari lady a bad reputation that can affect her marriage prospects. For expatriate women, marriage prospects were not threatened; however, combine this local gazing norm with the stereotype that white women are "sluts" and the admonition to avert your eyes made more sense. As Glenn reminds us, women are to remain "closed" in their social and moral roles, and as Rosemarie Garland-Thomson, author of *Staring: How We Look*, notes, "A gentleman's stare damages others; a lady's stare damages herself" because being the gazing subject "imperils a lady by opening up her engagement with the world" (70). Expatriate women in Qatar were told to avoid eye contact that could be judged inappropriate by local norms and in order to combat stereotyped assumptions about them as immoral outsiders. Even as it protected their reputations as tropes representing the excesses of the white West, avoiding eye contact erased women by rendering them invisible as subjects.

Being paradoxically invisible and hypervisible led to struggles in sensemaking. As Ashley illustrates, we look for stories we can tell ourselves and that we can share with each other about how to best represent ourselves and our identities, but a narrative explanation is sometimes out of reach.

> I don't dress poorly or show a lot of skin, but that doesn't matter. I go out in my workout clothes and [men are] throwing[26] their numbers at me, asking me to get in the car. It's just how they are here. It's the local, Qatari men. I also get the bad part of [the attention], too.

---

25. My Qatari female students taught me that in their society, a *woman* was sexually experienced (married, divorced, or socially scorned for immorality), so I had to adjust my Western feminist vocabulary. While I resisted calling female students *girls*, I made an effort to call them *ladies* even though for me the term carried outdated and fallacious connotations of normative femininity, patriarchal morality, and binary gender roles.

26. She means this literally. Men would write their mobile numbers on paper and throw the paper at her. Men could also "throw" solicitations digitally through social media and instant messaging tools, seeking out contacts from other users nearby.

*And I think they equate the way I look to maybe be like an Eastern European prostitute. —Ashley*

Ashley was seeking a logical explanation for being harassed, resorting to the traditional gender-discriminating narrative about clothing and skin, amplified by local modesty norms, yet she still struggled to interpret the level of attention she persistently received. That the men were Qatari was an assumption Ashley made as a result of their external identity markers, especially in regards national dress, even though the *thobe* and *ghutra* were widely available for anyone in the region to wear. Just as notions of being Western were conflated with white, notions of being Qatari were conflated with a traditionally dressed, seemingly wealthy Arab phenotype. When I asked Ashley about this assumption, she said a companion of hers was able to speak the Qatari dialect of Arabic to help ward off the harassment in some situations, and those exchanges were another way she confirmed her belief that her aggressors were local. To be fair, however, the ability to learn the dialect, like the national dress, was not confined strictly to locals. The "Eastern European prostitute" comment was meant literally and was partly a function of identities Ashley perceived she was being assigned. She had fair skin and hair, was young, and was often unaccompanied by a male. Her reasoning that she was being assigned the prostitute identity was based on media reports of some Gulf Arab locations, particularly Dubai, being hotspots for the sex trade specializing in Eastern European women (see Chakarova).

Reflective of Qatar being a hybrid transnational scene, interview responses framed the male gaze in two different cultural and socio-economic contexts: the aggressive attention of Qatari or other wealthy men versus the open, silent stare of the labor worker. Both heightened women's feelings of vulnerability, and in this section, I focus on the aggressive attention emboldened by socio-economic power. In these stories, the novelty of being white/Western, independent women was a source of dangerous vulnerability. Even as they resisted quick assumptions and tried to allow space for differences in cultural non-verbal cues, my interviewees experienced how "curiosity is interest headed towards possession" (Garland-Thomson 47) due to their hypervisibility:

*The first four months I was here, I used to go out. Go to the clubs, see what they're all about. But no. When the same people who met me at one place, I also see at the next place and the next place and the next place.*[27] *And they knew my name. That was when I was like, "Nope. I'm finished." It's the same people at all these places, and they don't forget you. It's Somalians and other [North Africans] that are looking for entertainment here. They've lived here their entire lives. They want to meet up and hangout with expat girls, Qatar Airways chicks, you know. It was like I was in the middle of a bad fad situation. They probably know every young girl in Doha. They want to make friends with all of them and do whatever. It was like "Nope!" So that makes what happened lately in the news with that British young teacher*[28] *who got killed even worse. —Jessica*

*I've been approached a couple of times to go home with Qataris (laughing). I was at Hardee's once, eating by myself, and a guy comes up. He doesn't speak English. I knew better than to speak to him in Arabic because I knew he would get excited. So we talked in some bad English. He asked me if I had a house, and I told him yes, I live here. And through broken English, I realized that he wanted me to go home with him. I said no. And he told me, "No, it's okay. We'll go home tonight, and I'll take you back tomorrow." And I said "No, no, no." I told him that I'm married, that I have a husband. And he tells me, "No, it's okay." And I'm like, "No, it's not okay." So he finally left. –Emily*

*[Qatari men will] stop behind me and take pictures of my butt. They'll tell me to get in the car. It's just a daily occurrence. I used to park in the parking lot, and they'd pull their car in right behind me so I couldn't get out, forcing me to talk to them. . . . As a single woman it's different than it is when you have kids. It's a different*

---

27. Bars in expensive Western-owned hotels were the only places where alcohol was served in public. As the population of white-collar expatriates was relatively small and the prices of the drinks and food further restricted access, a small sub-community ended up frequenting the establishments.

28. Jessica is referring to the 2014 case of Lauren Patterson, a British expatriate teacher who was raped and murdered, and whose body was burned by a Qatari national. Questions over the identification, prosecution, and consequences for Patterson's murderer were a major source of concern for expatriate women, who feared that justice would not be served to a Qatari. See Ruth Sherlock's reporting in *The Telegraph*.

*world, like they're starving for this girl contact and they don't know when to stop. —Ashley*

Jessica, Emily, and Ashley offered similar stories of men desperate to interact with young white/Western women. Later in the interview, Jessica wished she could "be a stranger" again, invisible to the solicitous male gaze. These stories of vulnerability locate women—by the storytellers themselves—amid the tensions of male possession/consumption and basic freedoms. As my interviewees sought to participate in public lives through driving, going to clubs, and eating in restaurants, men tried to trap them—quite literally corner them—and "take [them] home" to use them for "entertainment." Stories of harassment told by younger interviewees were disturbing. As Jessica commented, being perceived as young and unmarried exacerbated their visibility as targets. While Jessica's feelings of vulnerability pushed her to limit herself socially, Emily met vulnerability with rhetorical agency as she argued back and took control of the situation by, for example, choosing to speak English instead of Arabic so as not to further pique male curiosity. Ashley experienced the most extreme version of this harassment, including one situation that ended with one offender being deported.

Hair color as specifically enhancing vulnerable visibility was a topic with multiple interviewees. Mary, the mother of teenage daughters, reported her naturally blond-haired daughter was so disturbed by being the object of public gaze that she dyed her hair brown and indeed perceived herself as less visible with darker hair. Lisa interpreted how she was treated as a response to her blond hair and, by troped extension, her white/Western identity: "Qatari men have been very rude to me. Maybe that's because I'm a blonde. Well, maybe not. Okay, this is what I've felt: they resent us because we have autonomy. We can do what we want to and we're a bad example for their women." Ashley had worked for a short time at the local university that was more conservative and traditional regarding gender norms of dress, behavior, and segregation. Her hair style was called out as a symbol of her assumed morals:

*I'm always very conservative in my dress. Purposefully, because when I came from the local university, I did cover completely. I didn't wear an abaya, but I did wear something over my shoulders as well, and I always wore my hair up. I wore my hair down one day in a year and a half, and a colleague came up to me and said, "You know we all think you are as loose as your hair is." And I was like "okay, I'm putting it up!" (laughing) That was the one day I wore my hair down and never again. —Ashley*

Although she reacted with good humor, Ashley used her colleague's comment as an insight regarding the reality of local modesty norms. Although public rhetoric such as the "Reflect Your Respect" campaign seemed to clearly state what those norms were—and made no mention of hair—they were also a source of lingering confusion. Boundaries of appropriate dress and behavior for expatriates seemed to shift, heightening uncertainty about the lines of modesty and local morality to which we should conform. Our conversation focused on what public modesty campaigns *said* (e.g., to cover from shoulders to knees) versus what they *meant* (e.g., that we really should cover to our elbows and calves and keep our hair up). We wanted to respect our hosts and moderate our visibility as foreigners and as women, but our uncertainty and confusion added to our feelings of vulnerability.

To live a feminist life, whether by choice or by survival, means "acquir[ing] words to describe what we come up against" (Ahmed, *Living* 34). Through their storytelling, my interviewees revealed the pervasive, substantive, and complex ways that visibility occurs in and is shaped by being white foreign agents. Some of their stories—of being policed regarding their dress and hair, of being sexually harassed—are just another strain of the same exhausting songs sung in the USA and all over the world. Other stories reflect the challenges of the scene, where their presence is an embodied trope of modernization: women in the workplace, expatriate diversity, Western education. As visible symbols caught in the simultaneous change of progress and conservatism of tradition, my interviewees were vulnerable to resentment because of their autonomy and the encroachment of the "white devil" they represented. Ahmed's reflection is an apt response to these stories: "These are complicated scenarios: you can receive some benefits by adapting yourself to a system that is, at another level, compromising your capacity to inhabit a world on more equal terms" (*Living* 36).

The experiences described in this section reflect one aspect of the paradoxical scene, situated at a shifting intersection of tradition and modernity. The simultaneous privileging and harassment result from the conflicting messages emerging from a mixture of people, attitudes, and logics about women's places in public spaces. A clear local shift in narrative regarding women's roles had not yet formed. In other words, local logics regarding gender were all over the place because the mix of people and values were all over the place, oscillating between self-modernization and conservation of tradition. Adapting to the vulnerability of their visibility (and invisibility) did not yield specific new rhetorical feminist tactics. Our responses were the same as they always have been: we spoke back and claimed our space when we could, and we withdrew to invisibility when we did not sense the agency to respond. Despite not developing any new tactics, however, being conscious of our vulnerability, particularly as it was set amidst our significant privilege as white Westerners, was a source of feminist becoming because it pushed us to consider other vulnerable populations in our daily lives.

## Transnational Staring as Rhetorical Listening

The men who felt empowered to harass women in the previous section were not the only men in Qatar, and they were not the only source of the gaze that my interviewees and I became keenly aware of. In this last section, I focus on the persistently present gaze of the expatriate laborers present in great numbers. This gaze, as a form of staring, occurs across not only gender and racial/ethnic differences but also linguistic, cultural, and enormous socio-economic chasms. Because of its particular nature, I call it the *transnational stare*. Eleven out of twelve interviewees brought up being stared at by laborers and described it as uncomfortable because the nature of the staring was difficult to read. I remember sitting in traffic, looking up through the vehicle window, and finding dozens of laborer eyes staring at me. A few were taking photos of my young daughter from their higher vantage point in the bus next to our car. The staring could be prolonged, and my participants and I struggled with how to react. Michelle and Melissa provided sample stories and comments:

> *Here, you have to be very careful. . . . If a man is just looking at you, he could be just looking, but you smiling or whatever could be taken as something else. Women aren't forward like that [here], and [smiling] is seen as forward, I think. So considering if it's a local man, a Western man, it's very different. An Asian man, it's very different. But I had to become very aware of where and how I react to that [staring]. In the US, my immediate response is to smile, say hi, acknowledge someone's looking at you, but here that might not be appropriate. —Michelle*

> *So one of the coping mechanisms when I'm in public . . . because there's a bit of staring and that can be can be uncomfortable . . . when I'm out especially by myself, I have a bubble around me. So I basically—for example, let's say I'm at the grocery looking at fruits and vegetables—I'm here with the fruits and vegetables (motioning with her hands to indicate a narrowed space just around her) in my bubble and that's it, and so there might be a perception of "she's arrogant, rude, not friendly." I'm not, so I think that that's sort of something I established early on to cope with being uncomfortable, a little bit out of my comfort zone, and people looking at you. —Melissa*

Both of these women, when confronted with the transnational stare, felt a sense of intrusion and were compelled to "take care" in their reactions. As Ahmed writes, it can be "too much. Not to be assaulted: maybe you might try to close yourself off, to withdraw from proximity, from proximity to a potential" (*Living* 23–24). While Melissa had developed a strategy for shielding herself, Michelle tried to contextualize and read the gaze. To do this, she grappled with varied cultural logics of seeing and being seen as she carefully considered her available repertoire of re-actions. [29] Her story foregrounds questions of being appropriate and how she wanted to represent herself and the entailments of her white female identity. She came to understand that decisions had weight. Michelle later explained how she had to "realize that it's nothing aggressive, that there's no malice meant in it. It's not offensive." In the absence of malice or sexual domination, what remained was a perceived curiosity, perhaps mixed with anxiety over difference and fear concerning power, as re-vealed earlier in Patricia's story of being a jiggling infidel. Melissa created a bubble of personal space around herself as a means of blocking out or denying the presence of the stare.

As told above, Mary's blonde teenage daughter dyed her hair brown, and Ashley kept her hair in a ponytail or bun, not just in response to

---

29. Although focusing on Qatar, I acknowledge the obvious point that the male gaze is present across most cultures. As I was in the midst of this study, a public service announcement was published in India by Whistling Woods International, as part of a celebration of Indian cinema. The video, titled "Dekh Le," asks men in India to consider the effects and implications of leering at women by turning the leering around on the men through reflective props such as mirrored sunglasses. The culture of leering, staring, or gazing could have been imported with the sheer number of male Indian expatriates in Qatar.

harassment but also as a means of accommodating themselves in the eye of the transnational stare. A non-Muslim friend who had been in Doha for over ten years wore a *shayla* whenever she was in public; when I asked her why, she said it was because it helped reduce her visibility and made her less the object of the gaze.[30] Women covered their skin, changed their hair, covered their hair, built a bubble, hugged the wall, and responded with the silence of averted eyes: all were ways to "take up less space" (Ahmed, *Living* 25). Accommodating other people by withdrawing from view and taking up less space *could* be a rhetorical feminist tactic because shrinking one's white body could be a means of making more space for others at the table. However, it was not the intention at this point in the narrative. The point here was to hide from view as a means of self-protection as a response to feeling vulnerable to the male gaze and transnational stare.

Connections between power and gaze are undeniable, but what was interesting in Qatar's transnational scene was the question of whose stare was dominating whom. The country's significant gender imbalance had adult men outnumbering women five to one overall, ten to one in the workplace, and twenty to one on the streets. That imbalance amplified the presence of men. Finding myself as the only woman on a street as I was shopping, especially on Friday—the laborers' day off—was not unusual. Once, I was waiting on a store to open as a mosque let out its worshippers and found myself alone amidst a sea of at least a thousand men. Although they mostly ignored me, the sheer experience of being an Other among so many is certainly jarring and potentlally conscious raising. Expatriate laborers were also subject to local narratives that unfairly framed them—because of their sheer numbers and sheer male-ness—as a "menace" and a "threat to families . . . personal security and the general cultural integrity of Gulf Arabia" (Gardener 19). Although none of my interviewees use these degrading and fear-mongering words to describe the laborer population, its visible presence was undeniable.

---

30. Was it appropriation if the people who authentically wore the *hijab* were happy for non-Muslims to wear it and if it was worn to deflect attention? My Muslim students and colleagues alike were quick to compliment any move towards assimilating into the local culture as long as it was done in a positive spirit. The *hijab*'s meaning was deeply personal. For a Muslim woman to wear it probably meant a commitment to her religion, but for a non-Muslim to wear it meant it was simply a scarf. My colleagues and I had many conversations about appropriation versus assimilation, and I was not able to reach a clear and consistent conclusion.

The greatest problem my interviewees and I struggled with was making sense of the gaze's intent and power. Unlike most other studies of male gaze, my participants and I as objects of the transnational stare were not disadvantaged. We wielded economic and social power because we were white, and we had a reasonable degree of individual agency sometimes earned (through professional experience) and sometimes assigned (linked to whiteness and sometimes to gender). Our constraints—for example, being barred from speaking out against local systems—were imposed not by laborers but by our Qatari hosts. In contrast, laborers typically were denied most forms agency, including local economic power, freedom of movement, and options for speaking up or out. The local systems were designed to reduce them to being part of the scenic backdrop.

A primary form of agency that laborers could not always be denied, however, was *the agency of looking*. When the "menacing bachelors" did the gazing, they rendered themselves visible as subjects to white US-American expatriate women. In other words, rather than feeling the shame of being an object of the gaze, an expatriate woman *only saw the laborers when she herself was seen*, and in that moment of mutual transnational eye contact, what she saw—and may have felt the shame of—was her white privilege. The tempting response was to look away.

In Garland-Thomson's words, my participants and I were unable "to recognize, in anything but the most superficial manner, individuals amid the flood of mass-produced strangers," and we were easily overwhelmed (35). Our typical solution, as Garland-Thomson predicts, was "simply not to engage with them, to notice them as little as possible unless necessary, and to surround ourselves with shields of privacy" (35). Non-engagement was a *rhetorical* erasure of the laborers and perhaps of ourselves, a form of protection but also a form of disidentification or a *disavowal*, "an identification that has already *been made* and denied in the unconscious" (Ratcliffe, *Rhetorical Listening* 62). It was also a denial of our own privilege, granted by a violent and discriminatory system (117).

To return the stare of a man *we knew* to be trapped in a system compared to "modern slavery" was to be confronted with our own complicity in globalization's inequality. Yet our agency, our ability to work for any justice or even just basic humane treatment, was restricted, too. Qatar's regulations prevented us from social justice outside governmental charities. These organizations—while actively aiding Syria, Palestine, Egypt,

Haiti, the Philippines, Nepal, and other international sites—did not seem to be doing much to help those who were building the local streets, malls, compounds, and World Cup stadiums. One Christmas, my children's school organized a gift tree where we could leave basic supplies, food, and mobile phone cards for some workers, but the Ministry of Education shut down the project. Apparently, the Christian holiday was not the problem. Instead, the MoE told the school we were not allowed to have an independent charity project of any kind. Even as we were privileged guests in the country, the temporary and tenuous nature of our own positions as expatriates prevented us from challenging the system. We knew we were being surveilled, and offending a high-powered Qatari or disrupting public order and morality risked being deported or jailed ourselves. Our privileged status as guest residents ended when it was trumped by the privilege of Qatari citizens and their policies. Neither my interviewees nor I faulted the host government for wanting to control their own country, but our avoidance of meeting the transnational stare of the laborers was not simply a denial of our own complicity but also a recognition of our shared precarity.

Rather than dwell only on the oppression of objectification, Garland-Thomson's *Staring* engages feminist rhetorical practice of critical imagination as it reconceives of seeing and being seen as a potential process for interpersonal connections. She takes up staring as a form of open and honest curiosity, considering the topic from a broad perspective as well as through the lens of disability studies. Garland-Thomson defines a stare as "an intense visual exchange that makes meaning . . . more than just looking" (9) as opposed to the "gaze, which has been extensively defined as an oppressive act of disciplinary looking that subordinates its victim" (9). Differentiating between staring and gazing allows her to "bring forward the generative rather than the oppressive aspects of staring" (10). Garland-Thomson contrasts the curious stare from the unfocused, unseeing blank stare; the dramatic, gape-mouthed baroque stare; and the dominating stare, among others (9). In her terms, curiosity as a generative, open stance stops short of desire for domination.

When Garland-Thomson writes that "Each one of us ineluctably acquires one or more disabilities—naming them as variably as illness, disease, injury, old age, failure, dysfunction, or dependence" (19), she reminds her readers that in some point in all of our lives, we will find ourselves outside the ableist norms that structure the flows of our world. In amplifying the inclusion of us all, she invites application of her generative stance on staring. However, please understand that as I turn to her work, I fully recognize that none of my interviewees or I had visible disabilities, and we were not stared at in the same ways as those whose bodies are labeled this way. The visible disruption we created was by being women, white, and white women and resulted in being both invisible and hypervisible. Through that appearing and disappearing, we disturbed the local "routine visual landscape" of public spaces in Doha (20). As I take up Garland-Thomson's inspiring work into this expat narrative, I acknowledge my adaptation and re-application. By acknowledging the generative intersubjectivity that may happen between the seers and the seen, I hope to demonstrate my respect for Garland-Thomson's work rather than clumsily (mis)appropriate it.

In transnational spaces, staring is sometimes our only expression of curiosity. Verbal interaction is impeded or impossible due to linguistic, socio-cultural, and/or other scenic factors. I could not stop the bus to ask the men what they were thinking or why they took the photos of my daughter. Understanding through dialogue was often unfeasible. Of course, reasons for staring are highly individual and contextual—just because I learn why one person stares does not mean that the information is generalizable. Therefore, although "being stared at demands a response" (Garland-Thomson 3), the nature of that response—as Michelle tells us above—was difficult to determine. In this transcultural, nonverbal hybrid scene of seeing and being seen, a rhetorical feminist tactic materializes from interweaving of Garland-Thomson's stare of curiosity with Krista Ratcliffe's rhetorical listening.[31] Recasting the disconcerting transnational stare as potentially generative encourages starees to *look back* rather than retreat, and rhetorical listening reminds us to pause in a moment of contemplative nonidentification and to stand under the implications of the exchange.

Redefining gaze as generative and as engaging a listening position are rhetorical feminist tactics because they subvert the agonistic mastery of the hegemonic rhetorical tradition. Both moves reconceive of persuasion as embodied, based in dialogue, and achieved through multiple mo-

---

31. Krista Ratcliffe proposes rhetorical listening to re-establish the value of the aural as a means of productive participation in cross-cultural dialogues, particularly concerning the intersection of race and power ("Rhetorical Listening: A Trope for Interpretive Invention and a 'Code of Cross-Cultural Conduct'"). Her theory pushes back against the ocularcentrism of classical Western rhetorical theory (201), so I acknowledge that here I am re-turning to the privileging of sight/gaze, a move that Ratcliffe's original theory may resist.

dalities. Whereas meeting the eyes of the starer can reduce strangeness and bridge anonymity through a visual encounter, rhetorical listening engages in an interpretive pause and potential (re)invention—Ahmed's "beginning again"—as a means of becoming more familiar with others and ourselves. In sum, both Garland-Thomson's staring and Krista Ratcliffe's listening acknowledge that our identities are relational and interdependent. Both theories emphasize potential for learning, for building better understanding across difference. Ratcliffe's accountability logic is based in appreciating that "none of us lives autonomous lives . . . that we are indeed all members of the same village . . . [and] have a stake in each other's quality of life" (*Rhetorical Listening* 31). As such, being accountable means recognizing the Other—who may be erased or silent—as present in our shared world. Both listening and staring are complementary forms of invention, sources of rhetorical feminist sense(re)making. Rhetorical listening's examination of tropes in (visual) interaction can further inform the staree's repertoire of potential responses. Garland-Thomson's and Ratcliffe's theories work together so gracefully because they engage a wider range of rhetorical agency beyond the verbal, and they work together so powerfully because they are both designed for generative, transformative action. They behold rather than disavow.

These last stories, from Lisa and Amy illustrate what a new rhetorical feminist sense(re)making of "transnational stare as rhetorical listening" might yield. Their counter-narrative inspires my theory building because they offer an alternative to turning away.

> *These people [the laborers] don't see their families. I can see my girls whenever I want to. At least I recognize that. I have made myself say that to myself, to recognize our privilege. And again, you don't even think of them as men. They're [treated] like machines. And that's what I talk to myself about. I say, "you can't have that attitude." So I smile at the workers, and they smile back (laughing). Something that small thing makes a difference. —Lisa*

> *I remember one time, this happened not too long ago, I was sitting in traffic, and I looked over and it was a bus but it wasn't just packed full. And there was one guy in particular at the end, and he looked very young. And he was looking at me, so I noticed but I looked ahead, and the light was still red, and I looked back and he's still looking at me. I looked back at the light, and then after a few minutes, he's still just staring at me. But I did not feel it was*

> *weird, almost like he was just young, and I don't know what he was thinking. So then as the light turned green and we started to move, I just waved, really big. And he got the biggest grin on his face, and he waved back. And I couldn't help but think that was some kind of connection. He was acknowledged as a human being. So there wasn't any of that objectifying weirdness about it. —Amy*

Their stories illustrate the transformative power of rhetorical listening and generative staring as a way of reconceiving of agent identity in this transnational scene. It is a rhetorical feminist reassessment of how power and privilege shape interaction and a self-correction that denies the power of the systems seeking to reinforce division.

Meeting the transnational stare has generative potential: "Rather than passively wilting under intrusion and discomforting stares, a staree can take charge of a staring situation" (Garland-Thomson 84). Both Amy and Lisa rhetorically listened to "transpose a desire for mastery [performed in the white turning away or denial of oppression] into a self-conscious desire for receptivity [by acknowledging the presence of the Other]" (Ratcliffe, *Rhetorical Listening* 29). Amy was aware she could not read across cultural logics ("I didn't know what he was thinking"), yet she disavowed the menacing bachelor trope by recognizing her visual interlocutor as "very young." Lisa rejected that same trope by reinterpreting the starers' identities as fathers, sons, and brothers she identifies with through her own identity as a mother of daughters. Lisa also mentioned the "machines" comparison, less common but still present in the cluster of terms used to describe the workers (e.g., treated like "cords of wood," "not humans," "blue jump suits") all of them dehumanizing. By acknowledging their unjust treatment and lecturing herself that she must transform her views of the laborers, Lisa expressed awareness of her privilege. Amy's and Lisa's stories describe a re-cognition leading to transformative moments. Lisa resisted the social pressure to deny the laborers' humanity by rethinking the white status quo of looking away or retreating into a bubble. Both women hoped for a circuit of meaning making in their dyadic interchanges, a mutual acknowledgement and reduced "strangeness" across the socio-economic and gender divides.[32] Amy's last point on "that objectifying weirdness" could refer to what she

---

32. Although my interviewees did not know it, studies suggest smiling is "the opposite of staring as dominance display," because smiling mitigates hostility and (when reciprocated) indicates submission in the starer (Garland-Thomson 41). Their hope for a connection perhaps was more than naïve optimism.

perceived in his stare but could also refer to *Amy* resisting the urge to objectify *him*.

Emerging from these stories of paradoxical invisibility and hyper-visibility were literal and metaphorical eye openings with regard to rhetorical agency. Our time abroad inspired coming-to-consciousness regarding white privilege as one aspect of feminist becoming. Although the effects of privilege are often silent or unobserved—an *absence* of struggle—in the USA, living in Doha foregrounded whiteness and con-fronted us daily with our complicity in the local caste system. Staring that privilege in the face as well as seeing it stare back at us demanded our response, and because of the scenic constraints, our primary options were to meet the gaze or to retreat into an insulating bubble of denial. Based on the stories and observations from this study, we tended to os-cillate between both. Finding ways to reduce strangeness, disrupt tropes, make new meaning, and work towards accountability were rhetorical feminist tactics that some women adopted. Small acts seem trivial in the face of mass struggle, yet willful resistance (Ahmed, *Living*) must start somewhere. Through momentary *micro*-connections as human be-ings, as seemingly insignificant as smiling and waving across gender and socio-economic difference, we generated *micro*-reminders of shared hu-manity, and in doing so, challenged ourselves as USAmerican expatriate women to find ways to advocate for justice even within local constraints. In sum, our own struggles with questions of visibility and complicity set within the complexity of the transnational scene had the power to cata-lyze acts of micropraxis.

Simultaneous hypervisibility and invisibility affect the rhetor's status and functioning. Typically, being an actor means being visible in the scene. Locating opportunity to act and to have rhetorical agency means being available as a subject of other actors' gazes or stares. Agency is also a function of identity: we perceive our options for action in part based on who we perceive ourselves to be within the situation. However, iden-tifications are not only internal—they are also externally ascribed by those to whom we are visible. Although the agent is marked by the look-ers' identifications of her, what she does with those moments of being in view can be a source of not only agency but also praxis. Many expatriate women retreated from the stare in an effort to protect themselves and in an effort to present themselves as moral female representatives of the USA. Imagining themselves in bubbles of protection, they carried on with daily life, like Virginia Woolf's Mrs. Dalloway, they went "about maintaining the appearance of being fine, an appearance which is also a disappearance" (Ahmed, *Living* 63). Yet ironically, retreating from the stare and disavowing their roles in global inequity only reinforced systemic injustice.

We think of being feminist as standing up, claiming our space, being willful, but the nature of this transnational scene—the oscillation between USAmerican ideals and realities of limited power as well as precarity in the host country—meant adopting a variety of different tactics. Becoming feminist was a process of becoming aware of being both privileged and vulnerable, of rhetorical feminist sense(re)making by "finding another way to live in your body" (Ahmed, *Living* 30). Rather than having to "to wiggle about just to create room" (18), we sometimes reduced our spaces or muted ourselves. Being racialized and gendered bodies in another country was generative because rather than living in the comfortable denials of whiteness in the USA, we became much more aware of what it's like to be "a body that is not at home in the world" (13), even with our privileged status. Having experienced diminishment by being made or making ourselves invisible, some expatriate women took up Ahmed's "sweaty concepts" of transnational life as exigencies for feminist reflection. Recasting the transnational stare as an opportunity for rhetorical listening was a rhetorical feminist process of sense(re) making. Rather than accommodate the local caste system, some of us resisted it by looking back, by feeling the weight of our privilege, and by feeling the humanity and injustice of our scene. Grappling with visibility ourselves and re-cognition of the laborers' visibility led to us asking ourselves "then what can I *do*?" The simultaneously mundane and profound action of *looking back*—a refusal of comfortable denial and a turn towards the discomfort of recognizing our privilege—was the first step towards seeking out more substantive opportunities for agency. Beholding rather than disavowing. Because of the complicated scene and our own hypervisibility/invisibility within it, acts were to remain smaller, under the radar of the systems that controlled us; thus, the *micro* nature of the praxis we sought out.

So far, we have established the alchemic nature of the transnational scene and have considered how it set the stage for paradoxical experiences of hypervisibility and invisibility as well as how it inspired transformative feminist reflections regarding whiteness, privilege, and the Other. Adding to a broad view of what it's like to be an expatriate woman in Qatar, the next chapter recounts that *movement itself* emerged as a central narrative of agency. The primacy of free movement as power was revealed through storytelling imbued with anxiety over its equally present antithesis—unjust restraint—a vulnerability white USAmerican expatriate women witnessed through others yet also keenly felt themselves.

# 3 Freed and Restrained

*It's Qatar. Everything is negotiable. —Emily*

In traditional Burkean theory, an actor's agency is contained and constrained within the scene. In transnational spaces, rhetorical feminist agency is found through movement *across* scenes, across difference, and within (as well as across) complex local systems. Movement across scenes was the primary capability expatriate women learned and the means by which they acted, grew, reflected, created, and problem solved. Movement-as-agency amplifies the relational entanglements of power and identity: our bodies are understood relative to their locations, our realities as agents are perceived in relation to other agents, and our actions are implicated within the contexts of their settings. As we change scenes, our interior perceptions of self are transformed by forces external to us. In *Power Lines: On the Subject of Feminist Alliances*, Aimee Carrillo Rowe explains how "sites of our belonging constitute how we see the world, what we value, who we are becoming" (3). Moving within and among a wide variety of scenes expands our worldviews, even as these movements also inspire more nuanced critical thinking. We learn to recognize that our "be longings," or the connections we cultivate, constitute "a *politics of relation*" (26) that for feminist agents, requires ongoing (re)consideration of power and a persistent inclination towards accountability (34), especially for those advantaged by being white, by financial resources, and by positionings of prestige/power.[1]

---

1. Osland and Osland's earlier study of expatriates (thirty-three of thirty-five were men) identified "mediation paradoxes," one of which is "being freed from many of your own cultural rules and even from some of the host culture's norms but not being free at all from certain host-country customs that you must observe in order to be effective" (98). In comparison, white USAmerican

Encapsulating the relational themes that unfold to reveal paradoxes of movement and agency in this chapter is Sarah's story:

*This story goes in the top five hardest days in Doha as a woman. The semester had been a really hard time, and I was exhausted, and many procedural things were getting difficult and every time we tried to solve the problem, it wasn't working. My husband and I go to the airport to renew my e-gate card because the chip isn't working. I ask the person at the e-gate office, "can I pay to renew it and then go get the chip repaired?" Because of course, you cannot renew it and get it repaired in the same place. And she says, "No, no, no. You must get the chip fixed first. I cannot update it." Fine, so we go to the immigration department to get the chip fixed, but they say "Oh, no more. We've had too many people today. Come back tomorrow."*

*We go back the next day, first thing in the morning to the immigration department to get the chip fixed. We're there at 6:30 a.m., waiting in line, fourth in line. They get through the first three and the line just stops for some reason. For forty-five minutes, nothing is changing. We're the next people in line. We're getting more anxious. There's a lot to do, and we need to travel soon. Higher stress. We needed a break. —Sarah*

These first two paragraphs reveal lines of frustration extending from the scene at the branch campus (from chapter 1) into another bureaucratic scene, local governmental offices. "Procedural things" at work have made problem solving "difficult" and as a result, Sarah is "exhausted." She and her husband "need to travel soon" to get "a break" from the suffocating situation, but what they encountered when she goes to renew her e-gate card—the card that facilitates the exit permit process for being able to leave the country—was even "higher stress." The plastic card with electronic chip documenting her status as a legal resident and, there-

---

expatriate women were less concerned about effectiveness while being more concerned about how public social norms affected their status as invited guests and freedoms as resident actors within the legal and social systems. The nuanced differences seem to be a product of different locales as well as differences of participant gender identity. Osland and Osland's participants also resolved their paradoxical positioning through a common rationalization (106–107) whereas my participants settled into the paradox as a site of (un)learning as described in chapter 5.

fore, allowing her to enter and exit the country at will, was not working. Without a functioning e-gate card her travel was blocked. In trying to untangle this potential restraint on her movement, she faced additional struggles with state systems, the e-gate and immigration departments. She both understood the process (the need to renew and to get the chip repaired) and did not understand the process (the services were not logically located near each other, "too many people" made getting the repair impossible, the line ceased to move for no identifiable reason).

Sarah's story continues:

> *My husband is trying to be consoling. I also forgot to say that there was a woman's section and a men's section. Usually, if there's a family section, if there's a woman, then her husband can sit with her in the family section, but for some reason, this guard guy was under the impression that only women could sit here and only men could sit over there. We couldn't sit together. So as I'm not dealing well with all sorts of things, now I have to sit by myself. My husband is trying to console me from across the room. —Sarah*

In addition to struggling with the constraints of the bureaucratic system, Sarah had to navigate the local social norms and gender segregation systems that required her to be separated from her husband as she waited. They tried to bridge the gap through body language across the room, but restraints on where they were allowed to locate their bodies caused Sarah additional distress.

When their turn finally arrived, the frustrating impasse only escalated:

> *We finally get to explain to the Qatari woman at the immigration desk that the card doesn't work. She says that's because it's expired. Right. It is. We tell her it needs a new chip first before it can be renewed, but she doesn't seem to understand. We tell her again and again. She brings two men over who are of no help, and we just keep talking in circles. At some point, I was so frustrated and tired and stressed out that I start crying. Tears are streaming down my face, and immediately, no one would look at me. They were so uncomfortable. I've never seen anyone that uncomfortable. None of them would look at me. They wouldn't address me. They were only talking to my husband. —Sarah*

"Talking in circles" is communicative movement but is actually no movement at all, just an ensnaring of restraints, a lack of progress. Sarah's reaction to what she experienced as a dysfunctional rational system is emotional, and when the bureaucratic *logos* was faced with her *pathos* in response, she is rendered invisible.

> *I'm embarrassed, but I'm really frustrated, and this is the way I deal with it. I'm not one to yell out. I'm just overwhelmed. I need to step away from this environment for a while. Tears are streaming down my face and I'm trying to take deep breaths. They still won't look even in my general direction, avoiding any sort of eye contact. So they finally manage to fix my card, and she hands it to my husband. Then the woman looks at me and says "Um. Why are you crying? I'm a lady and I'm not crying." I just stared at her because there was nothing I could say. We're in a government institution, so how do you reply to that? I stared at her, and she immediately looked away . . . If I had said something . . . anything to come out of my mouth would have been rude and that would have been far worse. This was worse in a different way, that I was human. —Sarah*

When Sarah reappears as visible in the scene, it is only to be confronted with the Qatari immigration employee's comments on the nature of her emotional response. The precise meaning of those comments cannot be known, but the intent of the officer's question is less relevant than Sarah's reflection in response to it. She is fully aware that she was "in a government institution" and that to "have been rude . . . would have been far worse" than just staring at the other woman in return. The threat here is to her agency of movement: without the representative's help, Sarah and her husband will be barred from leaving the country. Even though Sarah did not understand the system-related struggles of getting her e-gate card updated, she quite clearly is aware that the card was critical to her freedom.

Sarah began the story by saying it was one of her worst days in Qatar "as a woman" and ended by saying that she was "human." To be human in this situation was to be vulnerable in the face of non-human (and sometimes inhumane) systems of policies, procedures, and laws. As will be described later in the chapter, categories of humans as "citizens" and "residents," were inscribed in the Qatar constitution and were a daily Othering aspect of expatriate life, so Sarah would have been hyper-conscious that her status as resident put her at a disadvantage and at the mercy of the immigration office. But to clarify, Sarah was also clear-eyed about her privileged status as a white USAmerican in Qatar. She reflected over that privilege in relation to laborers and People of Color multiple times throughout her interview. The vulnerability of being human here is a reflection of Sarah feeling the real nature of her precarious resident status as well as the threat to her ability to successfully navigate local systems and to move across national borders.

Weaving together scene, agent, and now agency: in this chapter, the primary paradox explored through participant stories is being simultaneously freed and restrained. Ironically, agency was *not* a matter of *belonging* or finding firm footing or claiming ground, but instead resulted from *non-belonging*, from moving between and among different spaces. Movement-as-agency was precarious, however, because civil liberties or freedoms we assumed in the USA were not certain in Qatar, in part because we were no longer fully citizens and instead were only residents. For white USAmerican expatriate women in Qatar, *non-belonging* was our independence as well as our constraint.

## Paradoxical Freedom and Restraint

The driving paradox in this chapter is simultaneous feelings of freedom and restraint.[2] Three aspects of movement-as-agency are explored here: crossing borders, navigating local systems, and negotiating justice. The scenes of these movements include the IBC but were more broadly set in the streets of Doha, where its congested, aggressive traffic was an anxiety-riddled (re)learning experience. Based on stories we told and heard, our paradoxical positioning of being simultaneously freed and restrained emerged. Additional contradictory positions informed that location, as we felt a persistent certain uncertainty and because of our permanently temporary status as outsider insiders.

---

2. After much pondering, I chose "freedom" because of its associations with license or authorization, a particular kind of power within contextualized rules and regulations. Freedom of movement requires rights of way and rights of access. "Rights" entail moral or legal authorization (rights as a citizen) and/or appropriate or sanctioned strategies for acting (a right way to do something). For expats, freedom was also understood as relational, as notions of our own power of movement as well as the looming threats of restraint were informed by stories of less privileged expats whose freedoms were more limited than ours.

## Crossing Borders

White USAmerican expatriate women gained confidence in their agency traversing a variety of borders. As a noun, a border crossing describes a specific location, most formally, the literal booth or checkpoint where an immigration officer checks paperwork and makes the decision about whether or not passage is permitted. As a verb, border crossing describes moving among different spaces, roles, and identities. Movement between languages, between gendered roles, between public and private, between identities: border crossing happens in the physical travel from place to place but also happens without much physical movement at all. Chapter 1 described the IBC as a borderland of intersections, where host and home systems yielded a scene ripe with paradoxical tensions despite— or perhaps due to—a formal legal agreement establishing the territory. Chapter 2 considered the transnational stare as a potential reframing of seeing and being seen across national, social, economic, and linguistic borders, a potential rhetorical feminist tactic for reassessing the gaze. In this section, movement across and among different spaces is explored through crossing of nation-state borders, adapting among multicultural borderlands, and developing across professional borders.

To begin, expatriation itself is a long-term commitment crossing between home and host spaces. The IBC's standard contract was for an initial two-year appointment with subsequent renewal on a yearly basis after that. Although an expatriate could continually renew her residency permit, actual immigration was almost impossible.[3] Even long-term residents who stayed in the country did not assimilate into Qatari society. Due to the small number of Qataris and to their own tribally influenced norms shaping the closed and private community, expatriates integrated into their expat communities instead. Lack of formal immigration and limited assimilation meant expats inhabited a persistent outsider-within status in a state of permanent temporariness. My interviewees and I all knew our time in the country was limited and contingent. The ques-

---

3. During my time as an expatriate, the Qatari government only offered a very small number of citizenship opportunities per year, usually to the children of marriages between a Qatari woman and a non-Qatari man. Some expatriates and their families—for example, from India, Pakistan, or other Gulf nations— had been in the state for generations but were still required to renew their residency permits every year or two. After I left, the laws were amended but still only allowed up to one hundred new citizens per year (Begum).

tion was not *if* but *when* we would move home or move on to another location.

When interviewees were asked what had brought them to Qatar, most said they came for their jobs, but additional factors—especially international experience, travel opportunities, and financial gain—motivated them, too. For some, moving was an act of liberation. Susan jokingly compared her move to Qatar to a mid-life crisis: "While other people buy a sports car, we move to the Middle East." A mid-life crisis typically is attributed to a sense of dissatisfaction, a loss of self-confidence, or a fear of missed opportunity, but the actual crisis results in some breaking of social expectations, a change breaching norms. For Mary, expatriation was an intentional move to escape the religious restraints of home: "when we lived in our home state [in the USA], I thought 'I have to get out of here.' I told my husband: 'This is a bubble. It's a Christian bubble. And it doesn't prepare kids to live in the world.'" Strong Christian values and practices guided Mary's life, but she felt that her homogenous home community would be a damaging limit to her children's perspectives. She said her family's expatriate experiences taught her children to resist stereotypes and labeling, to be open to new experiences, and to "see people for who they are." Both Susan's and Mary's metaphors are about escape and freedom from home norms. Susan and her partner rebelled against the narrative of the typical USAmerican life, particularly as they chose to relocate to the Middle East, a controversial location of the Other side of the Western/Islamic "clash." Mary rebelled against the limited perspectives of her religious community. These interviewees' longings were toward greater understanding of other perspectives, longings leading them to disrupt their previous belongings.

Once in Qatar, freedom of movement correlated to sponsorship. All expatriates were required to be sponsored by a Qatari individual or Qatari-owned business through the *kafala* system. Therefore, status as a temporary resident was tied to a specific employer who set your terms of sponsorship, including the inclusion or exclusion of a spousal or family residence permit. Some sponsors allowed more freedom than others. All twelve interviewees emphasized without prompting that, because of our IBC's Qatar Foundation sponsorship, we were among the most privileged in expat status. During the time of my study, QF granted us multi-exit visas allowing us to leave and re-enter the country as often as we wished without having to ask specific per-trip permission. The advantage of our multi-exit visa contrasted to known abuses of the *kafala* system, spread through many stories of employers confiscating laborers' and domestic workers' passports and not allowing them to leave the country at all, even to permanently return home. Melissa's comment represents our shared perspective: "The privilege I've felt is not necessarily because I'm American but is because of Qatar Foundation's role in my being here." Susan said it was a crucial feature of considering an overseas post: she advised those considering work in Qatar to "make sure to understand what it means to *not* have an exit permit" and to become aware of "all of those things we take for granted in the US and that most of us don't really realize until we get here." [4] Being able to come and go at will magnified our feelings of being free overall, even if we were reminded of our restraint at the airport each time we checked into or out of the country. Such stories may have been echoing in Sarah's ears as she struggled with her e-gate card.

Stories we heard about other sponsors who unethically and illegally confiscated their employees' passports and/or refused to grant exit visas gave us a counternarrative by which to gauge the privilege of our relative freedom. Amanda grew to recognize her advantages by witnessing the disadvantages of another: "I know someone who, by passport, is Indian. Her mom had come to Qatar, and they wanted to travel together, but because of the type of visa my acquaintance had, they couldn't leave the country. I don't ever have to really consider that." Frequent stories of barred travel into or out of Qatar triggered our growing awareness of and sensitivity to those same struggles when outsiders try to visit the USA:

> I knew a person of Filipino descent trying to go to the US, and they denied her visa because she didn't have enough of a reason to come back to Doha. They said, "Try again when you're married." And

---

4. At the time of my study, a home leave allowance additionally was required in all employment contracts, generally covering one round trip home per year (or sometimes once per two years) for each person or family sponsored. QF provided this benefit to their employees in the form of a stipend, a payment either monthly or once per year, so individual employees had the right to decide how the money should be used—to travel home, for tourism, or for other priorities. In addition, money was provided often by the IBC for professional development, including conferences, workshops, or training outside the country, so travel for employees was frequent and for varied reasons, including visits back to USA homes, tourism, and business. In other words, our freedom was supported both contractually and economically by our sponsors. We also heard stories of sponsors withholding home leave allowances from their employees.

*she did. She got married a year later, and she tried it and the visa was granted. [They let her visit the US after she was married] because her husband was here [in Qatar], so she had a reason to come back. —Amanda*

Free to exit Qatar at will, my interviewees and I also recognized being able to freely enter most other countries in the world was an agency based on national identity privilege. The instrument of that act was the US-American passport. Amy commented, "It's a privilege to have that navy-blue passport, and there's a lot power, a lot of bureaucracy behind that," and Susan provided a metaphor: "that blue passport is gold." Emily said, "As an American, you can go into pretty much any country.[5] There are a few places an American can't travel, but there are so many students I talk to who can't even get into a lot of countries because of their nationality." The relative freedom of movement we felt at home was assumed to extend beyond borders because of the USA's global political, economic, and military power and international partnerships. Our feelings of freedom and assumptions of unrestrained movement reflected our privilege as white people from the USA. We were not accustomed to being stopped at checkpoints, being questioned about our documentation status, or being told to "go back where you came from." Because of our privilege, these daily struggles in the USA were invisible to us. As an unconscious extension of white USAmerica's colonial history, we shared a presumed entitlement to go wherever we wanted. Being expatriates in Qatar made the fraught nature of immigration visible to us because there, we experienced being controlled by similar systems.

Inside Qatar, white USAmerican expatriate women felt the empowering agency of movement among cultures. Mary described an unexpected chance to witness a deeply valued Qatari heritage tradition: desert falconry.

*My daughter had five friends from the US visiting and we were on a day trip. We were at Al Zubara fort, and I saw a guy with his*

---

5. The number of countries that a USAmerican can visit (with or without a visa) varies based on political relationships and current affairs, but in general, USAmericans rank high in the world for border crossing power. In 2014—the time of this study—the USA ranked in the highest group for visa-free access. Along with Finland, Germany, Sweden, and the United Kingdom, we were able to access 147 out of 218 countries in the world. By comparison, passport holders from Afghanistan would only be allowed in twenty-eight countries without a visa (Henley and Partners).

*falcon in his car. So I was showing the kids the falcon and it was neat. Then, later we were driving back across the country on that road that cuts across the desert. We saw some camels and stopped to take pictures, and as I'm standing by the car, here comes this falcon and it flies right across our path at eye level. And here comes this Land Cruiser going a hundred miles an hour chasing the falcon. Then the Land Cruiser slams on it brakes. It's the same guy from the fort, and he doesn't speak any English. And [pointing to the falcon] he asks us "like?" And so I answered with the one Arabic word I really know—"Mumtaz!"—which means "fantastic!" or "great!" And my daughter was embarrassed, but I wanted him to know I loved the falcon. So he talks to my daughter in Arabic and invites us to their tent to show us their falcons. They were so sweet. First, they served us all tea. They only had three cups, so we had to drink our cup of tea and pass it to the next person. Then we all held the falcons, and they have a machine, a thing that has a little rope. They put meat on the end of the rope and the machine shoots it into the air. Then they let the falcons fly up there to get the meat off of it. It's so high up you can't see it. The falcon then brings it back down, and the men use their car battery to wind the rope back up. It's fascinating! We had the best time. It was a wonderful memory, and they were very hospitable. —Mary*

Multiple types of movement-as-agency appear in this story. Mary's expatriate daughter was free not only to enter the country herself but also to invite guests to visit on visas that were easy to obtain for USAmerican visitors. The family had the means—access to a large vehicle, time off of work, a driver's license, a feeling of freedom to travel around the country—to take a day trip. Mary had been taught about the roads that allowed access to the vast desert so she had the agency of being able to move through otherwise unfamiliar places. Once they met the locals, even just a word of Arabic was met with gratitude, but Mary's daughter's years of language lessons heightened their access. Her ability to move across languages prompted being invited into the insider scene of the local host's tent, the invitation to tea, and the close experience with the falcons. Being *gaijin* or third-sex (chapter 2) was another likely means by which they accessed these insider spaces. As known outsiders, the group was free to transgress what would have been firmer boundaries for other locals (e.g., Qatari women would not have been invited into a men's tent). Through these movements, Mary, her daughter, and their visitors also benefitted from cross-cultural insight into the important heritage practice of desert falconry and the Gulf Arab culture of hospitality, both defining features of Qatar. The local ritual of welcoming strangers, which grows out of Bedouin life and the need for shelter from harsh desert climate, created the space for the interaction, while the falcons, as a celebrated sporting tradition eagerly demonstrated to outsiders, provided the exigency for the intercultural interaction. Mary's story foregrounds the layered ways expatriates felt unrestrained in their movements and in the potential for access to new cultural spaces. None of my interviewees seemed to assume that they were entitled to this access. In fact, the tone was generally one of marveling at opportunity and gratitude for Qatari hospitality.

Bridging the borders of intercultural perspectives also occurred between professionals of similar status in the workplace. Michelle's story reveals one border based in white identity:

> *I had a work relationship with a person who was Pakistani, as close as a male Pakistani and a white chick can be. Totally work related but we had to go through some hard times together, and we had somewhat of a personal relationship, a trust relationship surely. And one time we were talking about a problem we were having together and how we were going to handle it. And I was like "Okay, please help me because I truly don't know how to go forward with this one thing. So tell me what I'm not seeing. Tell me what I need to do, so I can formulate my plan." And he was like "I would never say this to another white person . . ." and he shared with me what this other person was thinking that I have clearly never thought about. —Michelle*

Michelle's close working relationship features movement across local gendered and ethnic lines, where white is conflated with Western. The trust they established was a form of freedom because it allowed her to share workplace questions with him and allowed him to answer frankly. Information typically kept away from white people was shared with her, enhancing her perspectives. Having your mind opened to other knowledges feels like a form of freedom as it is experienced as an alleviation of being restrained by not knowing "how to go forward." Because she was able, therefore, to understand more about the local/insider views of the situation, she was empowered to strategize and act; however, the agency created by her colleague's intercultural mentorship also reinforced Michelle's outsider status. Without an insider guide, she knew she was at a disadvantage in the workplace.

Opportunities for professional growth were stated often in creative terms of movement-as-workplace-advancement. Patricia, who joined the IBC early in its existence, said "I created my job from the ground up," and Sarah compared her IBC work experience as being "given a clean slate" and "figuring out what to put on the canvas" that allowed her to "take it to the next level." Emphasizing personal agency at the center of the expatriate professional experience, Ashley reflected, "this place is what you make of it." As she was preparing to leave the IBC for a new job back in the USA, Susan described her time at the IBC as "the best but hardest job you've ever had. But also, potentially the most rewarding" because it allowed you to "build a resume at lightning speed." She went on to explain how her time at the IBC prepared her to take a step up in her field as she looked for a new job back in the US. Michelle agreed, crediting the diversity of the workplace with her substantial growth: "Working in [a multicultural/expatriate] environment made me a 300% better employee." Although they existed at a nexus of knowing and not knowing about the host contexts, the affordances of being employed at the IBC granted them agency to "move up the ladder," to pursue greater professional knowledge and development.

Our selves are (re)constituted through border-crossing movements. Carrillo Rowe reflects that her identity "is not 'the same' in all places" (25). Who we "are" at work differs from who we are at home, which differs from who we are with our parents, our partners, and our childhood friends. In other words, identity is "a function of where we place our bodies, and [as a consequence,] with whom we build our affective ties" (26). As a form of rhetorical feminist agency, voluntarily moving within and across transnational spaces was a source of empowerment. It generated opportunities to critically re-imagine and strategically contemplate— both forms of Royster and Kirsch's "feminist rhetorical practices"—the affiliations and identities we previously accepted and, perhaps, had not questioned. Because movement-as-agency calls to mind an "unmooring" (Carrillo Rowe 27) from previous affiliations, it invites transformation through new identifications, new disidentifications, and/or experiencing nonidentification or a sense of non-belonging, that floating space of in-betweenness at once both disconcerting and liberating.

Even as expatriate women's sense of self-efficacy was strengthened through intercultural and workplace mobilities, it was simultaneously threatened by experiences on the literal streets. The next section details how driving a vehicle in Qatar's capital city, Doha, proved a source of uncertainty, as well as an illustration of being both freed and restrained by the local systems.

## Navigating Systems

Navigation as a form of agency or mobility/capability centers on the *knowledge* to move effectively. The Latin verb *navigare* refers to sailing and to the art and science of using celestial bodies to guide movement. In contemporary terms, our instruments of navigation focus on the street: being able to function within the rules and norms of our shared roadways, as well as having various means of directing ourselves (street signs, maps, etc.). As Ahmed writes in *Living a Feminist Life,* traffic is analogous to power: it has directionality and orients our bodies in specific ways (43). "Rights of access" and "rights of way" dictate who is allowed to operate a vehicle and who is permitted to move in specific situations. Learning to navigate the roads of a new place foregrounded the paradoxical feelings of simultaneously knowing (basic traffic rules) and not knowing (local norms of the street), of being an insider (an experienced driver) and an outsider (in an unfamiliar local context). The rules and laws of the road keep the flow moving but if a rule is broken or a body's movement is not aligned in the proper direction, "You become an obstacle; an inconvenience" (45). Right-of-way or freedom movement for some (e.g., those with the green light) typically indicates constraint or lack of movement for others (those with the red light). Linear forward motion evokes masculine notions of progress while the feminine tends to yield (see Jørgensen). Being aware of where and how you are moving, being skilled at navigating the systems within which you move, knowing your rights of way: these are agencies of movement. Knowing when to take an alternative route to a destination, having the confidence to improvise, being willful enough to direct yourself against the flow: these are also agencies of movement, agencies that resist the systems that direct us. Savvy navigation is a feminist strategy.

An emergent rhetoric of traffic featured heavily in the comments and stories of project participants, as it was a source of constant stress. Coursing through Qatar's only metropolitan area, Doha's streets were both microcosm and metaphor for expatriate life. Multi-lane roads were congested and dangerous,[6] clogged with a diversity of vehicles: tractor-trailers and other heavy construction trucks, busses transporting workers, school buses, private vehicles, and taxis. Simultaneous vehicle speeds along any road might vary from 50 to 120 kilometers per hour (30 to 75 miles per hour), as slow gravel trucks lumbered in long lines down the only lane where they were legally permitted to drive while speeding passenger cars darted in and out between them. The fine for running a red light—an infraction caught on traffic cameras—was 10,000 QR (2,747 USD), leading speeding drivers to brake suddenly and often violently when lights turned yellow. Rear-end collisions were a frequent result. During the time of this study, multi-lane roundabouts featured heavily in road design, which added a layer of foreignness and complexity for many drivers coming from the USA where roundabouts are less common. Road signs followed European or British conventions and, therefore, were not immediately familiar but were reasonably easy to learn, and driving on the right-hand side of the road offered USAmericans the relief of not having to re-learn to drive on the left. The combination of familiar driver configuration, unfamiliar-but-translatable road signage, unfamiliar roundabouts, and dangerous congestion proved intimidating to many new expatriates. However, because the city sprawled, was not well designed for walking or biking, and had only limited public transportation, most could not avoid learning to navigate its streets.

Before beginning her expatriate life, Mary established a friendship with another expatriate woman already in Doha who had refused to drive due to anxiety over the aggressive, choked roads. Knowing how this decision limited her friend's mobilities, Mary addressed the intimidation head-on: "The second day after I had moved here, I took the keys and went out driving. I wanted to face that fear and get it out of the way. I wasn't going to live here and not drive." Melissa described traffic as "chaotic," where you expect to get cut off and rear-ended. My partner had moved to Doha three months before I did, and because he had conquered his fear of the chaotic streets, I confess to waiting over a week to get behind the wheel at all, and even then, feeling resistant and scared for weeks if not months.

The main systems controlling mobility in Doha traffic were a source of confusion rather than agency. In the USA, driving on public streets is

---

6. As an example, in May 2014 alone, 158,300 traffic violations were recorded for the 876,000 vehicles on Qatar's roads, an average of one violation per 5.5 cars (Walker).

governed institutionally by the local infrastructure and legal codes determining qualifications to operate a motorized vehicle on public roads, the rules and technologies for regulating traffic flows, and the policies for accountability (fines for infractions, for example). Yet even within this highly controlled system, multiple ways exist for maneuvering a vehicle and performing as part of the driving community. For example, local norms define safe space between vehicles, acceptable passing procedures, and appropriate uses of the horn, headlights, and emergency flashers. We also learn our driving communities' practices for right of way—who gets to go first—and rights of access or where it is acceptable to drive and/or park the vehicle.

Traffic systems in Doha were familiar enough to USAmerican drivers that they provided a seemingly comfortable foundation for learning to drive there. The US and Qatar shared many laws and their attendant norms: for example, emergency vehicles legally have the right of way and should be given plenty of space; we do not park on sidewalks or in bicycle lanes, or drive through a construction site; we do not turn left out of the far-right lane on a five-lane road; and we generally drive between the white or yellow lines marking the pavement. However, all of these codes were frequently and blatantly broken on the streets of Doha. The nonsensical daily chaos of traffic intimidated new drivers. In this sense, newly arrived expatriates were outsiders trying to make sense of the contradictions, where the material signs and underlying set of regulations indicated one set of expected behaviors but another set of totally different behaviors were frequently displayed. The paradoxical feeling of simultaneously understanding traffic rules and not understanding traffic practice was common and baffling.

Gaining access to independent mobility in Qatar required getting a driver's license, and that process was one early way USAmerican expatriates learned about privilege and status. Although women were allowed to drive (no driving ban based on gender), not all expatriates were afforded the opportunity to apply for a license. To control the rapidly growing number of vehicles on the road (or at least the policy was framed that way), Qatari officials in 2013 amended previous regulations in order to deny laborers driving privileges. At the time of this study, expatriates in certain professions and those not meeting specific qualifications—including income level—were prohibited from getting a license or owning a vehicle. Over one hundred job titles, including many technicians, machine operators, tailors, and cooks did not have the option of driving regardless of their other circumstances.[7] For those who were allowed a license, how you acquired the license varied. Some passport-nationalities simply converted their home country license into a Qatar license, but that option was not available for US citizens. Because of unclear wording and a rumored tit-for-tat problem between the US and Qatar embassy representatives years ago, US citizens had two choices for getting a Qatar license: take the driving test or use *wasta*.

Foregrounding the paradox of understanding and not understanding, Sarah shared extended stories about her experience trying to get her license. The driving tests were administered by representatives of the Doha driving schools, which presented an interesting conflict of interest as applicants who did not pass the test were required to attend the driving school at a cost of several hundred dollars per course. The driving tests were inconsistent at best, based on the comments my interviewees, colleagues, and students who had taken them. For example, one tester's requirements for how to approach and proceed through a roundabout differed from another's requirements. Most testers did not speak much English either, appropriate considering Doha's linguistic mix but an additional complication for monolingual USAmericans. Sarah described her experience in the preliminary road sign test:

> *And so to take the signs test. The signs look a little different. They're in Arabic but the most important difference is that they use different words than Americans would. So like they don't say "yield," they say "give way." I'm pretty sure the gentleman giving me the road sign test didn't speak English but I didn't realize this until afterwards. So he points to the sign and I tell him what it is, and me trying to be helpful, I'd say "Yield, stopping to let the other car pass." I kept trying to explain what the signs were, but he would say "No, you failed." But I was like "But those were all the right answers!" And so my husband says (laughing) "When you point to it, just say the same thing over and over again, even if it's wrong. If you say the wrong thing, just repeat it, because he's just looking to see if the repetition does in fact mean that you know what it is." And I'm like "But I'm trying to explain myself" and he's like "Don't do that.*

7. Lubuna Jeffin outlined these restrictions in an information guide available to both expatriates and visitors, and Walker comments on it in her story on a Ramadan safety campaign designed to reduce accidents. Additional commentary and reaction are in Doha News Team's "New Ban on Driver's Licenses for Laborers Met with Confusion and Skepticism."

> *That's what's getting you in trouble. That's why you failed the test."*
> *And so the gentleman hands me the sheet and says, "You study." And*
> *so we do it again, and I pass by doing this. Saying the same thing*
> *every time. —Sarah*

As the test moved onto the road, Sarah's linguistic and cultural confusion continued:

> *I get in the car and he points to me, "You." Okay, so I'm driving*
> *first. Again, this man doesn't speak English; he only speaks Arabic.*
> *So fortunately, my friend translated for me. I guess he didn't like*
> *where I put my hands on the steering wheel, so he immediately*
> *slapped my wrist, which was really surprising for a number of rea-*
> *sons. So we start, and I'm driving slowly because I don't understand*
> *him and I'm relying on someone to translate what he wants me to*
> *do, and then he starts saying in Arabic that's translated "You drive*
> *too slow." I think very few people have ever gotten in trouble on a*
> *driving test for driving too slow (laughing), but so be it. Finally, we*
> *go out on the road, and it's a very basic, boring test. And ultimately,*
> *the tester was like "You will pass, but you are not allowed to drive*
> *in roundabouts by yourself." And I'm like "Well that's great—you*
> *don't think I'm a 'strong driver' but you want me to take other*
> *people with me into the circle of death." —Sarah*

Sarah understood the requirements and process for getting the license, but she simultaneously struggled to make sense of the interactions she had with the tester. Her confusion extended beyond strict language differences; in the sign test, her success was predicated not on the accuracy of the answers but on the insistence of her tone. Her hesitance and desire to demonstrate caution were interpreted as lack of capability, so even though Sarah felt knowledgeable and reasonably confident about her Doha driving capabilities, what she communicated to the tester was only a barely passable level of competence. The implication was seemingly illogical, that she should have been *more aggressive* and taken *risks* in order to demonstrate *care*.

Rather than navigating the licensing system, many US expats appealed to *wasta* for help. The Arabic word *wasta* comes from a root word carrying connotations of "the middle" and being loosely defined as "connections," "clout" or "influence" (Feghali). It is a system of reciprocal networking, carrying associations similar to cronyism in the US, although it has a stronger connection to family in the Arabian Gulf.[8] Students and I had extended conversations about *wasta* in the classroom, and interpretations as well as opinions of it were mixed. Qatari students typically argued for differentiating between "good *wasta*" and "bad *wasta*." The former meant using social or familial connections to get a chance at earning a deserved opportunity or other advantage, while the latter was connected with unearned privilege. "Good *wasta*" was having your uncle who worked in a large multi-national company let you list him as a reference for a job in that same company. "Bad *wasta*" was having your uncle pressure the hiring supervisor to give you the job. International students viewed Qatari *wasta* as corrupt, the unfair local "good old boys" system. Regardless of the perspective, *wasta* meant relational lines of power. As expatriates employed by the IBC, we had a certain limited form of *wasta*. We could rely on the cultural capital of working for QF and on the privilege of being white Westerners, but we were also outsiders to the local community. That outsider status created complications for navigating local systems that controlled our movement. *Wasta* was also power set within the local patriarchy, so being women in that context sometimes worked to our favor (*gaijin*, third-sex) and sometimes worked against us (resentment over not conforming to deeper local social customs).

In the context of navigating the driver's licensing process, *wasta* meant knowing the right person, someone on good terms with your organization and willing to help you streamline the licensing process. Our IBC's *wasta* connection worked in the traffic department and USAmerican employees were often taken to him to have their US licenses hand-converted into a Qatari license via the signing of a special exemption form. My partner and I were both directed to use *wasta* to get our licenses and we did, but through rather different experiences. My husband was taken by the IBC connection directly to the head of the traffic department's

---

8. Gold and Naufal divide *wasta* into two types, intermediary and intercessory. Intermediary is primarily concerned with family affairs, while intercessory is "used as a form of advocacy or intervention to obtain a benefit or expedite a transaction" (59). Ahmed Amin Mohamed and Hadia Hamdy find *wasta* may have negative impacts on how those who use it are perceived, and Metcalfe ("Gender and Human Resource Management") considers *wasta* specifically in terms of gender segregation's effects on women in the workplace. Jouharah M. Abalkhail and Barbara Allan argue "appropriate" *wasta* can help with the progression of women's careers in Gulf Arab states. For an exploration of how *wasta* can influence career progression in the Middle East, see Haifa Tlaiss and Saleema Kauser.

office where he met with a man with an honorary title of *sheikh* indicating his position as leader. My partner and the *sheikh* shared tea, cookies made by the *sheikh*'s mom, and an engaging chat (in English), then his license conversion paperwork was signed with great hospitable friendliness. Tea with the *sheikh* was one of my partner's first stories about what it's like to live and work in Qatar.

Three months later when I arrived, the *sheikh* was out of the country. A different IBC representative was assigned to take me to the traffic department, to find the administrator who understood the licensing situation for USAmericans and who would find the one manager in the entire country given power to sign my form in the *sheikh*'s absence. On the first trip to the traffic department, my colleague—who was not as well versed in the system as the one who escorted my partner—fumbled and we ended up in the regular line for the license process. I was told I had no choice but to take the test, and when I consented, was told to come back on "Ladies Day," which was Tuesday only. The second visit in search of the manager was equally unsuccessful. Meanwhile, human resources back at the IBC begged me to be patient and not take the test, as I was all but guaranteed to fail and then have no option but to take the expensive, time-consuming, and potentially ineffective classes, which would not necessarily increase chances of passing the driving test.

On the third visit, my representative/translator called the colleague who had helped my husband, who called one of his traffic contacts (*wasta*) and found out the location where the manager was working for the day. We raced to catch him before he moved to another one of the dozen or so traffic offices or police stations in Doha. In the main traffic department office, my representative led me from group to group, all men in local *thobes* and *ghutras*. Each time, I was asked to stand ten feet away from the group, while as many as four or five men carried on lengthy discussions in Arabic. Other than the occasional head motion or side-eye in my direction, no one acknowledged my presence, and I stood awkwardly—both hypervisible and invisible—trying to figure out what to do with my body and face. Should I stand up tall and claim my space or slouch and shrink to look humble? Should I look angry or annoyed? Should I look sweet and helpless? Should I look unconcerned? I knew each of these conversations moved me into spaces of more influence—my colleague was negotiating our rights of access—as evidenced by our shift from public places like lobbies and into progressively more controlled and restricted offices. I was repeatedly told, "wait here." Finally,

I was taken into the manager's office location. He asked me in English, "do you know how to drive? do you want to drive here?" and I answered "yes." He signed my papers and dismissed me.

My partner's experience and my experience shared the *wasta* path but varied in part due to gender.[9] As a male, my partner experienced a different ease of mobility navigating the licensing system. He faced less complication because the *sheikh* was readily available, but because my husband was a USAmerican male, he was allowed immediate access and was treated with special hospitality. He remembers his trip to the traffic department as a wonderful first entry into Qatari culture and as a fore-shadowing of future interesting and exciting transnational opportunities. I recall my licensing process as full of stops and starts, being told to follow then stand silently. It was marked by the confusion of not knowing where we should go, frustration at being invisible on the margins, and annoyance at not understanding the local process, which seemed odd in comparison to just taking the tests, as would have been the typical path in the USA. My experience highlighted how much I did not know and how much of an outsider I was, even in terms of participating in a system I had been navigating for decades in the USA and even despite having IBC assistance with the local language and regulations.

Once our mobility was permitted through official licensing, US-American women faced traversing the clogged and hyper-masculine Doha streets. Aggressive drivers are part of every culture, but what made Qatar surprising for USAmerican expatriates was that right-of-way seemed to be tied to national identity. Particularly Gulf Arab men—or those *passing* as Gulf Arab men—behaved in ways meant to communicate that their rights took precedent over the rights of others. Gulf Arab men in public spaces were identified by the white *thobe* and *ghutra* and because they often drove expensive vehicles: large SUVs (especially Land Cruisers) and luxury cars. They claimed their privileged right of way by both tailgating and flashing their high-beam lights at drivers who were in what they deemed "their" spaces. It was not unusual to see a fast-moving Land Cruiser flashing its lights in your rear-view mirror and speeding up to ride your bumper—unearthly bright halogen lights fill-

---

9. Metcalfe finds *wasta* to be "strongly gendered" because its networks of "re-lationships are channelled through male connections" ("Gender and Human" 59). However, seeing *wasta* only as promoting gender-based inequality is short sighted because "in another sense it is also supporting the importance of . . . balance and equilibrium in social and work relations" (59).

ing the entirety of your vehicle—until you ceded the lane. Availability of another lane or, conversely, absolute gridlock did not seem to make a difference. The message was "I own this space and you will vacate it immediately."

Horns frequently indicated right-of-way as drivers honked at other drivers they perceived were not moving fast enough when red lights turned green and honked to indicate priority of movement in round-abouts. Other examples of right of way tied to right of access included driving on sidewalks and in reserved parking lanes to cut in front of a traffic line. These were daily occurrences. In reality not all aggressive drivers were Qatari men, but when other drivers experienced aggression—a rapidly approaching vehicle, flashing of high-beams in the rear-view mirror, a car butting in line having cut through parking lots or across a construction site or over a sidewalk—they took note of the apparent identity of the offensive driver. Those in national dress and in expensive cars were commonly named as most likely to behave aggressively.

Lisa's story is typical of tales told regarding aggressive Doha traffic and identity as well as sensemaking assigned in response to national dress:

> *I've had some overt aggressive things happen to me. And this was a Qatari man. He was an older man in a thobe. He had on the national dress. And he used his own vehicle to push my car over sideways because he wanted to get where I was. And I had made him mad. At first, I wouldn't move over because I couldn't move over to the right. You know the whole deal, the flashing of lights. And I couldn't because there was someone there. I had a real small car, and he actually pushed my car sideways with his Land Cruiser to get by. Like crashed my car (laughing). It was a shock. That was probably the most difficult experience I've had . . . I was in shock, and then I couldn't do anything about it. He was gone. I did file a report, but he was gone. There was nothing I could do. —Lisa*

Expressing similar themes of male aggression, Ashley's story describes the consequences her friend faced for expressing outrage by raising her middle finger[10] in response to this treatment:

---

10. As of this writing, Gulf Arabian norms prohibiting rude and insulting behavior have not changed: a 2015 article warns readers that using obscene emoji in the UAE can also get the texter arrested (Shibata).

> *When I arrived, five and a half years ago, [Qatari or Gulf Arab men] were rather upset about women driving. I was actually quite scared for my life several times, and one time, the person I was riding with, she actually made a little gesture to someone that was running us off the road, and she went to jail. She had to appear in Shari'a court because of this, and so I was constantly aware that I had to be careful just because I was a woman. —Ashley*

These stories demonstrate that mobility or movement-as-agency is not something white USAmerican expatriate women could take for granted. Even as they navigated the local systems and achieved a *legal right* to be on the roads, their presence and movement on those roads was simultaneously under threat. Lisa was technically free to move as she was obeying traffic laws, but her presence in a man's claimed space turned into her restraint as her car was shoved to the side to get her out of the way. Ashley's friend experienced literal confinement in jail as a result of her defensive (and locally offensive) finger gesture. Both Lisa and Ashley described overt violence on Doha's roads, leading to surprise and even fear for their lives. Similar stories of aggressive driving continued to circulate throughout my time there, as did persistent warnings that rude gestures in public places could lead to arrest.

While stories about traffic were common, my interviewees and I also shared stories of privilege and rights of access to public places. The previous chapter details Qatar's large population of male laborers, referred to as bachelors regardless of marital status because they were in the country without a spouse. Laborers' movements were strictly confined: they were denied access to driver's licenses, transported by employer-owned busses to and from the job site, and had very little time off of work. When they were off work, they were further barred from entering some of the local shopping and recreation areas, particularly malls where Gulf Arabs and privileged expatriates shopped. Jessica talked about this access according to national identity:

> *So going to a mall, walking past a security guard . . . I don't think anyone would ever stop me for any reason. But if I were an Indian guy—even a single male that makes money—I would look like every other Indian guy in Doha, so the guards would assume I am poor and a laborer. That poor laborer cannot get into the malls on Friday. But if a white, single man wanted to go to a mall on a Friday, he could walk right in because he looks like he has*

> *money. You're not going to tell this Western guy he cannot go in-*
> *side. —Jessica*

As she points out, skin tone and phenotypic features—perceived indicators of economic power—afforded or constrained access to shopping areas. The malls to which Jessica refers are not necessarily high end either. I lived a ten-minute drive from a mall that compared to any suburban mall in the USA and saw permanently posted signs outside the door about family hours on the weekends. "Family" was code for "'bachelors' not allowed."

A video by UndercoverJim on YouTube titled, "Boycott Qatar 2022 World Cup: Undercover Investigation" and posted October 9, 2010, includes a conversation with a security guard stopping South Asian male expatriates from entering the mall. The guard tells the white male questioner (presumably "UndercoverJim") "it's the rules of the management" that the mall is for Americans, Arabs, and families and that the South Asian male expatriates cannot enter "because we can read their faces" and "especially Asian people are not allowed in." By "read their faces," the Nepalese guard means he can identify national/ethnic origin by reading phenotype. This video serves as further evidence of the discrimination that was blatantly obvious to us on a daily basis. Brown skin was associated with poverty and some undefined yet dangerous "lack of morality" that meant those with it should be barred from moving in "family" spaces where women and children were present. White skin was a pass allowing access even when being a single male should have brought some kind of scrutiny.

Family day rules were inconsistently enforced, due perhaps to outcries such as UndercoverJim's. However, an article in *Doha News* illustrates that control of bachelor movements continued to be a source of concern. In November 2015, Doha's elected Central Municipal Council "recommended shopping centers put back into place a policy that prohibits blue-collar workers from entering malls on weekends" (Fahmy). Although Council members acknowledged laborers were typically married and sending money back to their home countries to support their families, "bachelors" was the word used to describe these brown expatriate men. While one Council member argued for allowing laborers to enjoy food and recreation on their single day off, another expressed concerns over the sheer number of men and their perceived gazing. He argued families in Doha deserved a safe place to retreat from the summer heat yet "crowds [of bachelors] sometimes make it uncomfortable for women and girls to simply walk around the mall, and sometimes men look at them inappropriately, which is against the customs and traditions of a conservative society like Qatar." The fact that most laborers spent long days in brutal heat did not seem to be of issue in determining who deserved comfortable weekend leisure activities. One suggested solution was to keep the bachelors out of family spaces, segregating them to purpose-built spaces such as a sports complex near their primary housing (called "the industrial area"). In the article, authorities cited "Law No. 15 of 2010 Prohibition of Workers Camps within Family Residential Areas" (Qatar, Al Meezran) as the rationale for limiting access to malls, beaches, and other public spaces where citizens could find laborers' presence overwhelming and offensive. The law was specifically designed to prohibit workers from *living* in "family residential areas" but in this council discourse, was being extended to include simply *being present or visible* in broader public spaces as well.

Storytelling about navigating the local streets illustrated our oscillation between perceiving ourselves as simultaneously free/privileged and restrained/disadvantaged. Our presence in certain places (e.g., malls) was in relation to the denial of others. The streets themselves were metaphoric of the diversity and uncertainty of life in Qatar and provided a catalyst for developing awareness of inequality as well as agencies of movement. Through the licensing process, fender benders, and survival on the aggressive streets, we engaged in rhetorical feminist space-claiming and resisted being immobilized. Despite being aware of the tenuous nature of participating in complex and often frustrating systems that we both understood and did not understand, we learned to function within them (via patience and sometimes *wasta*) and refused to be denied or pushed aside (as Lisa's car literally was). What expatriate women experienced in Doha traffic was Ahmed's powerful directional flow as well as Carrillo Rowe's politics of relation, and by living within them, the fraught nature of "fairness" and "justice"—often rendered invisible in the USA through the fog of white privilege—became clearer.

### Negotiating Justice

Sources of agency are socially constructed and situationally constrained by what is deemed fair, right, or just for the actors and for the scene. Agency is linked to justice. The idea of justice hearkens back to ancient Greece, when its etymological root, *diké*, originally identified an act but also designated something as right or proper in terms of local norms or conventions (Burke, *Grammar* 13). Burke explains, "The connection between these two orders of meaning [an "act" and being "right"] is revealed in our expression, 'That sort of thing just isn't done,' and in the fact that our word 'morality' comes from a Latin word for 'custom'" (15). As an indicator of "how we do things around here," justice-as-custom orients bodies, directs flows, structures cultural logics, and is a bellwether of social progress. What a community deems just indicates its collective longings, the shared inclinations and relations that form local values and structure local bonds. Conversely then, questioning or rejecting those terms can lead to a sense of estrangement, nonbelonging, or longing for other ways of being.

Apprehensions over justice or fair treatment—both for themselves and for other expatriates—were at the heart of my interviewees' expressions of anxiety over being simultaneously free and restrained. With growing awareness of pervasive systemic injustices and local norms that did not seem fair from their perspectives, they looked for sources of agency to work within and sometimes against the host country's social, cultural, and economic systems. They wanted to feel they were "doing the right thing," even if in the host country, "that sort of thing just isn't done." In other words, they looked for rhetorical feminist tactics to address the glaring systematic injustices witnessed on a daily basis. Working against local systems was not necessarily a matter of disrespecting the hosts but instead was a result of dissonant perspectives. Whereas the *realities* of Qatar's local systems grew out of a tribal history, my participants and I carried with us *ideals* of inclusion and equality under which all members of a community should be treated fairly and consistently. We as white USAmerican women struggled to negotiate between our home *mythos*—"liberty and justice for all"—and the actuality of the host's norms and attendant social, economic, and legal systems. Even as we knew USAmerican equality was an ideal rather than a reality, being in a location of visible and drastic inequality made injustice undeniable. As described in chapter 2, it was staring us in the face every day. We had to learn to make sense of it and then develop tactics for surviving within it and even resisting it. Yet even as we sought agency of movement within restraint, we were keenly aware of the tenuousness of our status as permanently temporary invited guests.

For USAmerican expatriate women what seemed to be at risk of relinquishment were *basic rights*, defined as access to a fair legal system and freedom to speak out against unfairness. Negotiating what justice meant and how it was or was not accessible to us as residents led to daily anxiety, as the following set of comments illustrates:

- "The concept of justice that Americans also take very seriously . . . My biggest fear here is that if something happens, will I get justice? Because I'm not a citizen, I'm not a respected citizen." —Michelle

- "You can't go to the government and fight them because it's not your country." —Emily

- "I had to control my temper; in reality, we don't have legal rights here. . . . You can't be yourself a lot of the time because we don't have any rights." —Ashley

- "My civil liberties in this country are not what they are at home. This is always in the back of my mind." —Patricia

Key in these quotations is being an outsider or non-citizen. Despite Qatar's constitutional declarations of rights, confusion reigned over what an expatriate could expect in the eyes of the law because some rights, such as the right to an education, pertained only to legal *citizens*,[11] while others, such as freedom from discrimination *should* apply to *all* people within their borders.[12] Creating further anxiety was the restriction on anything that violated "public order and morality." This specific phrase, from Qatar's Constitution Article 47, granting freedom of religion, leaves the door open to bar forms of behavior, insignia, or dress based on perceived effects on general "public order." Similarly, freedom of expression—intertwined with freedom of scientific research in Article 49—is tied to "conditions and circumstances set forth in the law." Law in Qatar is based on Shari'a (Article 1); therefore, understanding what breaches

---

11. Victoria Scott's "Twitter Debate Begins about What It Means to be 'Half Qatari'" explores rights and privilege of belonging in the Qatari community when one parent is not a Qatari national. Scott gives a tip-of-the-iceberg peek inside some of the complexities of the local tribal system. Sofia Al-Maria's memoir, *The Girl Who Fell to Earth*, is a first-hand account of the same.

12. Part of the confusion may stem from the difference between the US Bill of Rights that refers to "people," "person," and "persons" (even though at the time of its writing, only some USAmericans counted). The word "citizen" appears earlier in the US Constitution when describing qualifications for the branches of government, does not appear in the Bill of Rights, but makes a reappearance in Article XIV, "Rights Guaranteed: Privileges and Immunities of Citizenship, Due Process, and Equal Protection" (United States, National Archives).

public order and morality and what breaks the law meant being able to interpret actions and implications through the lens of Islam and its attendant values. Because my participants and I were outsiders to Islam and Shari'a, because we were residents but not citizens, and because legal processes were conducted in Arabic, we worried we would not have access to just processes. We simultaneously understood a legal system based on rights and values and did not understand the implications of the host system for access to fair treatment.

Anxieties over justice and its negotiation were compounded by stories expatriate women heard and told each other. Even if they happened to know that Qatar espoused an ideal of "freedom from discrimination" for all *people*, they also knew the reality to be different. Mary offered an example: "I know a couple of maids right now who are in jail, and then you hear the stories they tell about the jail, about people who are there for years without representation, assumed guilty. The injustices here are very hard for me." In addition to hearing stories of unfair treatment for disadvantaged expats, my interviewees and I knew our own privilege had clear limits. One story feeding expatriate uncertainty was about a white British female principal of a Doha international school—in fact, the school my kids attended—fired for asking a student about her head scarf (*hijab*). The Qatari parents of the teenager, present at the interaction, found the principal's question religiously offensive. Because the father leveraged connections (*wasta*) to the Supreme Education Council, the principal was fired and deported within days—despite denials of wrongdoing by school, public apology over what the school called a "misunderstanding," and lack of formal administrative due process (Doha News Team, "Report about Hijab-Wearing Student"). Other well-publicized stories, including the 2012 fire at Villaggio Mall that killed nineteen people including thirteen toddlers (Khatri) and the 2014 imprisonment of a USAmerican couple over the tragic death of their adopted daughter (Kovessy and Sheble), reinforced that the legal system in Qatar could be impenetrable to outsiders. The narrative emerging from these stories was that, despite our privileged status and regardless of our attempts to respect local laws and norms, we were always in jeopardy of being caught up in incomprehensible yet life-changing legal situations.

Stories circulated through the expatriate community, reinforcing the confusion of negotiating the host country justice system, even for those who were socially and economically advantaged. Perplexity was compounded by paradoxically understanding the scene as constructed of familiar elements—a constitution, traffic departments, a modern legal system, etc.—yet knowing through first-hand experience and stories of others that it did not necessarily function in a way that was comprehensible. Our own cultural logics sometimes overlapped and other times deviated significantly from those of the host country. We simultaneously understood and did not understand. We were included and excluded from the systems and the means of negotiating them. The result was expatriates who felt both empowered by their privilege and access to resources and vulnerable due to their identities and associations (or lack thereof).

Emily's epigraph at the beginning of this chapter, "It's Qatar. Everything is negotiable," is about movement or navigation among intercultural spaces. It also reflects the inevitable lack of clarity and stability experienced as outsiders to Qatar and insiders to the expatriate community. Everything seemed negotiable, which meant everything was uncertain. The uncertainty was a function of not knowing the rules, even as many of those rules echoed familiarly. Justice was understood by USAmerican expatriates in terms of their own home systems in the US, and trying to negotiate between what was known of home and what was both known and unknown in the host country was an ongoing struggle. Although rife with imperfection, inconsistency, and *wasta* of their own, the idealized conception of the USA's judicial and bureaucratic systems was a baseline against which Gulf Arab policies and practices were compared—fairly or not. As educated, white, heterosexual, neurotypical, economically advantaged citizens in the US, we had not experienced unfair treatment within our home systems.

## Movement as Transformative Agency

Paradoxical notions of being simultaneously freed and constrained are contextualized, embodied, and relational. Because we were white US-Americans, we experienced broad freedom of movement that *seemed* unrestrained. We felt empowered by being able to enter and exit the country with relative ease. Within the country, being IBC employees granted us further freedoms: our QF sponsorship had major benefits. Our identities allowed us freedom in some spaces and threatened restraint in others. Our perceived autonomy was relational: feeling empowered through "leveling up" at our jobs and/or learning to communicate across cultures was experienced in relation to the "bubbles" and strict professional hierarchies we had escaped back home.

"Crossing," "navigating," and "negotiating" empower the agent to act more efficiently and effectively within a scene. These forms of rhetorical agency are fuel for rhetorical feminist hope, a "can-do" attitude. Living in paradoxical freedom and restraint taught us to adapt in the face of certain uncertainty. Rather than feeling cornered or shut down, my interviewees described themselves as being "not afraid," "open," "more tolerant," "patient," and "humble." They reflected about how they had learned to "just roll with it," to "study faces," to "listen more," to "lower expectations," and to "find someone who can help" in confusing situations. All participants reflected on their significant experiences recognizing their privilege through perceiving the risks they must take as outsiders, as residents rather than citizens. Many stories about life in Qatar were told with humor, sharing our surprises and a sense of wonder at how life could be so familiar yet completely unfamiliar. Some stories revealed common apprehensions based in uncertainty.

Agencies of action (freedom of movement) proved transformative. Through struggling to navigate the complex local systems, we learned that being able to drive a car in Qatar was a product of a system of *wasta* we did not understand, a series of discussions in a language we did not understand, and a policy or permission system that treated people in arbitrary ways. It became crystal clear that we were outsiders to the local cultural logic, yet we were also becoming insiders to the effects of colonialism, of colorism, and of other -isms that structured the scene. That was "how it worked" in Qatar. It was "just what we did." At the same time, growing awareness of inequities confronted us with "the political, social, and spiritual effects of our choices and practices of belonging" (Carrillo Rowe 43) to the USAmerican expat community. Some had great freedoms and many others had greater restraints. On our daily commutes as we saw and were seen by the busses of tired laborers, our relative freedom rang with troubling clarity in relation to the demands and restraints put on others. Ahmed argues "we can become even more conscious of the world in this process of becoming conscious of injustices because we had been taught to overlook so much" (*Living* 31). Being white USAmerican expatriate women in Qatar and becoming aware of how we were both free and restrained triggered a mighty recognition of what we had been conditioned to overlook back at home. In our voluntary and privileged displacement, we literally and metaphorically were "knocked off course" (47). A tolerance for being knocked off course when the veil of injustice is lifted grows out of our "foundational feminist concepts" (Glenn, *Rhetorical Feminism* 1) of being willing to listen and be transformed by counternarratives. For expat women, recognition of simultaneously inhabiting privileged centers and vulnerable margins changed the course of how we navigated and negotiated our time in the host country.

By coming to understand movement-as-agency, we developed tactics for being patient, for tolerating uncertainty, and for being aware of both the power and the tenuous nature of our freedoms. We actively listened to, reflected over, and learned from stories we heard about others being restrained, and through those stories, we increased our attention to systems and notions of justice (and injustice). We also felt the vulnerability of being situated in systems we did not have access to (e.g., the secret branch campus agreement described in chapter 1) or did not understand (due to linguistic, legal, and other contextual differences). As we lived in the liminal space of transnational here-and-there, vulnerability proved a radical change from feeling at home in USAmerican systems. As another rhetorical feminist tactic, we sat with these anxieties, resisted giving up on Qatar as hopelessly confusing and unjust, and actively attended to the experience of being an outsider-within. In other words, even as expatriate women came to understand the impossible and paradoxical complexity of their rhetorical scene, they recommitted to persisting within it.

Patiently and hopefully sitting with the anxiety of uncertainty and vulnerability is one thing, but rhetorical feminist hope does not sit still—it reassesses and acts. In this way, some white USAmerican expatriate women sought action amidst their paradoxical freedom and restraint. Every barrier has its weak points; these can be crevices of possibility. And the quiet, persistent seeker can locate or even create them. These crevices, which are typically invisible to the privileged who don't need them, offer small spaces of movement within restraint. They can be sites of micropraxis because they allow little movements, which in and of themselves seem insignificant but when persistently pursued, can create the synergy and path for larger activity. Continuing the threads of previous chapters and working towards micropraxis as actionable outcome: the transnational scene established our awareness of paradoxical complexity that could be reassessed as generative in-between spaces, realization of our own hypervisibility and invisibility bared our complicity in unjust socio-economic systems and could motivate us to act rather than look away, and anxieties over our own precarious freedoms taught us to be more aware of others' struggles as well as strategic in our movements. The back-and-forth of transnational life (moving among different national spaces, working in hybridity) and our positioning as outsiders-within prevented expats from fully assimilating into the local systems. For those who were aware of them and resisted retreating from such recognition, our knapsacks of privilege grew heavier with time. The sum of these factors—positioning, motivation, awareness—generated the rhetorical feminist tactic of micropraxis. But before it is more fully considered, one last narrative of expatriate life needs telling.

The current chapter set white USAmerican expatriate women in motion, engaging in the privileges and precarities of moving within transnational scenes. In the final interpretative chapter up next, my participants' overarching shared narrative of expatriate life—driven by metaphors and a final round of storytelling—is laid out. It broadens the rhythm of expatriate life beyond the Qatar/IBC scene and takes up transnational flows across international borders and systems to consider what it's like to return as a transforming person back to previous life spaces. Lessons about persistence, about listening across complexity and difference, and about an open desire to learn were some of the rewards of expatriate life that we looked forward to bringing home with us when we returned to visit our communities back in the USA. However, those returns proved more challenging than anticipated, and our heroic journey outcomes went generally unfulfilled.

# 4 Belonging and Estranging

*Our life in Qatar doesn't come up. A lot of people think we're just crazy. —Susan*

Expatriates differ from long-term travelers because they move between and among spaces. Typical is relocating between home and host countries, but for longer term expatriates, movement is multiple, a back-and-forth between host and home, as well as business and personal trips to additional locations. A period of expatriation can have profound effects on an individual's identifications or perceptions of herself in relation to her communities. Common wisdom says traveling changes you, and if that is true, then expatriation invites radical transformation. Returning home amplifies change, shifting how we position ourselves as rhetors. The previous ease and naturalness of home becomes something else: a new mild discomfort of fit, an unanticipated dissonance alluding to the alchemical transformations brought on by living in complex transnational scenes. Feminist rhetors are familiar with the tensions of simultaneously belonging and not belonging. Women know the discomfort of our stories being disciplined into ill-fitting narratives. Often these are men's narratives. As Ahmed writes, "becoming feminist puts us in touch with a world through alienation from a world" (Ahmed, *Living* 43). In other words, facing the pain of not belonging (re)defines our belonging. Here, I explore the paradoxical tensions of simultaneously experiencing belonging and estranging when USAmerican expatriate women visited their home communities in the USA. These tensions were expressed through metaphors and similes as well as through storytelling, and in this chapter, I weave those bits and pieces into a proposed narrative. However, even as I propose the existence of the narrative, I trouble it.

After beginning with the shared narrative emerging from my interviews, I then move to examine what was perceived as the ongoing "boon" or reward of the expatriate life: lessons learned and unlearned due to living in culturally complex spaces. We were excited to bring these lessons back to our home communities. However, upon return, we were met with and became entangled in silence and rather than sharing our boons, we tucked them away. What we then perceived as "failed returns" led to a process of *estranging* from home, and the strain of these home (dis)identifications left USAmerican expatriate women feeling torn or "splinched," paradoxically comfortable anywhere yet at home nowhere.

## AN ADVENTURE NARRATIVE WITH UNCERTAIN RETURNS

In their interviews, white USAmerican expatriate women described life in Qatar within a narrative of *mythos*. Stories were not shared in terms of methods and rationality—potential *techne* and *logos* for work in transnational spaces—but instead were framed as excursions through risky, liminal, otherworldly spaces. The archetypal journey, as explicated in Joseph Campbell's *The Hero with a Thousand Faces*, is an ancient, well-worn path. It begins when a singular protagonist is called to adventure. He (because historically, it is always a "he") crosses a threshold and enters an alternative realm where, with the aid of magical friends, he survives challenges from dangerous world guardians, successfully traversing a road of trials. Time in the alternative realm helps the hero realize the power hidden within him, and he returns home to share the treasures or boons of his journey—specific tools and/or spiritual insights—with his community. Although Campbell's book ethnocentrically strips cultural myths and tales of their cultural and temporal contexts, the journey monomyth persists in Western popular culture as a sensemaking trope (e.g., *Star Wars*, *Lord of the Rings*, *Wonder Woman*, the *Bachelor* television series).

Considered through a critical lens, Campbell's journey is arguably the archetype of the colonial marauder, an invader who seeks out the help of indigenous folks from the world he has entered, a conqueror who takes what he finds of value then leaves. Perhaps it remains a popular narrative trope in the West because it centers the rugged individualist who succeeds through his own innovation and who denies—or indeed, never thinks of—the accountabilities created through those friendships or relationships required along the way. The hero's "survival" and the treasures looted from his journey are artifacts affirming his superiority. His journey is his heroic destiny, made manifest.

I invoke Campbell's work here because, as a trope, it undeniably persists in the ways expatriates continue to talk about their overseas experiences. They re-tread the well-worn path of Western exploration via contemporary bodies. Management scholar Joyce Osland located Campbell's journey narrative in the stories of expatriate business managers in the late 1980s. She interviewed thirty-three men and two women, whom I presume to be white as she does not indicate racial or ethnic affiliations. Her participants worked a variety of professional or non-labor jobs, and lived in a range of places, mostly Europe and the United Kingdom. Her study, *The Adventure of Working Abroad: Hero Tales from the Global Frontier*, aligns their stories with the stages of the monomyth via a discourse of mastery, heroics, and self-efficacy. Osland's work was concerned with motivations of expatriates and effects within the workplace. Her study was not undertaken from a critical perspective, and troubling aspects of transnational movements remained invisible, part of a naturalized and privileged center.

Over twenty years later, strains of that *mythos* linger in how my female interviewees and I describe our experiences, too. These echoes are a function of whiteness, Western-ness, and colonial thinking deeply embedded in our cultural logics, likely amplified by our location in the "exotic" and "dangerous" Middle East. As described in chapter 1 ("Meeting Home and Host Demands"), my faculty colleagues and I came to realize the undeniably colonial overtones of our situation, of the international branch campus and our work within it. Subsequently, we wrote about these struggles in scholarly articles and chapters. Despite these purposeful and critical endeavors, however, we were unaware of how our *daily* rhetorics, in which we described the "adventures" of living and teaching abroad, were gravitationally pulled to the masculinist monomythic trope. The following paragraphs describe and illustrate how the shared narrative and varied metaphors of white USAmerican expatriate life converged and diverged from the classic heroic *mythos*.

When recounting stories of their shared narrative calls to adventure, my interviewees made deliberate and non-deliberate use of journey metaphors. They were motivated by escaping from containers, particularly what several referred to as the "American bubble/box." Susan laughed that she and her husband considered their time as expatriates as the answer to their "mid-life crisis." A mid-life crisis generally marks a period in life when a person re-evaluates the nature of how their life has been constructed (e.g., job, marriage or family, etc.). The "crisis" point is when that situation is found to be too constraining—the "container" of one's life is no longer satisfactory amidst the looming approach of mortality. The most common motivation for "escaping" the USAmerican container was a desire for fresh perspectives, to "be given a clean slate" or a "blank canvas" through having "a new experience every day." Some pointedly noted the USAmerican bubble as one of "egocentr[ism]," "self-interest," and "entitlement"; they sought alternatives.

Embarking on their journeys, interviewees found help through a range of aides. Osland similarly concludes that the more successful expatriation experiences are supported through close relationships with aides from the host culture. For example, later in this chapter Amy describes the small but transformative moment she experienced simply sharing family stories and videos with a Qatari man after establishing a working relationship with him. For her, it was an invitation to glimpse beyond the persistent veil of privacy in the local community. I was also privileged to develop friendships with Qatari former students that led to me being invited to private family events, including weddings. My participants and I occasionally enjoyed collegial friendships with Qataris and other Gulf Arabs; however, beyond the friendly surface interactions inherent in a university campus environment, most cultural mentors were not from the host population. In fact, several expatriates working in fields other than education remarked to me that they had *never* interacted with a Qatari "local." As described in previous chapters, Qatari cultural practices foregrounded hospitality, yet outside of organized activities, Qatari families tended to be insular and private.

Therefore, "magical aides" from the broader expatriate community—at the IBC and in the compound—substituted as stand-in hosts open to outsiders, and participants found their welcome into it to be like "living in a bubble of privilege and safety," "a comfort zone of the American expatriate community," and "living in a small town." First connections for my participants tended to be with other USAmerican families or co-workers. Their comparative language foregrounded a key feature of Nira Yuval-Davis's "belonging," as an *ease* or a feeling of being in one's "natural" (if not always happy) space (10). Easy identification, living together as expatriates, and working for the same organization, generated a "comfort zone" of familiarity. Irony is found in the desire to escape one USAmerican bubble only to find comfort in another bubble eight thousand miles away.

In contrast to Campbell's hero relying on aides and mentors, my participants' figurative language also revealed a sense of isolation: "like being on an A team with no B team," "it's an island," "it's like being invisible," "it's like being in a shell of anxiety." One participant who had worked in a space outside the IBC described her Qatari-centric work location as "a zoo." In the context of her comments, she was describing a host organization as chaotic because she did not initially understand its norms for behavior. The interviewee who used this phrase uttered it in a tone of wonder, as if to describe how she found herself in a place that simultaneously both familiar (Same) and utterly unfamiliar (Other). Ahmed reminds us that, as feminists, "We can think of alienation then as wonder: we wonder about things; we marvel at their assembly" (Ahmed, *Living* 41). Although used colloquially to indicate lack of control, an actual zoo is certainly a hyper-controlled series of containers. The metaphor foregrounds contradictory lack of control *and* being highly controlled ("caged"). As the previous chapter illustrates, expatriate life can feel exactly like that—paradoxically, you have been "let loose" (beyond the constraints of your own country and beyond the tighter controls over tourist activity in the host country) to work and live in this new space, but then you also notice that, in new ways, your existence and work are highly controlled by the host government, by your IBC's shifting or nonsensical policies, and by your lack of full access to local norms. This same interviewee described her isolation when first living in Qatar, comparing that time to "living on an island." Her experience being in a location outside the IBC (even as her job was connected to the IBC) was unique among the interviewees, although she was not the only one to use language of isolation.

Being in the alternative realm or in the "belly of the whale" stage of Campbell's heroic journey meant expatriates had to learn to give up a previous sense of control and, as a result, reflexively (re)examine their home culture values and practices (Osland, *Adventure* 57). For Osland, valuable interaction with the host community meant living physically among members of that community. She condemns "well-to-do" exclusionary golden ghetto expat communities as an ethnocentric rejection of the host population and as spaces where expats "spend their time complaining about the locals and comparing unfavorably what they find abroad to what they left behind at home" (61). Leveling Osland's criticism towards expatriates in Qatar is a bit unfair. At the time of my study, the IBC contracted housing in a number of compounds to assure employees had places to live and because the IBC directly paid the rent for these houses as part of expatriate contracts (see chapter 1, "Revising the Private as Public"). Therefore, my participants and I did not have a choice to live beyond those options. That said, it *would* be fair to characterize the compounds and high-rise apartments, which ranged from what USAmericans would characterize as middle class to middle-upper class as "golden ghettos" because at the very least, they segregated expatriates and were of good size and quality. In comparison to the overcrowded and shabby camps where a vast majority of labor workers lived, our homes were certainly a source of privilege and socio-economic elevation.

The monomythic road of trials for my participants was paved with metaphors of battles and liminality as they experienced the challenges of oscillating between home and host spaces. In contrast to feelings of home and comfort found in the expat community as described above, living and working in Qatar was also compared to "being on the frontlines," "trial by fire," "working in the trenches," and "a clash of two extreme worlds coming together." Additional comparisons focused on the aid of the expatriate community—"living in a bubble of privilege and safety," "a comfort zone of the American expatriate community"—revealed a perceived "danger" outside of those safe borders. However, rather than the media's Huntingtonian "clash of civilizations" narrative, the danger of being an expatriate was one of the unknown and the unlearned, the risk of uncertainty and being unsure of what to do when negotiating life in host spaces. Unsolicited comparisons tended to occur within a range of contexts, from the workplace to the streets. As described in chapter 1, the IBC is a site of competing demands, incompatible values or practices, and daily cross-cultural adaptation. Because participants were often challenged to take on unexpected roles, battles were associated with feelings of isolation. One unsolicited metaphor compared work-life in Qatar to "being a superstar," but even a superstar on a stage is ultimately isolated in the powerful limelight.

Foregrounding liminality, life in Qatar was compared to "living in the land of almost," "the Twilight Zone," "a fantasy limbo world," "like one of those Choose Your Own Adventure books," "like living on another planet," and "like living a dream and living a nightmare." These six metaphors and similes reveal participants attempting to articulate the confusion of simultaneously understanding and not understanding their environment. In *Rhetorical Listening*, Ratcliffe engages Martin Heidegger, W.E.B. DuBois, and Toni Morrison to describe a "circling through time" she refers to as "*then-that-is-now*" (109–111). Her purpose is to invite us to listen to the ways tropes of whiteness cycle through our discursive practices, to discover ways to be accountable for how history haunts us. For expatriates in Qatar, liminality was a sort of "*there-that-is-here*," a comparative circling back between the knowns of the home country (*there*) and the unknowns of the host country (*here*). Working at the IBC was a daily practice in negotiating the *there-that-is-here* in the borderland created between the home institution and the host campus. Private and recreational spaces reminded expatriates much of city life in the USA, so the surface comparison made the *here* look much like the *there*. But then once the expat got settled and dug into daily life, the differences became more evident, and the *there-that-is-here* transfer of expectations from home to host began to disintegrate. For example, calling Qatar the "land of almost" compares expectations about daily life *here* back to the *there* of the USA, and concludes that Qatar perpetually almost gets there but never quite does. The constant construction and change of the city, the inconsistent availability of items at the grocery store, the ability of the government ministries to change the rules on what seemed like a whim, as well as the ideals and reality at work created a daily uncertainty. The "Twilight Zone" liminality of the *there-that-is-here* was reified when expatriates returned to the USA on visits, as they re-experienced familiarity of home in turn amplified the uncertainty of life abroad. "Living a dream and living a nightmare" reflects the powerful/powerless positioning discussed in chapter 3, and while the "Choose Your Own Adventure" comparison emphasizes the agencies of choice and movement, it also implies the uncertainty of not knowing what will happen as a result.

Six participants framed life in Qatar as a gamble where the outcome remains unpredictable: "like hiking on unfamiliar terrain at night without a map," "like a roller coaster," "like a crapshoot," "rolling the dice and reacting to the outcome," "like searching for oil," and "like biting into an apple and finding some of it good and some of it bruised." Beyond living in a state of uncertainty about daily life and expectations, these comparisons foreground risk and potentially conflicting or alternating feelings about their environment. Being on a roller coaster or playing a game of dice mixes moments of enjoyment and elation with moments of fear or disappointment. Before getting into the coaster car or picking up the dice, a participant acknowledges these risks, but comparisons that risk failure foreground the anxiety of uncertainty. Gambling metaphors frame uncertainty as foundational to the experience, echoing Osland's conclusion that "addiction to novelty" draws people to expatriate life (*Adventure* 152–53). Finally, one participant offered this rather unique metaphor when asked to "tell me what it's like": "It is like eating alligator meat and not being able to describe it to anyone who didn't come to the restaurant." Unlike the previous comparisons, this one does not center on risk or uncertainty. She knows what she has eaten and has no clear anxieties or regrets about the meal, but she cannot bridge the divide to help others understand it if they are not located in the same space. In this metaphor, even an expatriate who had worked abroad but in a different country would not be able to understand the Qatar/IBC experience.

In general, the heroic journey narrative features conquering the unknown, the "strange," the Other. Even as the hero is consumed by the journey (swallowed into "the belly of the whale"), she consumes and collects boons on the "road of trials." In "Eating the Other: Desire and Resistance," bell hooks critiques the commodification and consumption of Otherness, particularly ways that USAmerican movies, music, and fashion use desire and the contact between white bodies and the bodies of Others as a means of denying that People of Color continue to be devalued and oppressed in modern US culture. In sum, coming into intimate contact with the Other is mediated to show white people as accepting of diversity, even as it fails to hold white people accountable for using that contact as a means of reinforcing their own power. In my interviews, comparisons of their time in Qatar to "eating alligator meat," "the shiny new apple," "a cornucopia [of opportunity]," and "a thirst [for adventure] to be quenched" explicitly linked to consumption. Figures such as "searching for oil," "a Choose Your Own Adventure book," "a clean slate," and "a blank canvas" also related to consumption through commodification, as the host country became a means of fulfilling expatriate desires. As described above, the hunger or desire was to "escape" the USAmerican container of "egocentr[ism]," "self-interest," and "entitlement." While my interviewees and I found a means of escape, the host country provided another bubble of entitlement as we expatriates landed in the golden ghettos of our living spaces and on the island of hybrid territory inside the branch campus.

The transformative experience of Campbell's heroic journey involves a death and rebirth, and in Osland's version of the expatriate narrative, that rebirth is into a feeling of cultural mastery in the host space. Quite in contrast, my interviewees and I were reborn into embracing uncertainty and into a persistently open mindset, in part because we had fewer durable connections to the host (Qatari) culture than expected and in part because living in complexity taught us humility. As Michelle said, "any Westerner who says they understand the Arab mind is in a really dangerous place." By this she meant assumptions about how local systems work or how expatriate interactions will be interpreted cannot be taken for granted. Other interviewees talked about strategies of understanding but knew even those strategies could prove faulty. Another colleague put it this way: "As Americans, we will only ever understand the top five percent of the [local cultural and professional] iceberg. The rest is either hidden or beyond our ways of understanding." Both comments were made with clear tones of self-effacement. While expatriates in Qatar quickly learned that US media images of the Gulf region present a limited view of life there and that people can be very different but still ultimately want the same things—safety, dignity, and opportunity—they also learned that differences in professional situations and in private lives are real. Being abroad presented my participants (and me) with ample opportunities for Spivakian "unlearning," a perspective (and its attendant limitations) I return to in the next chapter. For those willing to listen and reflect, living abroad foregrounded the importance of acknowledging and celebrating difference—as transnational feminists and Women of Color have been telling white feminists for a long time.[1]

As they spent time in the liminal belly of the whale, USAmerican expatriate women's stories reflected a clear loss of control. However, the resulting uncertainty could be resolved as they paradoxically began to understand that they could *not* understand the host country. Grasping required letting go. Because they lived in a permanent space of uncertainty—including anxiety over expectations of fairness and justice—the

---

1. Although the message seems obvious for scholars in critical fields, it also stands in stark contrast to current books designed to help expatriates (e.g., Nyell's *Understanding Arabs: A Contemporary Guide to Arab Society*, in its fifth edition in 2012; Wunderle's *A Manual for American Servicemen in the Arab Middle East: Using Cultural Understanding to Defeat Adversaries and Win the Peace*; and Melamed and Aharsh's *Inside the Middle East: Making Sense of the Most Dangerous and Complicated Region on Earth*). Our own scholarship in intercultural communication, for example, when uncritically applying Hofstede's *Cultures Consequences* framework, falls into the same traps of essentializing large, dynamic, and diverse groups into reductive binaries.

broadening of perspectives was never complete. My interviewees and I never felt confident in our sensemaking of host systems. Positioned in an ongoing lenticular of *there-that-is-here*, we lived in a space of almost understanding. As one interviewee posted on social media, uncertainty "wears on you in ways you really don't expect," and as Amanda commented, "Everybody has their ending point, where it's like 'I've *had enough.'*" Whereas the traditional heroic journey ends with a death or letting go and a rebirth or taking on, that rebirth was not complete for the participants in this study, in part because they were still in the process of being expatriates. Therefore, they remained on the road of trials. Unlike a singular journey, however, expatriate life is neither linear nor unidirectional. Trips back to the USA were an annual occurrence for my participants and for me—some went home at least twice a year and others spent over a month in the US each summer. Although our final journey endings were not yet written, returning to visit family and friends created opportunities to communicate our broadened perspectives as they developed.

## Boons of (Ongoing) Life Abroad

All twelve interviewees said their perceptions of the Gulf Arab region were radically transformed by their lives in Qatar. Reading across their responses, common lessons or boons emerge, including increased open-mindedness, tolerance for complexity and uncertainty, broadened perspectives on the USA and the implications of being USAmerican, and a humbleness regarding their placement and roles within transnational systems. Ashley's comment is typical: "I learned a lot about Islam and a lot about the culture." Mary described how she and her children now "see the world more truthfully than the way it is portrayed to them in the US," are "not so narrow in their thinking," and are "not afraid to be friends with Muslims, Hindus, anyone." Amy described feeling blessed, "meeting people from all kinds of different places and cultures, really realizing how I'm in the 1% of privileged." Michelle addressed the vulnerability of learning to work in culturally complex environments: "you're very humble because you're working in this environment where you hope people are supportive because you don't understand the social fabric." Amy told a story of a conversation she had that was personally transformative:

> *I, an American woman, was sitting alone with a Qatari man where he was telling me stories about his daughter. He showed me a video*

*where you know he couldn't find her. And in the video, he walked around the house, so he had to tell me about the structure of his house. He was telling me, "In our houses our kitchens are outside, they're not in our homes, and so I found her in the kitchen sitting in a bucket of water, playing." It's just very human, how he told the story, how his face lit up, that it was funny, it was a story that you could have heard from a friend back home. And there's a connection there, a connection as parents, a connection that it was funny. I wouldn't necessarily call it a bonding moment, but for me, it was a real. It just tore one more layer off. . . . It punched one more hole in the anxiety and it helped me the next time to not be as anxious.—Amy*

What Amy compared to tearing off a layer refers to differences we apply to unknown Others; in this story that layer is the imaginary of what it's like to be Qatari. Due to local gender norms, Amy being alone with this adult Qatari male was unusual and was only permitted because it occurred in the hybrid spaces of Education ("Sin") City, away from the socially conservative gaze of the larger local community. This simple act of showing a short home (private sphere) video transcended multiple boundaries of gender, private/public, and socially acceptable interactions. The layer torn away was infused with Othering and anxieties of difference.

All interviewees described conscientious efforts to be more "open," "better listeners," "more patient," and readily "adaptive" to culturally complex situations. Ashley's comment revealed how she learned to oscillate between host country perspectives and home country perspectives in response to her mother's annoyance:

*My mom made me think about how I've been here long enough where my perception has changed and I don't question things really. Different things—I just sort of deal with it. But my mom doesn't want to deal with it and she doesn't think I should have to deal with it. So that was interesting. For example, my Qatari friend and her sister always have to go places together and have to get permission all the way up through the family from a bunch of different people in order to leave the house. My mom just really gets agitated by that because she does see the lack of freedom. Anyone can say whatever they want about it, but there is a lack of freedom. It's very restricting for the women. . . . I just feel like I understand the local women a little more. I see them with other women and I understand the emphasis here on reputation, where my mom doesn't see that part of it.—Ashley*

Ashley does not just "deal with it" but instead accepts the restriction—even in her dislike of it—because she has recontextualized it within local norms and practices concerning reputation. As IBC students explained to me, local unmarried women risk being socially ostracized if they refuse to conform to local norms, ranging from if/how the *abaya* and *shayla* are worn (strictly, loosely, or not at all) to their public cross-gender interactions. For example, men and women are kept fully segregated at the more traditional Qatar University, while co-ed education is the norm at Education City. Some families might let a young woman meet a potential spouse at a mall or restaurant, while other families will only allow controlled interactions at home under close supervision. Acceptance did not necessarily mean Ashley condoned her friends' limitations ("It's very restricting for them") but she knew that to maintain her friendships, she could not ask her Qatari friends to subvert the system. What might have seemed like agency for a USAmerican woman involved different risks for a Qatari woman.

Amanda shared another specific example of how her outlook had adapted:

*Being here definitely has made me a little more understanding. For instance, women not being able to drive 8 or 10 years ago.[2] In the past, I would have thought "Why would you not want to drive? Everyone wants to drive in the States!" But then trying to put yourself in their shoes, especially in traffic like this and the way parking is . . . if I had a driver, I wouldn't be driving. Why would you want to? It is a different perspective. In America it seems like if you don't want to do something like that everybody does, it's a bad thing, like you're putting yourself below other people. Here it's a choice. They can drive if they want.—Amanda*

Both Ashley and Amanda adjusted their cross-cultural gaze to oscillate between both sides, allowing for a view of both/and. For Ashley, it was no longer an issue of women being *either* free to leave the house *or not*, but instead was an issue of moving within the cultural constraints re-

2. To my own knowledge, women have never been legally forbidden from driving in Qatar, and I cannot find a date when women were "allowed" to drive. What has changed over time is the local social acceptance of women driving.

garding reputation. Local women were at once free and constrained—a paradoxical position to which Ashley could more empathetically relate due to her own experiences. For Amanda, the argument changed from being that women must drive because they *can* to being that a woman's decision about driving or not driving should be respected no matter what her choice. Control of a motor vehicle, a privilege we in the US treat as a right, is not the defining act of women's freedom or oppression. Amanda has substituted the "right to choose" for the "right to drive" above, as she describes how her perspectives on what counts as agency have changed. Transformation in her thinking is generated through her transnational positionality. Amanda's USAmerican positionality centers the agency of driving a vehicle and the freedom it confers, a freedom re-confirmed when Amanda drove on her visits back to the USA, to other countries, and because she preferred to drive her own car in Qatar. But her time in Qatar disrupted the binary of driving/freedom versus not-driving/restraint, and her perceptions of choice evolved. Through this learning (or what I reframe in the next chapter as *un*learning), my participants began to articulate "oppositional knowledges" or counterstories that resisted the master narrative of Gulf Arab women as universally and persistently oppressed, stories they wanted to share upon returning to visit their homes in the USA.

Increasing tolerance for complexities in their host spaces led to expatriates recognizing their own home country's contingencies and inconsistencies more easily. As a result, they became paradoxically more patriotic and more critical of the USA. Melissa said, "The questions that I'm asked make me think a lot about the US and how things are represented. . . . I look at things in the US a little more critically, in a different way." Amanda described it this way: "Most people that I've encountered here have actually put the US on a higher pedestal than I think it should be sometimes (laughing). Now having said that, I will tell you that I've probably become more patriotic since I've been here, but I'm not blind still [to the faults of the US]." Amy explained it is important for her "to feel like a global citizen with connections to the rest of the world that you just don't have when you're back home." She goes on to explain:

> *In some ways, I would not describe myself as patriotic anymore. I don't feel those ties. In some ways, that sense of patriotism and nationalism seems sort of cultish to me. On the other hand, I still get chills when I hear the US national anthem. . . . It's always going to*

> *be home. But I have more skepticism about patriotism and I defi-*
> *nitely look at it more critically than I used to.—Amy*

Patricia reflected on how her time in Qatar has changed her: "I think it may be a little challenging to transition back to the US. When I go back home for vacations, I am sometimes appalled at the increasing decadence of my home country."

The foregrounding of our privilege, by comparing ourselves to other expatriates in Qatar and by traveling to some places labeled in the West as "developing," where norms of daily life are markedly different than those in the US, pushed us to reflect on narratives of Western/USAmerican exceptionalism and the role in "saving" other nations. Sarah, who accompanied students residing in Qatar on a trip to Africa, told a story of her own transformation regarding assumptions of privilege:

> *I took IBC students to Uganda on a service trip there were a lot of interesting, eye-opening moments for me (laughing). I mean I knew students were privileged. But the way Americans are seen as coming in and telling people what to do. . . . That is more about privilege than nationality. . . . IBC Students would say, "We need to teach them how to wash their hands" or "We need to teach them how to do this." And I was thinking "You're from Pakistan. You're from Qatar. You're eighteen years old. What do you know about this that this forty-year-old man doesn't know? He's lived twice as long as you, so he must be doing something right. Why do you think you can tell other people how to live? In what ways can you partner with and not overlord over someone?" So for me, that was like "Duh. Of course. Your Dad's the general in the Pakistan army. You think you can tell people what to do. That's not just an American thing. That's because you come from this level of privilege, and I hadn't prepared you for that. I'll do better next time."—Sarah*

Student access to IBC education is often a product of economic and social privilege, so Sarah's observation may be on point. Additionally, students' brash go in and fix it and/or the save the [incompetent] world narrative certainly seems to re-enact some US foreign policy as well as private and non-profit savior efforts. Not being there and not talking to her students, only hypotheses are possible, but Sarah's story is an illustration of complexity not often voiced: privileged attitude transcends national identities. Recognizing she needed to resist reinforcing the white savior narrative, she learned she needed to "do better next time."

As a result, Sarah developed tactics for guiding students in stepping back from their entitled perspectives and in looking for relationships based on mutual respect and reciprocity.

Another major boon to the expatriate adventure was awareness of how USAmericans are perceived abroad. Expatriate women in Qatar felt responsible for how we, as ambassadors, represented the USA, and most described actively working against the "ugly American" stereotype. Reflecting on American economic and military power, Amy described her emerging awareness that "the US is very egocentric and very isolated, which is odd considering its role in the world." As a result, she "probably goes overboard to avoid the ugly American thing." Patricia explained she "didn't know how much the US was resented around the world until I came here. I don't try to explain US foreign policy. I just hope that I set an example of reason and compassion." Ashley also commented on the responsibility of representation, saying, "if I'm nice and they find out I'm an American, then all Americans are nice. But if I'm mean and I'm American, then they assume that all Americans are mean." Susan remarked on how assumptions of privilege were invasive: "I see a lot of bad behavior by Western, white people that feel they have a sense of entitlement. That's horrifying to me. Yet sometimes I feel that same sense of entitlement myself because I've lived here, and I'm appalled, you know? When that rears its ugly head." Melissa, who used her bubble as a strategy for countering hypervisibility and the gaze in chapter 2, reflected that doing so actually contradicted her other efforts at avoiding ugly American behavior. She and all the other interviewees described strategies, such as friendliness, listening, and generosity (in tipping, etc.) to re-present the USA in a better light.

At the end of the mythic journey, Osland's heroic expatriate businessperson had been reborn as a "master of two worlds," whose "understanding of two cultures is one of the boons they bring back to their companies and to the larger society" (*Adventure* 185). In contrast and despite developing extensive host-country strategies and tactics, USAmerican expatriate women in Qatar did not claim to feel a sense of bi-cultural mastery. To begin, as a transnational space, Qatar was not bi-cultural but richly multicultural. Also as described above, adjustment into the Qatari host community was limited—expatriates assimilated into multicultural "ghettos" that were privileged but also intentionally segregated from the local community *due to* the policies of the local community. "Culture" in Qatar was contextually dependent. At the IBC, the institutional culture was at the intersection of public university policy and local Qatari practice. At the traffic ministry, the culture was decidedly local. At the grocery store, in traffic, and in the compound or apartment building, the culture was most complex. Further disrupting feelings of expatriate confidence and competence was the paradoxical un/familiarity of Qatar. USAmerican expatriate women grew to understand they would never understand; indeed, "the only certainty is uncertainty." Rather than assume any sort of full cross-cultural understanding was possible, we sought to "stand under" the sometimes-confounding experiences of life abroad, "letting [host space] discourses wash over, through, and around us and then letting [those discourses] lie there to inform our politics and ethics" (Ratcliffe, *Rhetorical Listening* 28). The strain of long-term standing under, an ongoing process of oscillating between the *"there-that-is-here,"* manifested itself in the previous battle and liminality metaphors. Yet ironically, that long-term strain also translated into anticipated boons of greater patience, adaptability, and openness (also see chapter 3, "Movement as Transformative Agency"). Rather than speaking in terms of mastery or conquering, white USAmerican expatriate women were humble, reflective, and grateful to be (un)learning (see chapter 5).

Instead of the fully transformed rebirth metaphor of Campbell's master narrative, "splinched" is a more apt description for the experiences of my interviewees and me. In J.K. Rowling's *Harry Potter* series, when inexperienced witches or wizards use disapparition (disappearing) and apparition (appearing) to instantly move from one place to another, some parts of their bodies might not make the transition: "There was a horrible screech of pain and everybody looked around, terrified, to see Susan Bones of Hufflepuff wobbling . . . with her left leg still standing five feet from where she had started" (385). When Susan disappears and reappears a few feet away, one of her legs stays behind. Up to this point, I have been using Rose's feminist tactic of "oscillation" to describe the generative nature of expatriate perspectives, what Carrillo Rowe calls a "teetering between here and there, self and other, between power over and power with" (178). However, the feeling—upon return to our home country—of being splinched reveals that a moving back-and-forth between home and host is not sufficient because it is limited by being tied to movement itself. While movement is one form of feminist agency (chapter 3), the ability to focus from multiple perspectives *at the same time* is another. Therefore, building off of Rose's concept, I propose *lenticularity* as a unique rhetorical feminist positioning.

A lenticular image begins as two static images, but these are layered so the viewer can shift between them. They're common on all sorts of children's toys, pictures that move when you tilt them. If you hold the image just perfectly, both intertwined images are visible at once. A lenticular perspective emerges from existing in liminal, in-between spaces. In "Different Spaces," Michel Foucault's mirror operates similarly when his own reality and identity are jarred through a jump in perceived location: "I see myself where I am not. . . . I am over there where I am not. . . . I discover myself absent at the place where I am, since I see myself over there . . . I come back to myself . . . to reconstitute myself there where I am" (179). What Foucault describes is the movement from one reality to the other. However, a truly lenticular positioning can also settle in the space of both/and or here/there. In moments of lenticular positioning, we bridge two perspectives rather than locating ourselves in one or the other. When Amy experiences the transformative moment sharing family stories with the Qatari man, she experiences the lenticular perspectives of sameness *and* difference.

When Amanda reflects over her ability to keep one foot in the US-American perspective on the agency of driving a car, while at the same time, finding her footing on why women in Qatar would not *want* to drive, her ability to bring two cultural perceptions, is due to lenticular positioning. In these examples, each side is understood, yet Amy and Amanda locate themselves between the two rather than choosing one as primary and the other as secondary. Because it is about bridging and functioning within liminality and paradox, lenticularity also goes beyond the basic inclusivity of both/and. Lenticularity is not just an openness to perceive multiplicity, it is the ability to make decisions as a rhetorical agent in situations that exhibit complication. Lenticularity is the embodied agency and perceptive positioning of Anzaldúa's *mestiza* identity and *nepantlera* locationality, both disorienting and re-orienting to systems and symbolic processes (*Light in the Dark*).

A literal embodiment of lenticular positions—movement stopped between here and there—produces a strong sense of disorientation, even disintegration. Rowling's splinching is violent and messy, leaving anything from hair to full limbs in the original location where the disapparating took place. The wizard is not here *or* there but here *and* there, a *there-that-is-*[now]-*here*. In Rowling's world, splinching "occurs when the mind is insufficiently *determined*. You must concentrate continually upon your *destination*, and move, without haste, but with *deliberation* . . . (385–86). The partial transformation of expatriate life in Qatar marks it as a liminal existence full of determined deliberation, yet because expats learn to live in the persistence of certain uncertainty, a both/and outlook and set of lenticular tactics result. Being an outsider-within the host space may feel almost but never fully "right," yet because of this splinching, the return home to the USA no longer feels fully right either. Campbell's *mythos* and Osland's application to expatriates would have us believe our boon-toting heroes emerge fully transformed and empowered, but for USAmerican expatriate women moving between Qatar and their US homes communities, the transition is incomplete.

Expatriate splinching—I can say from my own experience—is awkward, painful, and feels like a pulling apart, yet it is also a powerful source of growth and insight. Anzaldúa movingly describes being the border-crossing, border-spanning *nepantlera*: "I disintegrate into hundreds of pieces, hundreds of separate awarenesses. . . . Yet while experiencing the many, I cohere as the one reconstituted and restructure my own unconscious urge toward wholeness" (*Light in the Dark* 50).[3] For several years—after I had adjusted to the initial shock of living abroad—I felt a keen sense of disintegrating, particularly when I would travel back home. It quite literally felt as if I might come apart into a million pieces, and at the time, I was confounded and could not put words to it. It was a sense of being both between and simultaneously in two worlds—a *there-that-is-here* from the USAmerican location. It also gave me vertigo. I felt like I might be losing my rational mind. What I realize in retrospect, and thanks to Anzaldúa's writing, is that I was coming undone and being remade through the intense, jarring loose from my previous lifeworld and my transformative (and never fully realized) adjustment to my new lifeworld. That jarring loose was most intensely felt when I returned home because home no longer felt like the stable, integrated place I had comfortably known it to be. During my time in Qatar, I knew other expatri-

---

3. Folx of all identities can be nepantleras: "All people in nepantla—Natives, immigrants, colored, white, queers, heterosexuals, from this side of the border, del otro lado—are personas de lugar, local people, and relate to the border and to the nepantla states in different ways" (Anzaldúa, *Light in the Dark* 57). However, the nature of experiences and perspectives would differ based on factors of assimilation (or lack thereof). Anzaldúa's "seven stages of conocimiento" open another compelling framework for the movements of transnational expatriate lives (*Light in the Dark* 121–156).

ates who could not endure the disorientation and stress of disintegration/ reintegration. They would stay a year or so and then begin looking to return back to the USA.

Lenticular positioning allows a vantage point for valuing interdependence, "a view from the cracks, rather than from any single culture or ideology" (Anzaldúa, *Light in the Dark* 82). When systems divide us into groups of insiders/outsiders, lenticular positioning plants our feet on the liminal thresholds of these divisions and pushes us to consider how ranges of difference also represent opportunities for coalition building (Carrillo Rowe). By bridging centers and margins, it is a disruptive as well as generative rhetorical feminist tactic, a refusal to acquiesce to the master narrative in the presence of counternarratives as well as a means of resisting simply choosing a new singular narrative with its own attendant margins. Lenticularity positions you here, there, in-between, and moving among all at once.

As heroic journeyers, white USAmerican expatriate women did not tread the path promised by Campbell's monomyth. Although they heeded the call to adventure and traveled a road of trials, they did not have clearly defined insider magical aides to mentor them through the process. Time in the belly of the whale led them to experience the transformative nature of living in paradoxical positioning: certain uncertainty, simultaneous power and vulnerability, competing privileged freedoms and threats of restraint. And through these alchemical moments, expatriate women persisted and adapted by opening up more than closing down, and in that process, became more aware of systemic injustice and the implications of their white privilege. Living as outsiders-within gave them a new vantage point from which to view their home communities, where they returned to visit as transformed *insiders-without*. Yet despite celebrating the discombobulating and gratifying growth of their adventures, and despite having boons to share with their families at home, efforts at fulfilling the narrative of the heroic return by "building bridges between cultures" (a metaphor used by participants) were a source of frustration. Rather than sharing the boons of our learning and growth, we became entangled in silence.

## Expatriate Women as (Silenced) Cultural Ambassadors

An ambassador is an emissary representing one group in conversation with another or multiple others.[4] Derived from a Latin root also yielding terms for servant (*ambactus*) and "to go on a mission" (*ambactiare*), an ambassador's goal is to work in relational borderlands. An ambassador can function in multiple modes: delivering or transmitting information; providing translation aimed at enhancing understanding; and/or shaping meaning directly by choosing the content, tropes, and tone through which to communicate. Her role is inherently political and certainly rhetorical, as she negotiates between or among parties. In choosing—consciously and unconsciously—what information to use or not use in her bridge building, the ambassador (re)constructs terms of belonging. In other words, moving between groups, she sets up notions of similarity and difference with regard to perceptions, values, and practices. In influencing how the process of learning about the Other takes place and how each group perceives the other, she facilitates the opening and closing of spaces for Burkean identification.

When in host spaces, my interviewees and I tried to understand (sometimes by Krista Ratcliffe's "standing under" and "laying alongside") multiple perspectives and ways of being, but for reasons discussed above, our levels of adjustment—rather than assimilation—into the host cultures were limited. Although oscillating and adapting between home and host spaces might help an ambassador serve both more successfully, ultimately, she must remain focused on the mission of serving her home when she knows she is permanently temporary in the host space. Although we wanted to build bridges, expatriates who expected to return home also felt compelled to reaffirm their ongoing primary belonging or loyalty to home. In the face of a persistent media focus on clashing civilizations of Islam and the West, USAmerican expatriate women faced big obstacles in their bridging work. Demonstrating too much host-ad-

---

4. The term "diplomat" could also be used here—the expatriate's cross-cultural diplomatic function. Both terms' modern uses imply official capacities normally associated with national governments. Where the Latin root for ambassador (ambactiāta) relates to service and missions, the Greek root for diplomat (διπλωμάτης, diplōmátēs) relates to a "folded paper" or accreditation to formally represent a governing body (Oxford English Dictionary). An association with service rather than licensure better fits the tone of how expatriates viewed their bridge building. Osland also mentions the ambassadorial inclination (*Adventure* 120–22).

aptation and empathy risked being accused of disloyalty to USAmerican ideals. For example, too much interest in Islam triggered worries over being converted or too much time on host soil was read as losing your USAmerican identity. One of my family members told me she worried my children had been gone too long and "would not understand what it means to be Texan." Although framed in terms of identity, concerns were centered on community belonging.

Despite the complexities of the ambassadorial role, my interviewees initially took to it with enthusiasm. Amy was anxious to share ways that her intercultural communication experiences had "punched holes" in her anxieties, and Mary purposefully moved her family abroad to escape the "bubble" of her home community. Empowered by the challenges and newly exercised sources of agency in their lives abroad, they had many stories to share. As Susan put it, "I live diversity!" She and others hoped to help "dispel myths" by sharing the boons of transnational life and learning. Although participants and I recognized the realities of our challenging and confusing lives in Qatar, most of us hoped to (re)define assumptions about the Middle East at home just as we sought to subvert the ugly American stereotype when abroad. We wanted to foreground the ideals of beneficial intercultural communication and collaboration shaping our transnational lives and to leverage our first-hand experiences as counterarguments to the clash narrative in the media. As described above, we approached the role with humble enthusiasm because, as Michelle observed, "Any Westerner who says they understand the Arab mind is in a really dangerous place." The "danger" was not one of avoidance but one of awareness and a reminder to be open-minded as well as willing to learn, self-assess, and self-correct.

When asked about how their stories regarding life in Qatar were received by home audiences, however, my participants were met with unexpected responses. Susan said she was not offered the space to discuss Qatar when visiting her home community in the USA: "It doesn't come up. A lot of people think we're just crazy." For those that did try to tell their stories back home, a common basic plot emerged: expat attempts to share experiences, expat grows frustrated by home community response, so expat engages strategies of silence. Ashley laughed as she said, "I'm generally positive about being here in Qatar, but it's funny, when I start talking about what it's like back home, at the end, people say, 'But I thought you said you liked it in Qatar.'" Although she found humor in the irony of how her stories were received, Ashley felt incapable of fully communicating the nuanced tangle of opportunities and challenges her expatriate life entailed. Even as she was positioned lenticularly in the both/and of knowing something of her home *and* about Qatar, she felt at a loss for how to articulate across that divide. Melissa had some success with close friends or close family members, with whom she could "have these conversations over sort of an extended period," but in contrast, "Everybody else, they don't get it. You know their eyes sort of glaze over very quickly and you know . . . let's talk about football or the weather." Patricia similarly reflected, "I don't tell stories much anymore. My stories seem to go in one ear and out the other. Six months, or a week, or a day, later, my 'listeners' have slipped back into believing their old stereotypes."

Emily commented on the growing divide between her transformative mobilities and the seemingly unchanging consistency of home: "It's difficult for me to talk to people. A lot of my friends and even my family have lived in the same town or same state all their lives, and there's just things that you can't explain." Eyes glazing over and gaps in common experiences were challenging to overcome. Emily went on to say that "There's just *things* that being in the US . . . it's very frustrating." Although Emily did not elaborate on what the "things" in the US are, from the broader context of her interview, she seemed to be referring to how her friends and family were limited to understanding the US in terms of how it is stereotypically narrated from within. The national *mythos* of power, opportunity, equality, and exceptionalism—the "shining city on a hill"—overshadowed and ultimately silenced what she knew to be the more complex, critical, and hypocritical ways the US was perceived abroad. She could not explain these nuanced understandings to her friends and family because doing so risked her being seen as disloyal to her home country. Belonging, as a USAmerican, means unwavering patriotism.

Frustration and defensiveness also emerged when expatriates realized the degree to which family and friends stubbornly clung to their prejudicial stereotypes and shut down the space for story sharing. Amanda said she must "constantly defend myself even being here [in an Islamic state]. When I defend it, they think I'm defending Islam like I'm on the verge of converting, which I'm not. I'm defending Muslims' right to it, and my parents don't quite get that. That's one of the reasons that especially with my parents that I don't discuss living here, because that's always where it ends up." Amanda defended the host population's human right to self-determination through an argument based on USAmerican value of religious choice and non-discrimination, extending a well-loved US civil liberty to decisions made by nation-states. But her family audience re-interpreted her argument as a dangerous sign she was being overly influenced by being in an Islamic country.[5] Michelle's family was also concerned about her sense of identity and belonging:

> *I have to be very careful to not say the word "home" in front of my mother. I messed up once [referring to Doha as home] and she said "Here is your home" because we were in my home state. So now I have to be very careful to not say "when I go home" or "when I'm home." For her, my identity is in my home state. It's not Doha. But for me, that's . . . I don't know if it's been that way for a while and I'm now just thinking about it or if it suddenly happened because I've been here for a long time. But it happened to me this summer that I really started thinking that I don't identify with my home any more. It's a place I visit when I come back to the United States and it's where my loved ones are.—Michelle*

More overt resistance based on racist stereotypes also emerged as typical. Jessica said, "I have family that is very country, very hick. They say, 'What are you doing out there with those *Ay-rabs?*' And I'm like 'what?' I don't even want to engage in that conversation because they already have their opinion." Mary also described working to change attitudes back home: "Arab people are not like they are portrayed on TV, as terrorists. That's what I try hard to portray to people in the US, to my friends, to my family. Because they are all very prejudiced." Lisa's story is a good representative of interviewees' shared narrative:

> *It makes some people mad that I'm over here. And you've probably heard this, "Why are you teaching those people how to blow up the world?" And that's just ignorance. I just laugh and say, "Oh come on. We're building bridges between our cultures. We're making things better in the world. How are we ever going to get along if we don't know each other?" That's usually my answer. And—these are not people related to me! (laughing)—they'll say things like, "You're using our money, our tax payer money." And I say "That is so not true." So I tell them the correct story on that.—Lisa*

---

5. I could critique Amanda's argument in terms of how well it does or does not function as an extension, but the point here is the way she perceives trying to "build bridges" by relating USAmerican civil liberties to her host nation.

Fueled by the clash of cultures narrative and general xenophobia concerning all parts of the Middle East or Arab world, questions of whether or not the USAmerican IBC should even be participating in Education City extend beyond Jessica's family. Worries that the IBC is "funding terrorist education" stretch back to the opening of the campus in 2003, and although the university has re-emphasized that it operates off Qatar Foundation funding rather than state tax monies, confusion persists. For example, a former student of the home university campus (and former chair of a conservative student group) worries "his university is educating radical extremists" (Nakano). He says, "It's very concerning that public resources are potentially assisting those who want to attack America, destroy Western values and terrorize others." Angelo Codevilla, a former Professor of International Relations at Boston University, writing for *Security Studies Group*, believes Qatar has strategically "capitalized on the US foreign policy establishment's predispositions to Progressive ideology and to meddling" and is using the branch campuses as a ruse to cover their support of terrorist activities. Presenting a slightly more balanced perspective, R.G. Ratcliffe, a writer for a prominent state magazine, blogs about the challenges of the IBC pursuing an educational mission while positioned inside a controversial nation-state. Ratcliffe ponders, "just how did the first state-run university of [this state] become wedded to such a questionable state of affairs?" Despite over a decade of growing development and success, and despite a clear vision supported by vast investments (both economic and socio-political) from Qatar Foundation, efforts to budge the dominant terrorist/clash narrative in the USA seem Sisyphean.

Even when storytelling was allowed back home, interviewees reported learning to stay silent. Sarah described feeling like "one of those dolls where you pull the cord out of its back" when discussing her time in Qatar. She commented that "people always ask the same questions, so even our extended family who don't know as much about Qatar, we know what they're going to ask: Is it safe? How many people live there? Why are they so rich?" Because she felt the questions came from narrow perceptions based on the stereotypes, Sarah sometimes chose silence over ambassadorial sharing. Talking about her funny but frustrating experience with her driver's license testing as told in chapter 3, Sarah said, "I wrote a really long blog entry about this but then decided not to post it. I didn't feel comfortable putting that on the Internet even though I wanted to share the experience with friends and family in the States. But the complexity and anxiety that came with that experience—they would never understand or appreciate." I had the same experience. For the first year or so we were in Qatar, I kept a blog of cross-cultural interaction, but as we adjusted to expat life, it became more of a travel blog for places outside of Qatar. Three years into our time abroad, I stopped blogging completely. Like Sarah, my impetus for stopping was my own inability to tell a story capturing the nuance of the situation, to find the humor in life abroad without seeming to put down my hosts and colleagues for outside readers.

In *Unspoken: A Rhetoric of Silence*, Glenn establishes the reciprocal interdependence of words and silence, laying out for readers a "constellation of symbolic [silence] strategies that (like spoken language) serve many functions" (18). She invites readers to consider how "silence and silencing also provide new pathways and new methods for expanding the rhetorical tradition" including "a chance to readjust relations of power" (153). When returning to the US on visits to friends and family, white US-American expatriate women reported wanting to *speak*, to share the valuable and complex learning experienced abroad, but instead they learned they would encounter or choose to engage silence. Through the stories told above, their framework of rhetorical silence emerges and includes both "silence as a strategic choice [and] silence as an enforced position" (13). Engaging silence as *strategic choice*, expatriate rhetors responded to their audience's inability to relate because their listeners had not been in similar scenic borderlands of un/familiarity and un/certainty. Strategic silence was the response to realizing they could not adequately—within the time and other home contexts allotted—describe their experiences in ways that they felt fairly represented life abroad and to realizing even audiences who attempted to listen would likely not sufficiently relate to the stories long enough to stay interested.

Expatriates' purposeful silences reveal an ultimate failure of bridge-building. Silences were also strategic in their protective role. If the expatriate kept talking, she risked alienating her friends and family and being judged as "spoiled" or entitled as she endlessly rattled on about her travels and international experiences. As Amanda said, "I don't want to be singled out with, 'Oh, let's hear about your international stories.' I don't want to be *that* person." Silence also protected the expat from misleading her audience with inadequate or misunderstood stories, as when Ashley shared that people who heard her stories thought she did not like living in Qatar. As ambassadors, expatriate women wanted to represent their home and host parties in overall positive (if complicated) lights. However, doing so back in the USA was made more difficult because of stronger competing negative narratives.

The complexity of the Qatar expatriate narrative was challenging to share, but upon return to USAmerican soil, it faced an even greater hurdle—one that ultimately rendered it mute—as an insufficient counter-narrative to Islamophobia and the master narrative "clash of civilizations." In other words, the clash narrative deafened potential listeners and limited or destroyed potential for reforming identifications. The "Islam-as-Terrorist" versus the "West-as-Moral-Authority" binary demands a clear standpoint and unlimited Western allegiance, a line in the sand drawn in George W. Bush's televised post-9/11 speech declaring, "Every nation, in every region, now has a decision to make. Either you are with us, or you are with the terrorists." If you belong and are "with us" as an "American," your position must be singular and sure, not multiple and complex. To defend a woman's right *not* to drive or to *not* be bothered by the headscarf demonstrates wavering conviction. In Glenn's terms, what emerges is "a *differend*—one party simply cannot voice his or her complaints or point because the other party insists on speaking within a different language game or genre of discourse" (*Unspoken* 6). The consequences of persistent silencing "often inculcates a muted group as subaltern, inadequate if not worthless" (27). White USAmerican expatriate women confronted the paradox of being both powerful and powerless when abroad, and by traveling the uncertain and challenging road of trials, broadened our perspectives and grew in confidence through their experiences. However, when we returned home hoping to build bridges and share our boons, we were instead marginalized.

Addressing damaging stereotypes to combat injustice is central to feminist work. Glenn paraphrases bell hooks when she says, "Resistance can be nothing more (or less) than 'talking back'" (*Unspoken* 26). We have a myriad of ways to speak beyond verbal utterances. At the time of my study, ten of the twelve participants had no immediate plans to leave the IBC and Qatar. In other words, the silencing they faced at home might be partially understood to have indeed triggered a response: their "talking back" was performed by "*going* back" to Qatar.

## Paradoxical Belonging and Estranging

The expatriate's return home was experienced as a splinching prompting development of a lenticular perspective. Through the oscillation of transnational movement, she learned to exist in a liminal threshold between host and home spaces. However, while her body fully made the trip back to the USA, her insights were silenced. A significant part of her was cut off, not permitted the space to share her ambassadorial boon. The feeling of being splinched—partially cut off—triggered *estranging* from home. In Ahmed's *Strange Encounters* the figure of "the stranger" is "an effect of processes of inclusion and exclusion, or incorporation and expulsion, that constitute the boundaries of bodies and communities" (6). In other words, being labeled as a stranger is being labeled as an outsider, a disidentification or disavowal. Ahmed is concerned with how insiders with power recognize or assign strangerhood—a dark and dangerous identity—to some bodies but not to others. Being an expatriate and returning home can lead to a sort of reversal. Upon returning and finding silence, the expatriate learns that she carries with her a *shadow* of xenophobic strangeness and a dark denial of alternatives to the clash narrative haunting those closest to her at home. She also begins to recognize herself as becoming a stranger—a self-estranging—from home family and communities. Her life in the host space has changed the terms of belonging in her home location, and her feelings of belonging to home as a "natural space" (Yuval-Davis 35) are disrupted both by the silent reception and by the expatriate knowing she will be returning to the host space soon. Rose's Sameness and Otherness have intertwined. She is not only self-estranging through her own transformative expat life but is also being estranged by the silence of her reception. Competing tensions of belonging and estranging from home are experienced as paradoxical: ultimately, she finds herself in the liminal in-between, "at ease anywhere yet belonging nowhere" (Osland and Osland 100).

Caught between spaces of belonging, the expat begins to perceive herself as "charged" with a danger of Otherness (Ahmed, "Making Strangers"). While Ahmed is specifically ruminating over racialized bodies, the taint or haunting fear attached to shadowy figures functions transnationally, too. As described above, the shadow of the ugly American stereotype haunted us abroad, while the shadow of Islamic influence haunted us at home. When Ashley began to understand the pressures on Qatari women to uphold patriarchal standards, her mother became agitated because she saw women's restrictions as unfair and worried Ashley's time in the host nation tainted her USAmerican views of gender equality. When Amanda tried to explain host practices, her parents accused her of defending Islam, as if she were in danger of conversion. Michelle could not shift her view of home because to consider Qatar "home" was not acceptable to her mother. Although the story Michelle shared does not explicitly say what the source of that objection is, it may be in part that her mother fears losing Michelle to the Other. A general taint of danger associated with the region also existed. Anytime a major threat of violence or escalation occurred (e.g., the ramping up of Iran's nuclear program or the Arab spring of 2011), friends and family sent me messages urging me to bring my family home to safety. An unfortunate irony to this situation was that their pleas would themselves be tainted by other headlines of mass shootings by (white) USAmericans against USAmericans, violence that seemed to be happening with alarming, increasing frequency on assumed "safer" soil of home.

For the families of expatriates, home was a sanctified space, but as the expatriate was shaped by transnational experiences, her feelings of belonging shifted and her lenticular positioning became clearer. Ahmed writes, "home becomes associated with stasis, boundaries, identity and fixity. Home is implicitly constructed as a purified space of belonging in which the subject . . . is so at ease that she or he does not think" (*Strange* 87). The movement inherent in expatriate life flipped this narrative, making the fixity and the ease of homegrown stereotypes and assumptions seem odd. For the expatriate who was constantly engaged in movement and difference abroad, being in a space "uncontaminated by movement, desire or difference" (88) became strange. Then facing the silent and silencing reception of family and friends further pushed the expatriate away from the identification and belonging of home. Returning expatriates perceived home through a new lens of paradoxical incongruity. Their new sensemaking shifted, to be based on stories of uncertainty, challenges, agency, and (un)learning. Realizing this new incongruity but not being able to share it amplified the process of estranging. Even as coming home became awkward or frustrating, my interviewees and I did not feel compelled to reject our most important social ties. Instead, we closed off some parts of our lives to home while leaving others open. In doing so, we became splinched between the *there-that-is-here*.

Previous chapters laid a foundation for how a transnational scene (Qatar and the branch campus) substantially shifted or re-set expatriate life. As agents within that complex scene, women were challenged by competing accountabilities, unjust social systems, and unfamiliar legal systems. As white/Westerners, they were hypervisible, and as women they were often rendered invisible. Living paradoxically in home/host spaces, in/visibility, and freedom/ restraint developed their awareness of a lenticular positioning. Although the scene often felt constraining, it also expanded their perspectives. In large part, it amplified the advantages of being white, of living a comfortable life, and of having a trustworthy host sponsorship.

So what did we *do* with that privilege? As this chapter has revealed, efforts to translate it back to our home communities were not successful. Upon returning to Qatar, then, did we sit in our golden ghettos, grateful for our status and pitying those who did not share it? Sometimes, I confess, yes, we did. But we also sought out ways to subvert host systems that confronted us with injustice on a daily basis. We learned to leverage our oscillating visibility and our simultaneous power and powerlessness in small acts of resistance. As the upcoming final chapter explicates, white USAmerican women developed a rhetorical feminist tactic for *doing* something, a strategic means of promoting hope (Glenn, *Rhetorical Feminism* 5): micropraxis.

# 5 Unlearning, Learning, and Micropraxis

يا رايح عالجبل جيب معاك ولو حجر

*Who are going to the mountain bring something back, even if it is a stone.*

—Arab Proverb

I have been to the mountain, spent six years there, returned to the USA, and this project is the small boon . . . or perhaps the stone . . . of a long journey. Our worlds were rhetorically constructed within liminal scenes that were simultaneously traditional and modern, ideal and real, where the private became the public. In these scenes, we were hypervisible because of our whiteness, exotic because of our white femaleness, and erased because we were women. We came to understand the power that accompanied visual presence could be cleverly leveraged through positioning ourselves in the shadows. We also learned the power of movement, of being challenged to navigate systems that were confusingly familiar as well as unfamiliar, where our only certainty was uncertainty. Through these perspectives, we embraced being "in a constant state of response, reassessment, and self-correction" (Glenn, *Rhetorical Feminism* 4) and learned to pause, reflect, and respect a wider variety of cultural logics (Ratcliffe, *Rhetorical Listening*).

Weaving our stories into this narrative illustrates how adopting a lenticular outlook between paradoxical positionings, being willing to question and make new sense of our environments and ourselves, and choosing to view uncertainty as generative rather than limiting are rhetorical feminist tactics. Stories we told about "what it's like" reveal our willfulness, which was feminist even if we were not always conscious of being so. We were "stand[ing] on the edge of [our own] becoming" (Carrillo Rowe 178). As expatriates struggling to fit into the community and to find our footing on new ground, we committed to "foundational feminist concepts" as we embraced a shared openness to new (and confusing or even troubling) experiences, as we sought out "authentic dialogue and deliberation" among cultural perspectives, and when we chose to face—rather than turn away from—an "interrogation of the [socio-economic caste system's] status quo" in our host country (Glenn, *Rhetorical Feminism* 1). We displayed "feminist tendencies," most importantly, "a willingness to keep going despite or even because of what we have come up against" (Ahmed, *Living* 6). Living in systemic injustice, seeing our complicity in the eyes of the laborers toiling in the sun, became a question of accountability and pushed us to do *something*. Yet considering our own status as outsiders, as invited guests who could also be uninvited, we struggled with contradictory feelings of power and precarity.

Rather than shutting down in the face of contradictory positioning at the intersection of two seemingly incongruous realities, expatriate women turned to hope, creating small spaces for opportunity. What my participants demonstrated was this: when the scene prevents "big" acts, feminist agents can leverage their paradoxical (in)visibility to take advantage of the liminal threshold between power and powerlessness. Power is not present as a binary but as a shifting current of opportunities. Ahmed writes about how we sometimes change direction to "go with the flow" while other times we continue to resist the flow even though that puts us under pressure. She says, "We need a feminist account of such techniques of redirection" (*Living* 50). This final chapter is one accounting. I call small acts of purposeful agency within paradox "micropraxis." It is defined, illustrated, expanded, and troubled here.

## (Un)Learning through Sense(re)making

Moving across geographical locations and multicultural spaces is jarring, often experienced as culture shock but also an opportunity for unlearning. Donna Landry and Gerald MacLean emphasize the "injunction to 'unlearn'" is "one of the most powerful tasks set readers by Spivak's writing and teaching" (4).[1] To unlearn is not a project of complete reversal. It

---

1. Spivak subsequently complicates unlearning and says that although her original idea was "more about how to behave as a subject of knowledge within the

is not to forget, erase, or deny. Instead, unlearning is a rhetorical feminist process of sense(re)making, a disrupting and a challenging to the narratives that have guided our assumptions. It involves listening to tropes, to narratives that prescribe our individual and community identities to us. Unlearning occurs in transformative moments: "When you begin to put the pieces together, it can feel magical: the wonder of the clicking moment, when things that had previously been otherwise begin to make sense, when things fit into place. You blink and the world reappears" (Ahmed, *Living* 29). Unlearning is a genuine risk. It threatens estranging us from basic feelings of belonging: "becoming feminist puts us in touch with a world through alienation from a world" (Ahmed, *Living* 43). It is an undoing of the sensemaking that has previously held us together— the stories we tell ourselves "in order to live."

Didion's *White Album* essays are about her lived experiences witnessing the social and cultural revolutions of the USA in the 1960s and 1970s. It is no accident that her writing would resonate with me as an expat working to make sense of my life and my participants' lives abroad. Didion did some border crossing of her own when she displaced herself by immersing herself in the counter-culture of her time. The phantasmagoria anchored in her previous narrative became unmoored in that alternative space, unveiling anew the incongruent (paradoxical) nature of life. In that dream-like incongruence, she experienced the shifting perspective between what she had known and what she was coming to know, and her writing spoke to readers from that liminality.

What Didion describes is her own unlearning. Although her writings have this process in common with USAmerican expatriate women in Qatar, the nature and products of the unlearning differ. Spivak's unlearning is concerned with divides of privilege—social, economic, racial/ethnic, national, and gender. For Spivak, living in unexamined privilege is a "loss" and unlearning "constitutes a double recognition" that our advantages may have "prevented us from gaining a certain kind of Other knowledge" (Landry and MacLean 4). Analysis of Didion's positioning in the counter-culture of later twentieth-century California is beyond

---

institution of neocolonial learning" but that over time and consideration, her focus had become more about ethics and about the nature of learning and the complication of "the suspension of learning, without legitimizing it by reversal" (Darius, et al. 25). She recommends a process at the heart of expatriate life: "check[ing] out your theoretical presuppositions by testing them in areas" very different from where they were originally learned (25).

the scope of this project, but her essays do not foreground economic and national caste divides comparable to those experienced by expatriates in early twenty-first century Qatar. Although Didion, my participants, and I all experienced an unraveling of our previous narratives, living in the hybridity, uncertainty, and drastic inequality of transnational spaces amplified and intensified our resulting transformations.

The subjects of our sense(re)making were ourselves. Having a "blank canvas" at work because there is "no precedent" could be seen as working in complete uncertainty, an enormous risk when annual review time rolls around. Instead, my interviewees learned to redefine the "zoo" as a site of re-examining how we value time and intercultural collaboration. We made new sense out of our shifting visibilities. In the USA, feminists constantly battle erasure and being denied space to speak and act, but even within a culture where gendered harassment was common, my interviewees re-learned to leverage visibility and invisibility as agency. As Ahmed writes, "Feminism: how we survive the consequences of what we come up against by offering new ways of understanding what we come up against" (*Living* 22). Sense(re)making was a rhetorical feminist tactic that refused to accept the reality, the invisibility, and the restraint as pure deficiencies.

Key to transformative unlearning and relearning in transnational spaces was adopting an oscillating perspective, which is also a rhetorical feminist perspective. In a Foucauldian mirror, my participants and I saw ourselves here in Qatar and there in the US simultaneously. Crossing borders and negotiating complex situations, we gained confidence. Moreover, moving back and forth between the ideals of being USAmerican (e.g., "all men are created equal," "honest pay for honest work," "pull yourself up by your bootstraps") and the realities of the host labor conditions engaged us in reflection. Looking into the thousands of laboring faces visible but ultimately mute and inaccessible—and knowing that thousands more domestic laborers also were silent as well as hidden from sight—was an intense daily reminder of white privilege. Expatriate women tried to listen through what they could see, but ultimately, they knew that they could not confidently read across such cultural and socio-economic inequities. Nevertheless, our sudden and prolonged immersive awareness of privilege invited us to the "double recognition" of "unlearning our privilege as our loss" (Landry and MacLean 4). Although privilege could *not* be unlearned or set aside, recognition of positioning and power, as well as personal experience with inequity could at least trigger the reflective sense(re)making process. At the same time, expatriate women knew we were tenuously and permanently temporary as guests of the host nation. Through our own experiences with the local systems and through hearing frequent experiences of swift and uncertain justice, we recognized our disadvantages as part of Qatar's resident (non-citizen) population. Although we saw unjust practices on a daily basis, we did not feel empowered to respond in overt ways.

Previous scholarship has established the fundamental uncertainty and paradox central to expatriate life, but the themes revealed here are particular to Qatar as a context. White USAmerican expatriate women living in Germany or England would not experience the same hypervis-ibility/invisibility described here because Gulf Arab norms of dress and gender influence the situation. Expatriate women living and working in Central America, in South America, on the African continent, or in Asia would experience in/visibility differently. While being simultaneously free and restrained is common, the ways it is experienced in Qatar as related to access and movement are amplified by the local context, for example, through the *kafala* system of sponsorship. Qatar's path to mod-ernization—not Westernization—affected white USAmerican women's experiences by inviting them to be insiders as privileged employees and guest residents of the country but permanently keeping them as cultural outsiders. To modernize was to invite influence, but to refuse Western-ization was to hold that influence at arm's length. An expatriate as-signment where the home and host cultural norms align would yield different outcomes.

What can be taken away from an otherwise particularized study? What can readers who have not lived in different regions or nations learn? What does this project add to our notions of feminist rhetorics and rhetorical feminism? The big lesson is actually rather small.

## MICROPRAXIS AS AGENCY IN COMPLEXITY

My interviewees and I expressed enormous gratitude for the opportuni-ties being at the IBC and in Qatar offered, but mixed with that gratitude was frustration over the treatment of less privileged expatriate popula-tions, particularly those who were visible on the streets (construction laborers) and invisible within our living spaces (domestic laborers). Our reactions echoed the reactions of white women in the USA when faced with the realities of white supremacy, economic injustice, and political division. Some of us retreated to our bubbles or golden ghettos, "to contemplate others' sufferings from 'safe' places without engaging them with deep feeling" (Anzaldúa, *Light in the Dark* 79). Sometimes we resigned to having no agency in the overwhelming and systemic levels of socio-economic disparity and what appeared, from outside observation, as collective local indifference to the system and its effects. Others simply could not accept the local norms and persisted in finding ways to resist or to act, striving to "really listen, we must put our corazones y razones (feeling and intellect) in our manos and extend them to others" (79). Mary stated her philosophy of confronting the overwhelming gaps this way: "I cannot help them all, but I can help the one in front of me." By "them," she means men and women trapped in Qatar by unethical employers and/or by economic struggles. In other words, moves to address injustice were *ad hoc*. When expat women shared stories about helping others, the tellings were incidental and more of a comment on daily life, void of self-congratulatory back patting and humble bragging. Awareness of and attention to disparities were a product of unlearning, a feminist inclination towards "asking ethical questions about how to live in an unjust and unequal world" (Ahmed, *Living* 1). The sheer scope of the host scene, especially the number of laborers being contained and controlled, confronted us daily with a persistence forcing us to reflect, reconsider, and try to (un)learn about this largest population in the country. It challenged us to face the Other and to "surrender ourselves to those interstitial spaces" (Carrillo Rowe 197) that related us as humans yet separated us through inequality. Unlearning was not a denial but rather an acknowledgement and source of questioning about our places in the system.

Obviously, we were complicit in our privilege, but what could we *do* with those advantages that we had, amidst the uncertainty and risk of our own temporariness? What actions were possible? How could our status as privileged, mobile, in/visible guests be leveraged? Based on the stories told by my participants and events I witnessed firsthand, I propose that agents who are caught in corners can leverage those dead ends in small but potentially meaningful ways.

**Defining Micropraxis**

As previewed in the introduction, micro*praxis* is a rhetorical feminist tactic performed through purposeful small acts of respect, relationality, and reciprocity designed to in/visibly acknowledge, resist, and/or subvert injustices and narratives of oppression targeted at marginalized people(s). Functioning both as framework and practice, acts of micropraxis seek to acknowledge intersubjectivity in opposition to systemic injustice. As an outcome of this study, it is offered as a countermove to microaggressions, the everyday slights undermining the dignity of marginalized or under-represented populations (Sue, et al. 271), a.k.a., diminishment and death by a thousand small cuts. Just as microaggressions seem on the surface to be insignificant, an act of micropraxis is small and ensues beneath the radar of those unfair systems and those who reinforce them. A sig-nificant difference between microaggressions and micropraxis, however, is intentionality. Whereas microaggressions may be either intentional or unintentional, micropraxis is motivated by a willfulness to subvert or transgress.

*Praxis* is "the processes of mediation through which theory and prac-tice become deeply interwoven with one another" (Swarr and Nagar 6). Transnational feminist praxis requires culturally contextualized knowl-edges and an open willingness to work across difference to confront is-sues of systemic injustice. It is also a reflective and reflexive practice, pushing agents to examine how their own backgrounds and assump-tions influence their positioning, the potential for and choices of action, and the variety of outcomes and consequences. For academics and other researchers working in transnational situations, "such reflections have frequently revolved around the limits and possibilities of writing, as well as positionality, intellectual and political accountability, and representa-tion" (6). Here, praxis began in an understanding or a personal theory of the transnational space and developed into imagining and identifying the opportunities and constraints appearing in any particular situation to shape possibilities for action. In general, expatriate women were con-fronted with and remained deeply aware of their precarious positioning as well as potential consequences of their actions. Such risks ranged from personal embarrassment or causing a scene in public to trouble at work, legal actions (including jail), or deportation. Such risks implicated not only the agent attempting the micropraxis act but also the receiver(s) of that act.

Derald Wing Sue describes microaggressions as perpetrated both consciously and unconsciously (29). On both levels, they are "reflec-tions of marginality and/or a worldview of inclusion/exclusion, superi-ority/inferiority, desirability/undesirability, or normality/abnormality" (Sue, et. al. 14). Conversely, micropraxis must be *purposeful*, mindful and intentional. It is not "random acts of kindness" because micropraxis is intended to acknowledge and to potentially resist or subvert. Whereas microaggressions reify exclusion, micropraxis complicates binary and biased systems by disrupting who is deemed "worthy." While micropraxis as individual acts cannot undo systemic injustice, it is performed as a conscious resistance to the flows that maintain the systems through segregation and discrimination.

Micropraxis invisibly and/or visibly acknowledges, resists, and/or subverts injustices. It evokes unlearning via re-viewing and reassessing the power of our attention: "If a world can be what we learn not to notice, noticing becomes a form of political labor. What do we learn not to notice? . . . If we have been taught to turn away, we have to learn to turn toward" (Ahmed, *Living* 32). Visibility may be engaged when, for example, gazing back as described in chapter 2. Amy, as a white US-American expatriate woman, was visible to the expatriate laborer, and through his gaze, the laborer rendered himself visible to her. Acknowledging co-visibility and intersubjectivity was a small, and perhaps in the moment, seemingly insignificant act. Yet micropraxis also challenged expatriate woman to continually re-confront their privilege within the local systems of injustice. The incongruity of "feeling wrong is what brings a wrong home," what makes it undeniable (Ahmed, *Living* 28). Daily re-cognition inspired generative feminist agency for white expat women, prompting them to look for or create ways to acknowledge, resist, subvert.

In a framework and practice of micropraxis, invisibility becomes a source of agency. Because acts are small, they can benefit from being less visible. For example, one November, Mary learned about twelve Filipina domestic workers sheltering at the Philippines embassy. They had fled to the embassy after having been abused by their host families but were without money to leave the country. They were trapped in the embassy and would have been arrested if caught in public; they had no homes and few possessions, and were sleeping on the embassy floor. Because Mary knew she could not use public channels to advocate for justice, she sought help in less visible ways. She talked to many of her colleagues (including me) individually behind closed doors and collaborated with a woman who had privately interviewed some of the domestic workers about their situations. Through individual efforts and group presentations (held in expatriates' homes) that included the workers' testimonies, Mary and her friend were able to gather enough donations to buy flights for all of the stranded domestic workers in time to celebrate Christmas with their families. Mary's tactics illustrated how staying invisible—avoiding the attention of the embassies and press, for example—protected vulnerable women and supported their successful return home.

The effects of micro*aggressions* include indignity (Sue 5), further marginalization (14), exhaustion (15–16), and shutting down/shutting out conversation (19), and a resulting "conspiracy of silence" (20). In contrast, the goals of micro*praxis* are to support or grow dignity, to address and reduce marginalization, the offset exhaustion, and to open conversation at multiple levels. Such efforts require more than random acts of kindness. In the definition of micropraxis above, *respect, relationality, and reciprocity* come from Shawn Wilson's *Research Is Ceremony*, which provides a paradigm for more ethical cross-cultural and indigenous research. Respect is rooted in deep listening and silencing one's own assumptions of understanding or expertise (58). In culturally complex spaces, listening is difficult or even sometimes seems impossible due to language barriers and/or to ways that systems keep people separated. In chapter 2, I proposed, as one strategy, using Garland-Thomson's theory of generative staring as one means of trying to listen rhetorically across cultural and socio-economic divides. Relationality is an ongoing process of observation and rapport building that acts as a form of accountability underpinning all relationships (Wilson 40–42). Relationality extends beyond individual friendships or collaborations out to the greater community, tacking out to include broader contexts and patterns of being, relating, and knowing. Reciprocity is not about an exchange of gifts or an obsession with equal value. Instead, it focuses on the interconnectedness of the human experience and accountability to the power dynamics in any relationship.

Opportunities for micropraxis do not require crossing nation-state borders or even travel at all because "in a multicultural society, we cross into each other's worlds all the time…We are mutually complicitous" (Anzaldúa, *Light in the Dark* 79). Ellen Cushman's "The Rhetorician as an Agent of Social Change" includes the author's reflections over her relationships with students and civic partners around Troy, New York being rooted in reciprocity while resisting the potential domination emerging when the two sides of a give-and-take situation are not equally advantaged. Her concept of reciprocity "includes an open and conscious negotiation of the power structures reproduced during the give-and-take" and is concerned with "a self-critical, conscious navigation" of the interactions (16). Similar to the list of ways Cushman experienced the gifts of reciprocity (17), expatriate women in Qatar did not expect an explicit exchange. Instead, they understood that they were already receiving from others by the very nature of the city and its infrastructure being built and of the significant services and hospitality provided. They knew, for example, that while their Qatari hosts extended generous hospitality, it was expatriates from India, Nepal, Pakistan, pan-Arabia, the Philippines and other areas that created the living and work places, as well as provided the actual materials, spaces, and services facilitating that welcome.

## Demonstrating Micropraxis

What does micropraxis look like? Contextualized in the transnational space of Qatar, it included small acts like unusually generous tipping and/or taking time to ask labor and domestic workers about their families and situations. It included inquiring further when intuition told you something may be an issue and helping people seek out safe sources of advice or help.

Let me pause to further unpack generous tipping as an example because these moves, as *small acts*, seem on the surface rather trivial. In Qatar, generous tipping is considered culturally appropriate, and inherent in practicing micropraxis was knowing about local cultural norms. In other countries, tipping at all may be considered inappropriate or even insulting. Service itself is also embedded in all aspects of life in Qatar. For example, at the time of my study, no self-service gas stations existed. Each pump had a serviceperson—usually part of the South Asian expatriate labor population—who pumped gas and washed the windshield. When I asked other expats how much to tip, answers ranged from "not at all" to "the equivalent of a dollar" (three or four Qatari Riyal). The advice to tip "not at all" came from an IBC co-worker, himself from India, who argued that generous tipping could make service-people spoiled and entitled.

As I was chatting informally about this project with my colleagues, I learned that we all tended to tip about five times more than I had been advised (~15 Riyal or 4.12 USD, about thirty percent of the cost of filling the tank). Another factor affecting a decision to tip generously was how the specific business handled tips. Did they distribute the tips fairly back to the workers, or did the manager and owner keep a share or even keep all of the tips? Asking the service person about how tipping worked in the specific establishment was a good idea, but in Qatar, language barriers or even the physical context of the interaction (e.g., the manager standing close by) could have prevented these questions. If a manager were to hear how a serviceperson responded, the nature of the response could jeopardize the serviceperson's standing in the workplace, and because employers in Qatar were sponsors of residency, being fired meant risk of deportation. The practice of tipping—although seemingly trivial—foregrounded the highly situated and political nature of small, well-intentioned but potentially perilous acts.

Because Qatar's traditional social norms emphasized privacy and separation by gender and socio-economic status, labor and service workers were often treated as nameless and faceless, what one interviewee compared to being treated like "cords of wood." During my time there, begging or panhandling were illegal and aggressively prevented through fines, jail time, and/or deportation. For expats in less dire economic situations, micropraxis was being prepared to not turn away when a stranger was brave (or desperate) enough to ask for help. The following is an example of micropraxis as inquiring based on intuition: a colleague at another IBC became curious about how contract laborers who worked at the branch managed to live on relatively meager salaries, when he knew they often sent money back to their home countries to support their families. Through conversations, he learned many were subsisting on only the most basic rice and bread-based diet. As a result, he (a white, USAmerican male) proposed that his IBC start hosting a weekly lunch for these contract staff. Although he could not directly address the Qatari contractor's unjust wages himself, he worked within the system and within the IBC budget to try to make some small improvement to the situation.

A colleague and I engaged in micropraxis in our IBC classrooms by designing curricula where students had the advantage. For example, my colleague chose to teach poetry written in Arabic by Palestinian authors. Although the book included English translation, that process often muddled important aspects of the poetry. Her students could understand the original language and the political contexts of the work while she had to rely on them to help her (re)consider the lesser quality of the translation. When I taught a literature class, I assigned a memoir by Qatari-American author Sophia Al-Maria. Although it was written in English, many of Al-Maria's stories were complicated by local social norms meaning that sometimes how her stories were received by my students confused me. Although I thought I had a growing knowledge of local norms—even after four years of living in Qatar—much was still lost on me, and students sometimes voluntarily helped me by explaining them.

In some sense, the micropraxis moves emerging from this study are betrayals. Carrillo Rowe, writing about transracial feminist alliances in academia, reminds us that "Our feminism [arises] from our betrayals, not our investments in innocence" (179). Many of the acts I heard about, witnessed, or participated in were transgressive. We betrayed the host nation's philanthropic systems by doggedly insisting they were locally insufficient and working outside of them. We betrayed the sponsorship system that allowed our own presence in the country by affirming its inadequacy and discriminatory effects. We betrayed our own disciplinary expertise and Qatar Foundation's desire for us to help it import Western education by decentering the classroom. Even in these betrayals, however, we knew that we were still implicated in an unjust system and that we were neither perfect nor even sufficient in our attempts at resistance. These small acts did not support our innocence but rather were humble attempts to account for our complicity.

More broadly, micropraxis for my participants and I meant not giving in to the exhaustion of living in a confusing and sometimes nerve-racking place. As one participant posted on social media, "Living here [in Qatar], you have to be careful of everything all the time. It wears on you in ways you really don't expect." Similarly, Ahmed describes the weight of the vulnerable and violent experiences that brought her to feminism: "they seem to accumulate over time, gathering like things in a bag, but the bag is your body, so that you feel like you are carrying more and more weight. The past becomes heavy" (*Living* 23). Cushman also encourages academics to attend to "ways in which people use language and literacy to challenge and alter the circumstances of daily life" ("Rhetorician" 12). White USAmerican expatriate women in Qatar developed their own local literacies for reading complex intercultural scenes and for deciding when, if, and how to act. Cushman provides a number of efforts she herself made to support individuals in her local community (13–14), further examples of micropraxis. She explains that the types of social change she supported "would be overlooked or underestimated with the emancipatory theories we currently use" (14). In other words, these acts were not visible. Sometimes invisibility is *necessary* for engaging these forms of agency at all.

## Extending Micropraxis

Small acts of social justice are not a new idea. However, naming them as micropraxis identifies them as a rhetorical feminist tactic and creates the space within which to unpack when and how this form of agency works, to provide examples of micropraxis that can invite further extension and application of the idea, and finally, to step back and consider the potential positive and negative implications of the concept. Micropraxis is willful, a reclamation of agency. "The term *willfulness* is a charge not only in the sense of a burden and an accusation but also as a load and responsibility: it is how we carry something forward" (Ahmed, *Living* 81). By definition, micropraxis is what should be sought out as possible when larger, public acts of resistance, solidarity, or activism are not feasible, when more overt acts may risk the agent's or receiver's safety, constraint, and/or deportation. The real power of micropraxis is in its potential for concerted effort, how it can be extended or spread.

The structure of expatriate life in Qatar—breakdown of public/private, the golden ghettos—created spaces where stories of micropraxis could be shared. Because of the paradoxical intertwining of public and private, expatriates knew more about each other's lives. Our shared efforts at sensemaking about the social, political, economic, and cultural contexts at play inside Qatar provided a fertile field for conversations regarding the local caste systems, treatment of expatriates of all identities, and fears over potentially offending local customs and/or breaking local laws. Additionally, the simultaneous powerfulness/powerlessness of our shared status as outsiders-within meant we understood without major explanation the constraints we were up against when we saw something unjust and felt we had few options for doing anything about it.

My colleagues and friends did not realize they were seeking out similar forms of less visible or invisible agency, ways to address or resist local injustices without drawing attention to themselves. The unspoken collective "aim" was "to reside as well as [they could] in the spaces that [were] not intended for [them]" (Ahmed, *Living* 9). However, a pattern of behavior emerged through the stories told in their interviews and from my own observations and participation as an expat. Through these conduits, what I heard was the presence of feminist rhetorical "power lines" or "channels that may be deployed for resistive and transformative purposes. Power lines, like belonging, are generative: they offer the potential for an array of progressive renovations; they generate community and purpose; they are the vehicle of our [feminist] becoming" (Carrillo Rowe

178). However, rather than above ground lines on poles visibly moving energy through a network, expat powerlines were underground, not visible yet generating a current of motivation, of possibility, or creative resistance, and ultimately, of agency amidst uncertainty. Through tuning into these underground power lines, I heard my interviewees' love of and frustrations over living in the host country and reflections over how they leveraged their paradoxical positioning and oscillating perspectives as tools of feminist agency.

Those who deride micro*aggressions* claim calling out such acts is "making a mountain out of a mole hill" (Sue 6). In contrast, micro*praxis* is best extended when those who purposefully engage it *seek* to make a mountain out of their molehills, when they share their experiences and in turn show others how to add their own efforts. Figure 5 is my proposed continuum of micropraxis activity.[2] It is inspired by a process for developing relationships that support philanthropic giving, and I chose this model because it focuses on the development of the individual actor but moves towards creating and sustaining a community of influence. In other words, it begins with "me" but moves towards the power of "us."

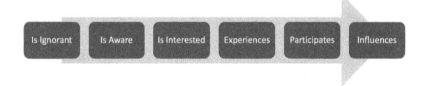

Figure 5. A continuum illustrates the progression of awareness and engagement in micropraxis. Image created by the author.

Using myself as an example, I will walk through each phase. Upon arrival as an expatriate, I was generally *ignorant* of the social, economic, political, legal, and cultural contexts of the host state. Primarily, I felt the joy of my unexamined privilege working for the IBC and being sponsored by QF. Expatriates who came from other backgrounds likely would not have arrived with my level of ignorance and would not necessarily have felt the same naïve bliss I felt. Because of the sheer magnitude of the visible caste system and the confusing mixed messages emerging

---

2. This chart was inspired by the "Donor Continuum Chart" created by Advancement Resources, a philanthropic training, research, and consultation group.

from settling into paradoxical spaces, I became *aware* of the glaring inequities of my new host home.

My awareness turned to *interest*. Interest is awareness fueled by curiosity and concern. As I began asking questions, satisfying answers proved challenging. As I sought knowledge about the hundreds of thousands of "bachelors" and about the large population of domestic workers and their treatment, for example, I struggled to locate information. Qatar news sources stuck to reporting on other areas of the Gulf or to pre-approved press releases. Information beyond basic census statistics was hard to find. I began listening to and even (when appropriate) soliciting stories told by co-workers, by domestic workers, and by other expats in spaces like compound playgrounds and children's schools or activities. I engaged in long reflections when driving, meeting the gaze of people I could not know, questioning my ignorant assumptions about globalism's opportunities, and in doing so began working through a process of (un) learning and disrupting the comfort of my privilege. While constantly tempted and sometimes persuaded to retreat back into my easy, protective golden bubble of accepting the status quo, I persisted in questioning how the country operated, at whose expense, and at whose gain. Interest opened doors to conversations about what other expats have done in the face of shared concerns and constraints. However, interest only gets us halfway through the continuum.

If micropraxis is to have its best potential effects, then agents must learn how to participate in and ultimately influence others to undertake small acts building respect, relationality, and reciprocity. That may be through *experiencing* them with other people who are more knowledgeable in what risks to take and how to navigate the local systems. I experienced micropraxis with Mary when she shared with me her work to get the Filipina domestic workers back home. Michelle helped me experience micropraxis when she told me about hiring a male colleague to subvert local gender codes. Stories of others working against systems of inequity opened my eyes regarding how to find similar openings for agency in my own life. Their creative willfulness was contagious: "as a collective source of energy, [it was] a way of being sparked into life by others" (Ahmed, *Living* 77). Because of their role-modeling and encouragement, I began *participating* by taking quiet risks in the classroom as described above and in my home spaces. For example, I lent an expat domestic worker money so her mother could get cancer treatments back in her home country. She could not afford money from the compound's loan shark who charged an interest rate of one hundred percent per month. When she approached me, I asked questions and talked through the situation carefully with her, but I would not have been as comfortable with it if I had not heard stories from others about helping in similar ways. I lent her the money interest-free, and she paid it back. I cannot know that all situations of mutual trust turned out positively, but because of stories I had heard, I was willing to consider the risk.

Watching others and finding spaces for micropraxis can lead to *influencing* others, by encouraging them to seek out their own opportunities and/or organizing larger collaborative efforts that still function under the radar of risk. Mary's story about the Filipina domestic workers trapped at the embassy is a clear example of the latter. Working with my colleague to disrupt the Western-centric nature of our teaching materials was another instance of micropraxis influence at work. However, the linear nature of figure 5 is inaccurate, because even when one has experienced, practiced, and influenced others, she still remains open to being influenced herself, to learning about new spaces and ways to re-think, resist, and address injustice. For example, even late in my tenure at the IBC, my colleagues continued to inspire me to think about micropraxis as identifying, resisting, and/or subverting harmful colonizing practices associated with the IBC (see Rudd). The goal of micropraxis is to "normalize" such small daily acts, to shift our notions of the "routine" (see Cushman, "Rhetorician" 12, 14). Then through informal sharing, coordination may emerge and "Like tender green shoots growing out of the cracks, they eventually overturn foundations" (Anzaldúa, *Light in the Dark* 84). In other words, it is through social circulation—a feminist rhetorical practice—that the power of micropraxis is realized.

Micropraxis is a generative form of Karlyn Kohrs Campbell's promiscuous and protean agency, as a rhetorical force it has "an equal capacity for transcendence, resistance, and destruction" (8). The protean nature of agency is its adaptability. What begins as destructive (looking away) can be transformed into something generative (looking back). Agency is tied to community and context, as agents "are best described as 'points of articulation' rather than originators" (5). She means this in terms of not being able to initiate an action outside of the local or scenic constraints; however, "points of articulation" can also extend to connections among agents supporting and encouraging particular forms of agency. In other words, agency is "communal, social, cooperative, and participatory" (3). As a form of agency, micropraxis requires savvy understanding of the surrounding contexts. It compels agents to "negotiate among institutional powers" (5). In this project, powers included bureaucracies that overlapped even as they competed with or contradicted one another. The result was that the transnational space felt at once familiar *and* foreign. Agents felt compelled to act but were often unsure of how to navigate complex systems that put them at risk. Therefore, micropraxis as a form of agency required an "artfulness" or the "skills to respond to contingencies" and in situations where "there [were] no precise or universal precepts" even though "skilled practitioners [could become] alert to recurring patterns" and learn which "forms" (what K. Campbell calls "texts") of action were feasible (7). The nature of that generative act may be small yet significant. Micropraxis offers transformative potential for individuals, but its bigger power is in (re)defining a community through collaborative power.

Small acts still entail risk, but because the power lines of micropraxis are less visible, its power might accumulate faster than the negative effects it chances. Because micropraxis acts can be distributed among individuals, a less coordinated or *ad hoc* collective agency, it has the potential to create impact before it is noticed. As Ahmed writes, "Feminists who gather together are dangerous" (*Living* 18). The delicious and hope-driven danger comes in the possible collaborative power of their energies, agencies, and acts. Carrillo Rowe describes white feminist academics who strategically use their identities as a means of accountability: "These white allies practice 'responsibility' in ways that 'ab-use' both the identities they inherit as white women and the institutional locations they occupy as academic feminists" (194).[3] In other words, women can leverage their knowledge of their communities and their power within those communities as a means of affecting feminist change, as a means of advancing inclusivity, equality, collaboration, reciprocity, and respect. In taking potentially subversive risks, white feminists can demonstrate their relational accountability to others and put some skin in the game of promoting justice. After all, what is the alternative? Retreating into our golden bubbles is cowardly, a cop-out that only re-enacts ways white feminists have failed others too many times. Expatriate women—indeed

---

3. Carrillo Rowe is quoting one of her participants. The term "ab-use," however, comes from "Spivak's call to postcolonial intellectuals to 'use the Enlightenment from below"—to 'ab-use' the academic structures we so intimately inhabit for the purpose of transforming them—provides a point of entry for imagining the contradictory work of transracial belonging" (187).

for white women living in privilege everywhere—all "have a stake in . . . anti-racist work," work that must be undertaken to "save our souls" (Carrillo Rowe 45).

Aligning with the principles of transnational feminism, micropraxis foregrounds the effects of globalization, rejects a singular narrative of subjectivity and/or experience with inequality, and invites collaboration. Implemented with care, it can resist the fallacy of "first world" women speaking for "third world" women and the myth of "global sisterhood." Micropraxis must be highly contextualized. It centers on listening yet proceeds to action. In the introduction to their edited collection, *Critical Transnational Feminist Praxis*, Amanda Lock Swarr and Rachi Nagar advocate for "grounding feminisms in activist communities everywhere" as "a means to interrogate all forms of implicit and explicit relations of power (e.g., racist/classist/caste-ist), and to contest those power relations through ongoing processes of self-critique and collective reflection" (5). They critique transnational *academic* feminist work as disconnected from the lived realities on the ground and as purposefully separating theory, method, process, and product (6–7). Micropraxis addresses these concerns by growing out of lived experiences on the streets and in the living and working spaces of Doha. It also teases out an implicit and typically unnoticed practice that has the potential to be of greater effect if it is unveiled and shared.

In summary, micropraxis engages in the principles of feminist rhetorical practice (Royster and Kirsch) and transnational feminist praxis (Swarr and Nagar). As a rhetorical feminist tactic, it . . .

- prioritizes listening and mindful awareness of inequalities resulting from globalization,

- is highly contextualized and specific,

- engages critical imagination in brainstorming options and tools for action, mindful of how hybridity constrains and permits action,

- engages strategic contemplation in identifying people who need help and seeks out ways to be inclusive of all voices,

- negotiates strategically between subversion/risk-taking and leveraging privilege/agency,

- may engage networks but is not broadly organized into programs or movements, although more structured (narrative) praxis may emerge,

- cannot be or does not seek to be highly visible,
- benefits from social circulation.

Finally, micropraxis is a means of feminist becoming, a tactic borne of striving to unlearn privilege as a loss and confronting one's complicity even as one is ensnared in unjust systems. It does not require the claiming of a feminist card and engages the feminist principles that transcend gender.

## Troubling Micropraxis

In complex transnational spaces, haunted by the effects of globalization and regional colonization, "good intentions" are dangerous.[4] A generation of white feminism—guilty of too often speaking for Others and of making homogenizing assumptions that marginalize rather than elevate—has proven that. Mindful that critique is a healthy part of developing any idea, this last section considers the potential negative applications and impacts of adopting micropraxis as one means of addressing injustice.

To begin, the process of becoming aware of systemic injustices and becoming savvy about when and how to address them in small ways is marked by ongoing challenges. Ignorance or inadequate understanding of a community can lead to misinterpretations and clumsiness at best, and to offensive, unethical, or legal problems at worst. Acts designed to help can harm. A colleague visiting during a conference decided he wanted to learn more about Qatar's labor workers, so he impulsively sneaked on board a bus taking a group of workers back to their living quarters at the end of the day. Although he was an uninvited guest, the workers, mostly Indian, Pakistani, and Nepalese, shared their food with him and engaged him in conversation with him throughout the night. Eventually, the Qatar police arrived at the camp and questioned the visitor extensively. He risked going to jail for being in a space where he was not allowed. The police's concerns, according to my colleague, were that he was a journalist writing an exposé about the workers' living conditions. Once he was able to convince the police otherwise, he was released but forced to leave the camp. My colleague's decision to engage his identity privilege (being white, male, USAmerican) to find out more about

---

4. Arabella Lyon as well as Paul Gorski have both written about the challenges of transnational education and of decolonizing efforts in the teaching of writing. Too often these efforts end up revealed as misdirected.

the lives of the laborers was some combination of admirable (learning more directly through first-hand conversation) and foolish (entitled to assume that his risks were minimal). He was lucky to not go to jail as he was trespassing when he entered the bus and camp, and he was lucky not to get any of the laborers in trouble for allowing him in their living spaces. The body this colleague inhabited and the passport he carried allowed him passage others might not have been granted.[5]

The small-scale, less-visible nature of micropraxis's design is both its power and its limitation. When restorative activities are not shared or visible, others cannot be motivated by them, and an individual trying to assert agency in the name of positive change can be hobbled by fear, isolation, and exhaustion. Working alone or in a de-centralized way, individuals may take risks and face consequences alone. In contrast, larger scale, collaborative projects (community organizing, demonstrations) leverage a broader range of knowledge and support. People bring different perspectives on the issue and potential actions to the group, meaning activities can be better thought out, even if they must be less immediately responsive than individual actions.

In addition to these challenges, micropraxis must not be simply an excuse to assuage individual feelings of guilt. Well-intentioned acts can unwittingly reinforce oppression. Simultaneously meaning well while also doing further harm is a central topic in critical transnational scholarship. Swarr and Nagar comment that feminist efforts in transnational contexts—no matter how well intentioned—often only reproduce hierarchies elevating the academic theorist and subjugating the subaltern subjects (7). Raka Shome's *Diana and Beyond: White Femininity, National Identity, and Contemporary Media Culture* critiques media imagery of Princess Diana and other celebrities in the late twentieth and early twenty-first centuries, focusing on tropes such as "global motherhood" and about "white femininity [as] a *dependent* formation . . . [whose] privilege is constantly dependent on the cancellation or negation not just of the nonwhite female body" (42). She concludes, "Privileged white women end up offering models of citizenship, responsibility, and civic engagement that individualizes the notion of citizenly and global belonging as it delinks these concepts from any notion of collectivity and state support" (206). Shome's critique resonates. Even located in spaces outside

---

5. Although minor by comparison, see Cushman's story of her own miscommunication, where friendliness was mistaken for flirting, as another example ("Rhetorician" 21).

the USA, my participants and I were cognizant of our roles representing USAmerican ideals, and we as individuals sought to act in ways that affirmed a shared "notion of citizenly and global belonging." As she spotlights, we also were ultimately powerless to ask any state body to address our concerns. As residents with limited power, we were purposefully and fully segregated from the civic (citizen) sphere of the country. The acts of micropraxis emerging here admittedly "rearticulate old, formations of racism and classism" (206) because our positioning within the larger systems limited or prevented us from influencing how those formations were reinforced in the host space.

Rather than a completed, infallible, finalized product, I propose micropraxis as an emergent tactic of rhetorical feminism and of feminist rhetorical practices, of imagination and contemplation, entangled with as well as motivated by concerns of identity, in/visibility, and agency. Further study of micropraxis as a feasible framework and practice would include reflexive questions regarding privilege and contexts, and would ask how women, Women of Color, People of Color, folx of varying gender and sexual identities, people with different abilities and disabilities, and those along shifting centers and margins leverage their positioning to overcome obstacles such as paradoxical positioning. In "'Under Western Eyes' Revisited," Chandra Mohanty asks, "What would it mean to be attentive to the micropolitics of everyday life as well as to the larger processes that recolonize the culture and identities of people across the globe?" (508–09). Micropraxis by its nature engages micropolitics, and when shared and coordinated at larger levels, is another way to encourage feminist rhetoricians to be attentive to larger ongoing processes shaping our scenes.

This narrative of white USAmerican expatriate women, as well as the framework of micropraxis it yields, is about the generative agency growing out of a feminist framing of liminal and paradoxical positioning, oscillating perspectives, and sense(re)making amidst uncertainty. Bringing us all back to the US and other Western/white spaces, stories we learned to doubt, lessons we unlearned, and sense we have re-made in spaces *out there* must translate back to *in here*, to home, to our communities where we have more power to make a difference. "We must be (indeed it is our job to be) haunted—and motivated—by the myriad forms of global inequity and our negotiated positions within them" (Swarr and Nagar 208). Even in our own home countries, we are intercultural bordercrossers facing our troubled systems, feeling limited (and empowered) by our identities, and seeking out agency and engagement. We face uncertainties and witness injustices. Like the expatriates in this study, we must persist in being more critical, more imaginative, and more strategic in our roles as feminist and rhetorical agents. Rather than retreat into the comfortable bubbles of our lives, our storytelling and our shared narratives must encourage ongoing accountability through (re)cognition of small (and large) opportunities for resistance, assistance, and change.

# Appendix: Interview Questions

## I. Background Questions

1. In what type of industry and position do you work? (No company name, just industry type.)

2. Briefly explain how you came to the region. For example, did you move to this region for this job or for another job? Did you take a job or change jobs after moving?

3. How long have you been in the Gulf Region?

4. Briefly describe any other expatriate experience (nations, years, general industries or capacities)?

5. Describe any expat-specific training or preparation you received before moving here? For example, did you receive any training from the organization? Did you read any books about expatriate life and/or about Qatar?

## II. Agency in the Workplace

1. Generally describe the people you work with on a daily basis (number of people; types such as colleagues, students, or clients; genders; nationalities, etc.).

2. What are the greatest areas of stress in your workplace?

3. Do you see your professional ethos/power/agency the same here as you saw it in the US?

4. What approaches do you use to managing and/or motivating others in the workplace? How do these compare to strategies you used in the USA (similarities? differences?)?

5. Do you think your approaches to working with, managing, and/or motivating people in the workplace are influenced by your gender?

## III. Narratives about Living and Working in the Arabian Gulf

1. *Before moving here,* did you talk to colleagues about their experiences in this region? If yes, please explain.

2. Do you remember any specific stories or descriptions of Qatar that you heard before coming here? Did those impact or inform your views of the region? If so, in what ways? If not, then why?

3. *Now that you have been here a while,* do you talk to other people about coming to work in Qatar? If so, have you talked to female colleagues? What do they ask about most? Please explain.

4. Because many people that come to or hear about Qatar have never been to the Middle East or to the Gulf Arab region, we often find ourselves having to compare it to something else. I'm interested in the metaphors, similes, analogies we use to describe Qatar to potential colleagues (and/or perhaps to family or friends who have not been here). Fill in the blank (as many times as you wish): "Living and/or working here is like _____."

5. Please explain your comparison(s).

6. If I were a female asking you to tell me some stories about working and living in this region, what would you say? Tell me some of the stories you tell others? Use some detail—describe the people or places or things that stood out to you.

7. How do these stories seem to be received (how do you see the listeners react)?

## IV. Reflection and Identity

1. How do you feel about living and working here? How do you describe your quality of life?

2. How does living and/or working here compare to what you imagined?

3. How do you think others in this region perceive you?

4. Has living and working here influenced your perceptions of . . .

   • the region and/or its people? Please explain?

   • yourself and/or your role(s) as a professional? Please explain?

   • yourself and/or your role(s) as an American? Please explain?

   • yourself and/or your role(s) as a woman? Please explain?

   • yourself as a "white"? (Is being "white" in the Arabian Gulf different than being "white" in the US?) Please explain?

5. Has this experience changed the way you understand communication? Culture? Leadership?

## V. Thinking Forward

1. Do you anticipate returning to the USA from here? If not, then where might you go?

2. If or when you do return to the US, how do you think that transition back will be?

# Works Cited and Consulted

Abalkhail, Jouharah M., and Barbara Allan. "'*Wasta*' and Women's Careers in the Arab Gulf States." *Gender in Management: An International Journal*, vol. 31, no. 3, 2016, pp. 162–80.

Abdulhadi, Rabab, Evenlyn Alsultany, and Nadine Naber, editors. *Arab and Arab American Feminisms: Gender, Violence, and Belonging*. Syracuse UP, 2011.

Adler, Nancy. "Pacific Basin Managers: A *Gaijin*, Not a Woman." *Human Resource Management*, vol. 26, no. 2, 1987, pp. 169–91.

—. "Women Do Not Want International Careers: and Other Myths About International Management." *Organizational Dynamics*, vol. 13, no. 2, 1984, pp. 66–79.

Advancement Resources. "Donor Continuum Chart." *Advancement Resources*, 2015.

*Agreement to Continue to Operate the Undergraduate and Graduate Programs at Texas A&M University of Qatar*. Texas A&M University, 2011.

Ahmed, Sara. *Living a Feminist Life*. Duke UP, 2017.

—. "Making Strangers." *Feminist Killjoys*, 4 Aug. 2014. feministkilljoys.com/2014/08/04/ making-strangers/.

—. *Strange Encounters: Embodied Others in Post-Coloniality*. Routledge, 2000.

Ajrouch, Kristine J. "Gender, Race, and Symbolic Boundaries: Contested Spaces of Identity among Arab American Adolescents." *Sociological Perspectives*, vol. 47, no. 4, 2004, pp. 371–91.

Alexander, M. Jacqui, and Chandra Talpade Mohanty. "Cartographies of Knowledge and Power: Transnational Feminisms as Radical Praxis." *Critical Transnational Feminist Praxis*, edited by Amanda Lock Swarr and Richa Nagar, SUNY P, 2010, pp. 23–45.

Al-Maria, Sophia. *The Girl Who Fell to Earth*. Singapore Books, 2012.

Al-Qaradhawi, Sheikh Yusuf. "Shaking Hands with Women: An Islamic Perspective." *Islam Online Archive*, 2008, www.suhaibwebb.com/islam-studies/faqs-and-fatwas/shaking-hands-with-a-non-mahram-dr-yusuf-al-qaradawi/.

Al-Qassemi, Sultan. "Tribalism in the Arabian Peninsula: It Is a Family Affair." *Jadaliyya*, 1 Feb 2012, www.jadaliyya.com/Details/25199/Tribalism-in-the-Arabian-Peninsula-It-Is-a-Family-Affair.

Altman, Yochanan, and Susan Shortland. "Women and International Assignments: Taking Stock—A 25-Year Review." *Human Resource Management*, vol. 47, no. 2, 2008, pp. 199–16.

"Ambassador." *Oxford English Dictionary*, www.oed.com.

Ames, Paul. "Will Slaves Build Qatar's World Cup?" *PRI*, 9 May 2013, www.pri.org/stories/2013–05–09/will-slaves-build-qatars-world-cup.

Amnesty International. "Qatar: Migrant Workers Still at Risk of Abuse Despite Reforms." *Amnesty International*, 12 Dec. 2016, www.amnesty.org/en/press-releases/2016/12/qatar-migrant-workers-still-at-risk-of-abuse-despite-reforms/.

Anderson, Nick. "Qataris Say Texas A&M Pact for Doha Branch Should Remain Secret." *Washington Post*, 6 Jan. 2016, www.washingtonpost.com/news/grade-point/wp/2016/01/06/qataris-say-texas-am-pact-for-doha-branch-should-remain-secret.

Andresen, Maike, Torsten Biemann, and Marshall Wilson Pattie. "What Makes Them Move Abroad? Reviewing and Exploring Differences Between Self-Initiated and Assigned Expatriation." *The International Journal of Human Resource Management*, vol. 26, no. 7, 2015, pp. 932–47.

Anzaldúa, Gloria. *Borderlands/La Frontera: The New Mestiza*. Aunt Lute, 1999.

—. *Light in the Dark/Luz en lo Oscuro: Rewriting Identity, Spirituality, Reality*, edited by AnaLouise Keating, Duke UP, 2015.

Aristotle. *Rhetorica*. Translated by W. Rhys Roberts. *The Basic Works of Aristotle*, edited by Richard McKeon, The Modern Library, 2001.

Arnander, Primrose and Ashkhain Skipwith. *Unload Your Own Donkey and Other Arabic Sayings with English Equivalents*. Stacey International, 2002.

Badran, Margot. "Between Secular and Islamic Feminisms: Reflections on the Middle East and Beyond." *Journal of Middle Eastern Women's Studies*, vol. 1, no. 1, 2003, pp. 6–28.

—. "Understanding Islam, Islamism, and Islamic Feminism." *Journal of Women's History*, vol. 13, no. 1, 2001, pp. 47–52.

Bahry, Louay, and Phebe Marr. "Qatari Women: A New Generation of Leaders?" *Middle East Policy*, vol. 12, no. 2, 2005, pp. 104–19.

Begum, Rothna. "Qatar's Permanent Residency Law a Step Forward but Discrimination Remains." *Human Rights Watch*, 11 Sept. 2018, www.hrw.org/news/2018/09/11/qatars-permanent-residency-law-step-forward-discrimination-remains.

bint Nasser, Sheikha Moza. "From Illusions to Clashes to an Awakening of Alliances: Constructing Understanding Between 'Islam' and the 'West.'" The Chatham House, 14 Feb. 2007, The Chatham House, London, England.

—. "Remarks of Her Highness Sheikha Moza bint Nasser Al Missned." 2005, Oxford Center for Islamic Studies, Oxford, England.

Bitzer, Lloyd F. "The Rhetorical Situation." *Philosophy & Rhetoric*, vol. 1, no. 1, 1992, pp. 1–14.

Boje, David M. *Narrative Methods for Organizational and Communication Research*. Sage, 2001.

Burke, Kenneth. *Attitudes Toward History*. 1937. 3rd ed., U of California P, 1984.

—. *A Grammar of Motives*. 1945. U of California P, 1969.

—. *A Rhetoric of Motives*. 1950. U of California P, 1969.

Bush, George W. "Address to the Joint Session of the 107th Congress." Joint Session of Congress, 20 Sept. 2001, United States Capitol, Washington D.C. Keynote Address.

Caligiuri, Paula M., and Wayne F. Cascio. "Can We Send Her There? Maximizing the Success of Western Women on Global Assignments." *Journal of World Business*, vol. 33, no. 4, 1998, pp. 394–416.

Campbell, Joseph. *Hero with a Thousand Faces*. 3rd ed., New World Library, 2008.

Campbell, Karlyn Kohrs. "Agency: Promiscuous and Protean." *Communication and Critical/Cultural Studies*, vol. 2, no. 1, 2005, pp.1–19.

Carrillo Rowe, Aimee. *Power Lines: On the Subject of Feminist Alliances*. Duke UP, 2008.

Chakarova, Mimi. "Dubai Night: Night Secrets." *Frontline World Rough Cut*. PBS, 13 Sept 2007, www.pbs.org/frontlineworld/rough/2007/09/dubai_sex_for_s.html.

Cicero. *On the Ideal Orator*. Translated by James M. May and Jakob Weiss, Oxford UP, 2001.

Clandinin, D. Jean. *Engaging in Narrative Inquiry*. Routledge, 2013.

Codevilla, Angelo. "For Years, Qatar Has Been Corrupting the National Security Deep State," *Security Studies Group*, 23 June 2017, securitystudies.org/qatar-is-corrupting-the-national-security-deep-state/.

Cole, Nina, and Yvonne McNulty. "Why Do Female Expatriates 'Fit-In' Better Than Males? An Analysis of Self-Transcendence and Socio-Cultural Adjustment." *Cross Cultural Management: An International Journal*, vol. 18, no. 2, 2011, pp. 144–64.

Coles, Anne, and Katie Walsh. "From 'Trucial State' to 'Postcolonial' City? The Imaginative Geographies of British Expatriates in Dubai." *Journal of Ethnic and Migration Studies*, vol. 36, no. 8, 2010, pp. 1317–33.

Collins, Patricia Hill. *Black Feminist Thought*. Routledge, 2000.

Collins, Patricia Hill, and Sirma Bilge. *Intersectionality*. John Wiley and Sons, 2016.

Crenshaw, Kimberlé. "Mapping the Margins: Intersectionality, Identity Politics, and Violence Against Women of Color." *Stanford Law Review*, vol. 43, no. 6, 1991, pp. 1241–99.

Croucher, Sheila. "Americans Abroad: A Global Diaspora?" *Journal of Transnational American Studies*, vol. 4, no. 2, 2012.

Cuonzo, Margaret. *Paradox*. MIT Press, 2014.

Cushman, Ellen. "Face, Skins, and the Identity Politics of Rereading Race." *Rhetoric Review,* vol. 24, no. 4, 2005, pp. 389–95.

—. "The Rhetorician as an Agent of Social Change." *College Composition and Communication*, vol. 47, no. 1, 1996, pp. 7–28.

Danius, Sara, Stefan Jonsson, and Gayatri Chakravorty Spivak. "An Interview with Gayatri Chakravorty Spivak." *boundary 2,* vol. 20, no. 2, 1993, pp. 24–50.

Daskalaki, Maria. "Personal Narratives and Cosmopolitan Identities: An Autobiographical Approach." *Journal of Management Inquiry*, vol. 21, no. 3, 2012, pp. 1–12.

Didion, Joan. *The White Album*. 1990. Farrar, Straus and Giroux, 2009.

"Diplomat." *Oxford English Dictionary*. www.oed.com.

D'Mello, Chantelle, and Victoria Scott. "Campaign For 'Modest Dress' Relaunches in Malls and Public Spaces." *Doha News*, 21 June 2014, dohanews.co/campaign-modest-dress-stages-relaunch-malls-public-spaces/.

Doha Debates. "This House Believes Dubai Is a Bad Idea." *Doha Debates*. 14 Dec. 2009. thedohadebates.com/debates/item/index6e76.html.

Doha News Team. "Live Blog: Sheikh Tamim Succeeds Father Sheikh Hamad as Emir of Qatar." *Doha News,* 25 June 2013, dohanews.co/qatar-prepares-for-power-transition/.

—. "New Ban on Driver's Licenses for Laborers Met with Confusion and Skepticism." *Doha News*, 3 July 2013, dohanews.co/post/54504851983/new-ban-on-drivers-licenses-for-laborers-met-with.

—. "Report about Hijab-Wearing Student Barred from Class Not Correct." *Doha News*, 12 Sept. 2012, dohanews.co/school-report-about-hijab-wearing-student-barred-from/.

Fahmy, Heba. "CMC Calls on Qatar's Malls to Revive 'Family Day' Policy." *Doha News*, 17 Nov. 2015, dohanews.co/cmc-calls-on-qatars-malls-to-revive-family-day-policy/.

Fanon, Frantz. *Black Skin, White Masks*. Grove Press, 2008.

Fechter, Anne-Meiki. "Gender, Empire, Global Capitalism: Colonial and Corporate Expatriate Wives." *Journal of Ethnic and Migration Studies*, vol. 36, no. 8, 2010, pp. 1279–97.

Fechter, Anne-Meiki, and Katie Walsh. "Examining 'Expatriate' continuities: Postcolonial Approaches to Mobile Professionals." *Journal of Ethnic and Migration Studies*, vol. 36, no. 8, 2010, pp. 1197–1210.

Feghali, Rena. "Wasta: Connections or Corruption in the Arab World?" *Global Investigator*, Nardello and Company, Apr. 2014.

Fernandes, Leela. *Transnational Feminism in the United States: Knowledge, Ethics, and Power*. New York UP, 2013.

Figenschou, Tine Ustad. "Young, Female, Western Researcher vs. Senior, Male, Al Jazeera Officials: Critical Reflections on Accessing and Interviewing Media Elites in Authoritarian Societies." *Media, Culture, and Society*, vol. 32, no. 6, 2010, pp. 961–78.

Fischlmayr, Iris. "Female Self-Perception as a Barrier to International Careers?" *International Journal of Human Resource Management*, vol. 13, no. 5, 2002, pp. 773–83.

Fisher, Walter. *Human Communication as Narration: Toward a Philosophy of Reason, Value, and Action*. Columbia, SC: U of South Carolina P, 1987.

Fitzgerald, Ceili, and Liza Howe-Walsh. "Self-Initiated Expatriates: An Interpretative Phenomenological Analysis of Professional Female Expatriates." *International Journal of Business and Management*, vol. 3, no. 10, 2008, pp. 156–75.

Foucault, Michel. "Different Spaces." *Aesthetics, Method, and Epistemology*. Translated by Robert Hurly, edited by James D. Faubion, New Press, 1998, pp. 175–85.

Fromherz, Allen J. *Qatar: A Modern History*. Georgetown UP, 2017.

Gannon, Martin J. *Paradoxes of Culture and Globalization*. Sage, 2008.

Gannon, Martin J., and Rajnandini Pillai. *Understanding Cultural Metaphors: Metaphorical Journeys Through 29 Nations, Clusters of Nations, Continents, and Diversity*. 4th ed., Sage, 2010.

Gardner, Andrew M. "Gulf Migration and the Family." *Journal of Arabian Studies*, vol. 1, no. 1, 2011, pp. 3–25.

Garland-Thomson, Rosemarie. *Staring: How We Look*. Oxford UP, 2009.

Glenn, Cheryl. *Rhetorical Feminism and This Thing Called Hope*. Southern Illinois UP, 2018.

—. *Rhetoric Retold: Regendering the Tradition from Antiquity through the Renaissance*. Southern Illinois UP, 1997.

—. *Unspoken: A Rhetoric of Silence*. Southern Illinois UP, 2004.

Gold, Gary D., and George S. Naufal. "Wasta: The Other Invisible Hand: A Case Study of University Students in the Gulf." *Journal of Arabian Studies*, vol. 2, no. 1, 2012, pp. 59–73.

Gorski, Paul C. "Good Intentions are Not Enough: A Decolonizing Intercultural Education." *Intercultural Education*, vol. 19, no. 6, 2008, pp. 515–25.

Gray, Matthew. *Qatar: Politics and the Challenges of Development*. Lynne Rienner Publishers, 2013.

Gross, Alan G. "Rhetoric, Narrative, and the Lifeworld: The Construction of Collective Identity." *Philosophy and Rhetoric*, vol. 43, no. 2, 2010, pp. 118–38.

Gross, Zoë. "(De)Constructing Whiteness, Power, and 'Others' with Access: International Development and Transnational Interracial Intimacies in East Africa." *Critical Race & Whiteness Studies*, vol. 11, no.1, 2015, pp. 1–19.

Hall, Edward T. *The Hidden Dimension*. Doubleday, 1966.

Harrison, Edelweiss C., and Snejina Michailova. "Working in the Middle East: Western Female Expatriates' Experiences in the United Arab Emirates." *The International Journal of Human Resource Management*, vol. 23, no. 4, 2012, pp. 625–44.

Hartl, Katharina. "The Expatriate Career Transition and Women Managers' Experiences." *Women in Management Review*, vol. 19, no. 1, 2004, pp. 40–51.

Henley and Partners. The Henley and Partners Visa Restrictions Index 2014: Global Travel Freedom at a Glance. *Henley Global*, www.henleyglobal.com/files/download/hvri/ HP%20Visa%20Restrictions%20Index%20141101. pdf. Accessed 24 Oct. 2017.

Hofstede, Geert. *Culture's Consequences: Comparing Values, Behaviors, Institutions, and Organizations Across Nations*. 2nd ed., Sage, 2001.

Holliday, Adrian. "Complexity in Cultural Identity." *Language and Intercultural Communication*, vol. 10, no. 2, 2010, pp. 165–77.

hooks, bell. "Eating the Other: Desire and Resistance." *Black Looks: Race and Representation*. South End Press, 1992, pp. 21–39.

Horvath, Agnes, Bjørn Thomassen, and Harald Wydra, editors. *Breaking Boundaries: Varieties of Liminality*. Berghahn Books, 2015.

Howman Wood, Cynthia. "Institutional Ethos: Replicating the Student Experience." *New Directions for Higher Education 2011*, vol. 155, 2011, pp. 29–39.

Human Rights Watch. "World Report 2013: Qatar." *Human Rights Watch*, www.hrw.org/world-report/2013/country-chapters/qatar. Accessed 9 Apr. 2018.

Hundle, Anneeth K., Ioana Szeman, and Joanna Pares Hoare. "What Is the *Transnational* in Transnational Feminist Research?" *Feminist Review*, vol. 121, no. 1, 2019, pp. 3–8.

Huntington, Samuel P. "The Clash of Civilizations?" *Foreign Affairs*, vol. 72, no. 3, 1993, pp. 22–49.

Insch, Gary S., Nancy McIntyre, and Nancy K. Napier. "The Expatriate Glass Ceiling: The Second Layer of Glass." *Journal of Business Ethics*, vol. 83, no. 1, 2008, pp. 19–28.

Janardhan, N. "Expatriates—A Liability?" *The Khaleej Times*, 14 Dec. 2009, www.khaleejtimes.com/editorials-columns/expatriates-a-liability.

Janssens, Maddy, Tineke Cappellen, and Patrizia Zanoni. "Successful Female Expatriates as Agents: Positioning Oneself through Gender, Hierarchy, and Culture." *Journal of World Business*, vol. 41, no. 2, 2006, pp. 133–48.

Jeffin, Lubuna. "Driving Restrictions in Qatar." 30 Jan. 2014. *Marhaba: Qatar's Premier Information Guide*, marhaba.com.qa/driving-restrictions-in-qatar/. Accessed 20 Apr. 2018.

Jørgensen, Anette Jerup. "The Culture of Automobility: How Interacting Drivers Relate to Legal Standards and to Each Other in Traffic." *Gendered Mobilities*, edited by Tanu Priya Uteng and Tim Cresswell. Ashgate, 2008, pp. 99–111.

Kahf, Mohja. "The Pity Committee and the Careful Reader." *Arab and Arab American Feminisms: Gender, Violence, and Belonging*, edited by Rabab Abdulhadi, Evelyn Alsultany, and Nadine Naber. Syracuse UP, 2011 pp. 111–23.

Kamrava, Mehran. *Qatar: Small State, Big Politics*. Cornell UP, 2015.

Kamuf, Peggy. "Replacing Feminist Criticism." *Diacritics*, vol. 12, no. 2, 1982, pp. 42–47.

Kennedy, Tammie M., Joyce Irene Middleton, Krista Ratcliffe, Kathleen Ethel Welch, Catherine Prendergast, Ira Shor, Thomas R. West, Ellen Cushman, Michelle Kendrick, and Lisa Albrecht. "Symposium: Whiteness Studies." *Rhetoric Review*, vol. 24, no. 4, 2005, pp. 359–402.

Khatri, Shabina S. "Villaggio Fire Appeals Hearings Postponed until Late October." *Doha News*, 10 June 2014, dohanews.co/villaggio-fire-appeals-hearings-postponed-late-october/.

Kirkscey, Russell. "From *Homo Narrans* to *Homo Attendens*: A Revision of the Narrative Paradigm." *Conference Papers—National Communication Association*, 2008.

Kovessy, Peter. "Qatar's Emir Signs New Cybercrime Legislation into Law." *Doha News*, 16 Sept. 2014, dohanews.co/qatars-emir-signs-law-new-cyber-crime-legislation/.

Kovessy, Peter, and Riham Sheble. "Judge Questions Confinement Allegations as Huangs' Appeal Continues," *Doha News*, 17 June 2014, dohanews.co/judge-questions-confinement-allegations-huangs-appeal-continues/.

Landry, Donna, and Gerald MacLean. "Introduction." *The Spivak Reader,* edited by Donna Landry and Gerald MacLean. Routledge, 1996, pp. 1–13.

Lauring, Jakob, and Jan Selmer. "Expatriate Compound Living: An Ethnographic Field Study." *The International Journal of Human Resource Management*, vol. 20, no. 7, 2009, pp. 1451–67.

Lewin, Tamar. "In Oil-Rich Middle East, Shades of the Ivy League." *New York Times*, 11 Feb. 2008, www.nytimes.com/2008/02/11/education/11global.html.

Lockerbie, John. *Catnaps.org*. www.catnaps.org/islamic/gulfarch1.html. Accessed 18 Apr. 2018.

Lyon, Arabella. "'You Fail': Plagiarism, the Ownership of Writing, and Transnational Conflicts." *College Composition and Communication*, vol. 61, no. 2, 2009, W222–39.

Mao, LuMing. "Reflective Encounters: Illustrating Comparative Rhetoric." *Style*, vol. 37, no. 4, 2003, pp. 401–24.

Martinez, Aja Y. "A Plea for Critical Race Theory Counterstory: Stock Story Versus Counterstory Dialogues Concerning Alejandra's 'Fit' in the Academy." *Composition Studies*, vol. 42, no. 2, 2014, pp. 33–55.

McIntosh, Peggy. "White Privilege and Male Privilege: A Personal Account of Coming to See Correspondences through Work in Women's Studies." *The Teacher in American Society: A Critical Anthology*, edited by Eugene F. Provenzo, Jr., Sage, 2011, pp. 121–34.

—. "White Privilege: Unpacking the Invisible Knapsack." Wellesley College Center for Research on Women, 1988.

McNay, Lois. *Gender and Agency: Reconfiguring the Subject in Feminist and Social Theory.* John Wiley and Sons, 2013.

McSweeney, Brendan. "Hofstede's Model of National Cultural Differences and Their Consequences: A Triumph of Faith—A Failure of Analysis." *Human Relations*, vol. 55, no. 1, 2002, pp. 89–118.

Melamed, Avi, and Luci Aharsh. *Inside the Middle East: Making Sense of the Most Dangerous and Complicated Region on Earth.* Skyhorse, 2016.

Mernissi, Fatima. *The Veil and the Male Elite: A Feminist Interpretation of Women's Rights in Islam.* Basic Books, 1991.

Metcalfe, Beverly Dawn. "Gender and Human Resource Management in the Middle East." *The International Journal of Human Resource Management*, vol. 18, no. 1, 2007, pp. 54–74.

—. "Women, Management and Globalization in the Middle East." *Journal of Business Ethics*, vol. 83, no. 1, 2008, pp. 85–100.

Miller-Idriss, Cynthia, and Elizabeth Hanauer. "Transnational Higher Education: Offshore Campuses in the Middle East." *Comparative Education*, vol. 47, no. 2, 2011, pp. 181–207.

Mohamed, Ahmed Amin, and Hadia Hamdy. "The Stigma of Wasta: The Effect of Wasta on Perceived Competence and Morality," Working Paper Series, German University in Cairo. *IDEAS Database of Economics*. January 2008. ideas.repec.org/p/guc/wpaper/5.html.

Mohan, Megha. "Ostracised and Fetishised: The Perils Of Travelling as a Young Black Woman." *BBNews*, 30 Apr. 2018, www.bbc.com/news/stories-43877568.

Mohanty, Chandra Talpade. "'Under Western Eyes' Revisited: Feminist Solidarity through Anticapitalist Struggles." *Signs: Journal of Women in Culture and Society*, vol. 28, no. 2, 2003, pp. 499–535.

Nakano, Hanna. "Are American Universities Funding Extremists' Education?" *Gulf News Journal*, 21 Apr. 2016, gulfnewsjournal.com/stories/510718132-are-american-universities-funding-extremists-education.

Napier, Nancy K., and Sully Taylor. "Experiences of Women Professionals Abroad: Comparisons across Japan, China and Turkey." *International Journal of Human Resource Management*, vol. 13, no. 5, 2002, pp. 837–51.

Nydell, Margaret. *Understanding Arabs: A Contemporary Guide to Arab Society.* 5th ed., Nicholas Brealey, 2012.

@oneofus_qa. *Twitter*, 2012, twitter.com/OneOfUs_qa.

Osland, Joyce. *The Adventure of Working Abroad: Hero Tales from the Global Frontier.* Jossey-Bass, 1995.

—. "The Journey Inward: Expatriate Hero Tales and Paradoxes." *Human Resources Management*, vol. 39, no. 2–3, 2000, pp. 227–38.

Osland, Joyce, and Allan Bird. "Beyond Sophisticated Stereotyping: Cultural Sensemaking in Context." *The Academy of Management Executive (1993–2005)*, vol. 14, no. 1, 2000, pp. 65–79.

Osland, Joyce, and Asbjorn Osland. "Expatriate Paradoxes and Cultural Involvement." *International Studies of Management and Organization*, vol. 35, no. 4, 2005–06, pp. 93–116.

Pattisson, Pete. "Revealed: Qatar's World Cup 'Slaves.'" *The Guardian*, 25 Sept. 2013, www.theguardian.com/world/2013/sep/25/revealed-qatars-world-cup-slaves.

Popper, Karl. *The Open Society and Its Enemies: Vol. 1 The Age of Plato*. Routledge, 2012.

Qatar. "Constitution of Qatar." *Hukoomi: Qatar E-Government*. portal.www.gov.qa. Accessed 9 Apr. 2018.

"Qatar." *OpenNet Initiative*, 6 Aug. 2009, opennet.net/research/profiles/qatar.

Qatar, Al Meezan. "Law No. 15 of 2010 Prohibition of Workers Camps within Family Residential Areas." *Al Meezan Qatar Legal Portal*, 19 Aug. 2010, www.almeezan.qa/LawArticles.aspx?LawTreeSectionID=8328&lawId=2510&language=en.

Qatar, Ministry of Development Planning and Statistics. *Labor Force Survey: The Second Quarter of 2013 (April-June)*. www.mdps.gov.qa/en/statistics/Statistical%20Releases/   Social/LaborForce/2013/Quarterly/Q2/LF_Q2_2013_AE.pdf. Accessed 9 Apr. 2018.

—. *Qatar National Vision 2030*. July 2008, www.mdps.gov.qa/en/qnv/Documents/QNV2030_English_v2.pdf.

Ratcliffe, Krista. *Rhetorical Listening: Identification, Gender, Whiteness*. Southern Illinois UP, 2005.

—. "Rhetorical Listening: A Trope for Interpretive Invention and a 'Code of Cross-Cultural Conduct.'" *College Composition and Communication*, vol. 51, no. 2, 1999, pp. 195–24.

Ratcliffe, R. G. "Hullabaloo, Qatar, Qatar!: Texas A&M at Qatar and Middle East Squabble" *Texas Monthly*, 9 June 2017, www.texasmonthly.com/burka-blog/hullabaloo-qatar-qatar-2/.

Rathmell, Andrew, and Kirsten Schulze. "Political Reform in the Gulf: The Case of Qatar." *Middle Eastern Studies*, vol. 36, no. 4, 2000, pp. 47–62.

Richardson, Julia, and Steve McKenna. "Exploring Relationships with Home and Host Countries: A Study of Self-Directed Expatriates." *Cross Cultural Management: An International Journal*, vol. 13, no. 1, 2006, pp. 6–22.

Rose, Gillian. *Feminism & Geography: The Limits of Geographical Knowledge*. U of Minnesota P, 1993.

Rossano, Federico, Penelope Brown, and Stephen C. Levinson. "Gaze, Questioning and Culture." *Conversation Analysis: Comparative Perspectives*, edited by Jack Sidnell, Cambridge UP, 2009, pp. 187–249.

Rostron, Magdalena. "Liberal Arts Education in Qatar: Intercultural Perspectives." *Intercultural Education*, vol. 20, no. 3, 2009, pp. 219–29.

Rowling, J. K. *Harry Potter and the Half-Blood Prince*. Scholastic, 2006.

Royster, Jacqueline Jones. "When the First Voice You Hear Is Not Your Own." *College Composition and Communication*, vol. 47, no. 1, 1996, pp. 29–40.

Royster, Jacqueline Jones, and Gesa E. Kirsch. *Feminist Rhetorical Practices: New Horizons for Rhetoric, Composition, and Literacy Studies*. Southern Illinois UP, 2012.

Rudd, LeeAnn Mysti. "'It makes us even angrier than we already are': Listening Rhetorically to Students' Responses to an Honor Code Imported to a Transnational University in the Middle East." *Journal of Global Literacies, Technologies, and Emerging Pedagogies*, vol. 4, no. 3, 2018, pp. 655–74.

Said, Edward W. *Culture and Imperialism*. Vintage, 2012.

Saudelli, Mary Gene. "Unveiling Third Space: A Case Study of International Educators in Dubai, United Arab Emirates." *Canadian Journal of Education*, vol. 35, no. 3, 2012, pp. 101–16.

Schwedler, Jillian. "The Third Gender: Western Female Researchers in the Middle East." *PS: Political Science and Politics*, vol. 39, no. 3, 2006, pp. 425–28.

Scott, Victoria. "Twitter Debate Begins about What It Means to be 'Half Qatari.'" *Doha News*, 22 June 2014, dohanews.co/twitter-debate-starts-means-half-qatari/.

Seshan, Ganesh. "Migrants in Qatar: A Socio-Economic Profile." *Journal of Arabian Studies*, vol. 2, no. 2, 2012, pp. 157–71.

Sherlock, Ruth. "Qatari Sentenced to Death Over Brutal Killing of British Teacher." *The Telegraph*. 27 Mar. 2014. www.telegraph.co.uk/news/world-news/middleeast/qatar/ 10726757/Qatari-sentenced-to-death-over-brutal-killing-of-British-teacher.html.

Shibata, Mary. "The Middle Finger Emoji Could Land You in Jail in the UAE." *Motherboard*, 18 June 2015, motherboard.vice.com/en_us/article/ypw9mw/ the-middle-finger-emoji-could-land-you-in-jail-in-the-uae.

Shome, Raka. *Diana and Beyond: White Femininity, National Identity, and Contemporary Media Culture*. U of Illinois P, 2014.

Small, Nancy. "Qatar's Globalized Citizenry and the *Majlis* Culture: Insights from Habermas's Theory of the Development of a Public Sphere." *Deconstructing Global Citizenship: Political, Cultural, and Ethical Perspectives*, edited by Hassan Bashir and Phillip W. Gray. Lexington Books, 2015, pp. 285–302.

—. "Risking Our Foundations: Honor, Codes, and Authoritarian Spaces." *Western Higher Education in Asia and the Middle East: Politics, Economics, and Pedagogy*, edited by Kevin Gray, Hassan Bashir, and Stephen Keck. Lexington Books, 2016, pp. 223–42.

Smith, Linda Tuhiwai. "On Tricky Ground: Researching the Native in the Age of Uncertainty." *The Sage Handbook of Qualitative Research*. 3rd ed., edited by Norman Denzin and Yvonna S. Lincoln, Sage, 2005, pp. 85–113.

Snoj, Jure. "Population of Qatar by Nationality—2017 Report." *Priya Dsouza Communications*, 7 Feb. 2017, priyadsouza.com/population-of-qatar-by-nationality-in-2017/.

Spivak, Gayatri Chakravorty. "Can the Subaltern Speak?" *Marxism and the Interpretation of Culture*, edited by Cary Nelson and Lawrence Grossberg. U of Illinois P, 1988, pp. 271–313.

Stalker, Brenda, and Sharon Mavin. "Learning and Development Experiences of Self-Initiated Expatriate Women in the United Arab Emirates." *Human Resource Development International*, vol. 14, no. 3, 2011, pp. 273–90.

Sue, Derald Wing. *Microaggressions in Everyday Life: Race, Gender, and Sexual Orientation*. Wiley and Sons, 2010.

Sue, Derald Wing, Christina M. Capodilupo, Gina C. Torino, Jennifer M. Bucceri, Aisha Holder, Kevin L. Nadal, and Marta Esquilin. "Racial Microaggressions in Everyday Life: Implications for Clinical Practice." *American Psychologist*, vol. 62, no. 4, 2007, 271–86.

Swarr, Amanda Lock, and Richa Nagar, editors. *Critical Transnational Feminist Praxis*. SUNY P, 2010.

Thomassen, Bjørn. *Liminality and the Modern: Living through the In-Between*. Routledge, 2016.

Tlaiss, Hayfaa, and Saleema Kauser. "The Importance of Wasta in the Career Success of Middle Eastern Managers." *Journal of European Industrial Training*, vol. 35, no. 5, 2011, pp. 467–86.

Twine, France Winddance, and Charles Gallagher. "The Future of Whiteness: A Map of the 'Third Wave.'" *Ethnic and Racial Studies*, vol. 31, no. 1, 2008, pp. 4–24.

UndercoverJim. "Boycott Qatar 2022 World Cup: Undercover Investigation." *YouTube*, 9 Oct. 2010, www.youtube.com/watch?v=VluY5SWfjSI. Accessed 20 Apr. 2018.

United States, Central Intelligence Agency. "Qatar." *The World Factbook*, 2 Apr. 2018, www.cia.gov/library/publications/the-world-factbook/geos/qa.html.

United States, National Archives. "The Constitution: Amendments 11–27." *National Archives*. www.archives.gov/founding-docs/amendments-11–27. Accessed 20 Apr. 2018.

—. *The Constitution of the United States: A Transcription*. National Archives. www.archives.gov/founding-docs/constitution-transcript. Accessed 20 Apr. 2018.

Vora, Neha. *Teach for Arabia: American Universities, Liberalism, and Transnational Qatar*. Stanford UP, 2019.

Walker, Lesley. "Qatar Road Accidents on Rise in May, New Government Report Shows." *Doha News*, 29 June 2014, dohanews.co/road-accidents-rise-ramadan-traffic-safety-campaign-launches/.

Weick, Karl. *Sensemaking in Organizations*. Sage, 1995.

Whistling Woods International. "Dekh Le." *YouTube*. 16 Dec. 2013. www.youtube.com/watch?v=SDYFqQZEdRA.

Willis, Rebecca. "The Use of Composite Narratives to Present Interview Findings." *Qualitative Research*, vol. 19, no. 4, pp. 471–80.

Wilson, Shawn. *Research Is Ceremony: Indigenous Research Methods*. Fernwood, 2009.

Witte, Anne E. "Making the Case for a Post-National Cultural Analysis of Organizations." *Journal of Management Inquiry*, vol. 21, no. 2, 2012, pp. 141–59.

Wunderle, William. D. *A Manual for American Servicemen in the Arab Middle East: Using Cultural Understanding to Defeat Adversaries and Win the Peace*. Skyhorse, 2008.

Yuval-Davis, Nira. *The Politics of Belonging: Intersectional Contestations*. Sage, 2011.

# Index

# About the Author

Nancy Small is an assistant professor and Director of First Year Writing at the University of Wyoming, where her work centers on a range of applications of storytelling as a rhetorical process and product. Her teaching and research engage topics of rhetorical feminism, public memory, qualitative research ethics, and intercultural communication. Her scholarly projects have been published in edited collections on education in the Middle East as well as in a range of scholarly outlets including *Peitho: Journal of the Coalition of Feminist Scholars in the History of Rhetoric & Composition; The Routledge Handbook of Gender and Communication;* and the *Journal of Technical Writing and Communication.*

www.ingramcontent.com/pod-product-compliance
Lightning Source LLC
LaVergne TN
LVHW042310110125
800979LV00004B/217